Morten Ougaard
THE GLOBALIZATION OF POLITICS
Power, Social Forces and Governance

Jørgen Dige Pedersen
GLOBALIZATION, DEVELOPMENT AND THE STATE
The Performance of India and Brazil Since 1990

Markus Perkmann and Ngai-Ling Sum
GLOBALIZATION, REGIONALIZATION AND CROSS–BORDER REGIONS

K. Ravi Raman (*editor*)
CORPORATE SOCIAL RESPONSIBILITY
Comparative Critiques

Ben Richardson
SUGAR: REFINED POWER IN A GLOBAL REGIME

Marc Schelhase
GLOBALIZATION, REGIONALIZATION AND BUSINESS
Conflict, Convergence and Influence

Herman M. Schwartz and Leonard Seabrooke (*editors*)
THE POLITICS OF HOUSING BOOMS AND BUSTS

Leonard Seabrooke
US POWER IN INTERNATIONAL FINANCE
The Victory of Dividends

Timothy J. Sinclair and Kenneth P. Thomas (*editors*)
STRUCTURE AND AGENCY IN INTERNATIONAL CAPITAL MOBILITY

J. P. Singh (*editor*)
INTERNATIONAL CULTURAL POLICIES AND POWER

Fredrik Söderbaum and Timothy M. Shaw (*editors*)
THEORIES OF NEW REGIONALISM

Susanne Soederberg, Georg Menz and Philip G. Cerny (*editors*)
INTERNALIZING GLOBALIZATION
The Rise of Neoliberalism and the Decline of National Varieties of Capitalism

Ritu Vij (*editor*)
GLOBALIZATION AND WELFARE
A Critical Reader

Matthew Watson
THE POLITICAL ECONOMY OF INTERNATIONAL CAPITAL MOBILITY

Owen Worth and Phoebe Moore
GLOBALIZATION AND THE 'NEW' SEMI-PERIPHERIES

International Political Economy Series
Series Standing Order ISBN 978–0–333–71708–0 hardcover
Series Standing Order ISBN 978–0–333–71110–1 paperback

You can receive future titles in this series as they are published by placing a standing order. Please contact your bookseller or, in case of difficulty, write to us at the address below with your name and address, the title of the series and one of the ISBNs quoted above.

Customer Services Department, Macmillan Distribution Ltd, Houndmills, Basingstoke, Hampshire RG21 6XS, England

---

International Cultural Policies and Power

Edited by

J. P. Singh

palgrave
macmillan

First published 2010 by
PALGRAVE MACMILLAN

Palgrave Macmillan in the UK is an imprint of Macmillan Publishers Limited,
registered in England, company number 785998, of Houndmills, Basingstoke,
Hampshire RG21 6XS.

Palgrave Macmillan in the US is a division of St Martin's Press LLC,
175 Fifth Avenue, New York, NY 10010.

Palgrave Macmillan is the global academic imprint of the above companies
and has companies and representatives throughout the world.

Palgrave® and Macmillan® are registered trademarks in the United States,
the United Kingdom, Europe and other countries.

ISBN 978-0-230-23527-4   hardback

This book is printed on paper suitable for recycling and made from fully
managed and sustained forest sources. Logging, pulping and manufacturing
processes are expected to conform to the environmental regulations of the
country of origin.

A catalogue record for this book is available from the British Library.

A catalog record for this book is available from the Library of Congress.

10   9   8   7   6   5   4   3   2   1
19   18   17   16   15   14   13   12   11   10

Printed and bound in Great Britain by
CPI Antony Rowe, Chippenham and Eastbourne

For Chuck

Contents

List of Figures		ix
List of Tables		x
Preface		xi
Notes on Contributors		xiii

1   Global Cultural Policies and Power   1
J. P. Singh

Part I   Politics, Power, Technologies

2   Cultural Policy and the Political Nature of Culture   19
Carole Rosenstein

3   The Arts, Culture, and Civil Society: Power Stations
in the Grids of Governance   29
Timothy W. Luke

4   Art–State Relations: Art and Power through the Lens
of International Treaties   36
Sandra Braman

5   Toward a Political Economy of Digital Culture: From
Organized Mass Consumption to Attention Rivalry   56
Jeffrey A. Hart

6   Playing with Power: The Cultural Impact of Prosumers   63
Bjarki Valtysson

Part II   Cultural Policies: US, EU, Japan

7   The Political Economy of Cultural Diversity
in Film and Television   77
Harvey Feigenbaum

8   An "Economic" Approach Toward the Trade
and Culture Debate: The US Position   84
Carol Balassa

9   Cultural Diplomacy: The Humanizing Factor   101
Cynthia P. Schneider

10   Power in European Union Cultural Policy   113
Patricia Dewey

11 Making Geography Matter in Cultural Policy Research:
    The Case of Regional Cultural Policy in Sweden   127
    Jenny Johannisson

12 The Importance of the Business Sector in Cultural Policy
    in Japan—A Model of Complementary Relationship
    with Government   140
    Nobuko Kawashima

Part III Cultural Voices: The Developing World

13 Coloniality, Identity and Cultural Policy   155
    Kevin V. Mulcahy

14 Valorization of World Cultural Heritage in Time of Globalization:
    Bridges Between Nations and Cultural Power   166
    Isabelle Brianso

15 Reality TV Shows, Private Television Networks and Social Change
    in India   181
    Lauhona Ganguly

16 "The Power to Narrate": Film Festivals, a Platform
    for Transnational Feminism?   194
    Jasmine Champenois

17 Everyday Cultural Politics, Syncretism, and Cultural Policy   203
    Dennis Galvan

Bibliography   214

Index   238

List of Figures

1.1   Instrumental and meta-power   7

5.1   Where do respondents get their national
      and international news?   58

10.1 Article 151 of the consolidated version of the
      Treaty on European Union   118

10.2 EU Institutions' roles in cultural policy decision-making 121

12.1 Total amount of spending for *méséna* by respondents
      1991–2007 (million yen)   145

15.1 Projected growth of Indian television industry   184

List of Tables

5.1   Old and new players in the cultural industries   57

11.1 Summary of the discourses used by institutional agents
      in the cultural policy (re)construction process
      in Göteborg 1991–8   131

Preface

The book provides a global survey of the implications of cultural industries and technologies for power and policies at local, societal, national, and international levels. It aims to integrate these perspectives into the study of political and social sciences. Especially political scientists by and large ignore cultural industries and technologies which are prominent in other disciplines. Cultural industries in this book covers fine and performing arts, publishing, heritage, films, music, television, design, and cultural tourism. Together, they make up one of the biggest sectors of any economy and are prominent in various policy debates such as in international trade profiles, copyrights issues, and economic development. Economics is merely the beginning, of course. The role of cultural industries in the realm of identity, aesthetics, and social voice carries us over to issues in anthropology, sociology, arts, and philosophy, to name a few other disciplines.

The book began as an all-day short course on "Cultural Industries, Technologies and Policies" at the American Political Science Association annual meeting in Philadelphia on August 30, 2006, where initial drafts of six of the chapters included in this volume were presented. Over three dozen scholars in attendance agreed that there was a need for a survey of issues covered in cultural policies for political scientists. However, it took a couple of years to find scholars from across the world who could translate the several sub-issues covered here in a language that would be useful for social sciences in general and political science in particular. In the early 1980s, there were a few political scientists who began to study comparative and international cultural policies but they soon left political science to teach their courses in arts management and cultural studies or communication programs. The result is that while courses in cultural policies are regularly taught in several social science and humanities programs, these courses are rarely taught in political science. We hope that this book will help in making cultural policy issues salient to political scientists who may find them an important subject of study.

I would like to thank several individuals and organizations that, in various ways, made the book possible. The Policy Studies Organization and two sections of the American Political Science Association—Information Technology and Politics; and Science, Technology and Environmental Politics—sponsored the workshop at the Philadelphia APSA. Tim Shaw, International Political Economy Series editor at Palgrave Macmillan, and Alexandra Webster, head of social sciences, provided enthusiastic support and a timely referee review for the project. Renee Takken, Manavalan

BhuvanaRaj, and Shalini Singh gave excellent and efficient production support. Sarah Thompson provided able research and editorial assistance at Georgetown University. Many thanks to Becky Jakob for proofreading and for preparing the Index. Anuj Narang also helped with the proofs. Students in my graduate seminar on Cultural Economics and Policies read several essays and gave important feedback. Most importantly, I thank the many scholars in this volume who rose to the challenge of writing essays that would make the subdiscipline of cultural policies and power accessible to social scientists.

Note: The applicant further agrees to print, or cause to be printed in every copy of the work, on the copyright page, separate acknowledgements page, or on the first page of such quotation covered by this permission, the following notice:

Notes on Contributors

Carol Balassa, Senior Fellow, The Curb Center for Art, Enterprise and Public Policy at Vanderbilt, Washington, DC, US.

Isabelle Brianso, *Centre d'Histoire Culturelle des Sociétés Contemporaines (CHCSC)* and *Laboratoire de recherche en management (LAREQUOI)*, Université Versailles Saint-Quentin en Yvelines (UVSQ), Versailles University ATER (Attachée Temporaire d'Enseignement et de Recherche) in communication and information sciences, France.

Sandra Braman, Professor, Department of Communication, University of Wisconsin-Milwaukee, US.

Jasmine Champenois, Executive Director, Department of Executive Education, Graduate Institute of International and Development Studies, Switzerland.

Patricia Dewey, Associate Professor, Arts and Administration Program; Director, Center for Community Arts and Cultural Policy, University of Oregon, Eugene, OR, US.

Harvey B. Feigenbaum, Professor, Political Science and International Affairs, The George Washington University, Washington, DC, US.

Dennis Galvan, Associate Professor of Political Science and International Studies, University of Oregon, Eugene, OR, US.

Lauhona Ganguly, PhD candidate, American University, Washington, DC; Part-time Faculty, The New School, New York, US.

Jeffrey A. Hart, Professor, Department of Political Science, Indiana University, Bloomington, IN, US.

Jenny Johannisson, Centre for Cultural Policy Research, Swedish School of Library and Information Science, University College of Borås, Sweden.

Nobuko Kawashima, Professor, Faculty of Economics, Doshisha University, Japan.

Timothy W. Luke, Distinguished Professor, Department of Political Science, Virginia Polytechnic Institute and State University, US.

Kevin V. Mulcahy, Sheldon Beychok Distinguished Professor of Political Science and Public Administration, Louisiana State University, Baton Rouge, US; Executive Editor, *Journal of Arts Management, Law and Society*.

Carole Rosenstein, Assistant Professor, Arts Management Program, George Mason University; Affiliated Scholar, Center on Nonprofits and Philanthropy at the Urban Institute, Washington, DC.

Ambassador Cynthia P. Schneider, Distinguished Professor in the Practice of Diplomacy, Georgetown University; Non-Resident Senior Scholar, Brookings Institution; Washington, DC, US; Co-Director, *Muslims on Screen and Television: A Cross Cultural Resource Center,* Los Angeles, CA.

J. P. Singh, Associate Professor, Communication, Culture and Technology Program, Georgetown University, Washington, DC, US.

Bjarki Valtysson, Assistant Professor, IT University of Copenhagen, Denmark.

1
Global Cultural Policies and Power
J. P. Singh

> But the women had been taught to recognize these reflec-
> tions as self and it was frightening now to even to think
> that, the very facts which set them apart as a group, as
> women, as a certain kind of person, were only myths.
> —*The schoolgirl Tambu reflecting on the patriarchal*
> *practices binding her female relatives in colonial Rhodesia.*
> *In Tsitsi Dungarembga's Nervous Conditions (1988, p. 138)*

Representations shape and change identity. The cavemen in Plato's parables
and the schoolgirl Tambu's female relatives mentioned above find their
identities—and thoughts and actions thereof—shaped and constrained
by such representations. The symbiotic relationship between changes in
identity and the circulation of creative representations seems obvious here.
Dangarembga's cultural representations also evoke the culture of everyday
life for the women of colonial Rhodesia.

In our world of pervasive information networks and intensely interactive
communication, the flows of cultural representations, centered on created aesthetic expressions, are growing exponentially. While most political
scientists ignore these cultural representations, the "cultural turn," or the
study of everyday life in general is now a legitimate area of inquiry in various disciplines after decades of neglect. There are two concepts of culture
at play here. Culture as everyday group life is an anthropological concept.
Nevertheless it is reflected in the creative and aesthetic expressions regulating, sustaining, or at times, contesting the shared understandings of the
meanings of cultures. This volume mostly attends to the understanding of
culture rooted in creative and aesthetic expressions, although the anthropological concept of culture often runs parallel to the generation of aesthetic
expressions.

This overview first attends to the context of the main contribution, regarding the politics of cultural industries, in this volume. Next, it outlines the
specific value of going beyond instrumental types of power understandings

1

to account for transformational dimensions that lead to identity and interest formation. Finally, the chapter provides a few guidelines to understanding the governance of cultural industries, otherwise known as cultural policies, both in the developed and developing worlds. The multiple layers of governance and the plurality of actors involved showcase complex patterns of policy-formation ranging from European Union's singular quest for a common identity to the syncretic and hybrid forms of identity evolution throughout the world.

Contribution and concepts

Cultural politics and policies examined in this volume are not only a microcosm of all kinds of politics and policies—of the "who did what to whom" variety—but they are also unique, precisely because they attend to cultural representations and understandings. Cultural politics make salient issues of identity and expression, inclusion and exclusion, voice and silence, and the power of symbols. Arts and entertainment evoke collective memories and shape our understanding of the present. Cultural policies attend to the instruments and institutions governing arts and entertainment. Institutions vary from government, intergovernmental, civil society, and private actors from local to global levels. Instruments governing cultural industries and expressions include copyright, trademarks, heritage measures, archiving, subsidies, grants, taxation, philanthropy, trade tariffs, and international conventions and treaties. Other politics and policies might reveal similar facets. But, perhaps, not all of them are as visible and important as art, creativity, and cultural industries. Political scientists who spend hours listening to music or gazing at historical monuments but have struggled to accommodate these "passions" into their scholarship might be especially interested in the following pages. This volume is of course of direct interest to those who have been following the rise of cultural industries globally and the way these industries have been situated politically to address various forms of identity politics. As the following chapters evidence, cultural trade disputes between the US and the EU, the rise of reality TV in India, or nationalist arts in Mexico are all representative of broader political trends, thereby providing a window of opportunity to study them.

This volume emphasizes the importance of international cultural politics and policies to political scientists, especially in the US. The study of the politics and policies of cultural industries, understood in this chapter as the economic organization of aesthetic expressions—referring to production, distribution, consumption, and archiving or preservation—is common in most countries. However, students of cultural industries in political science, or even the social sciences, in the US are hard to find. In general, the economic value of these industries to the national social and economic well-being is often applauded globally. In European and other contexts, cultural industries are often well represented in scholarship and in policy making—in cultural ministries and a variety of institutions—but often these industries grow up under state patronage systems and their economic value is underestimated. This book does not try to resolve the fraught debates over the role of cultural politics and policies in various contexts. It merely makes them salient in order to make future scholarship well aware of these concerns.

This volume brings together an eclectic set of 16 original and one readapted chapter on cultural politics and policies from around the world. The interdisciplinary and intentionally global team of scholars and practitioners in this volume spans various theoretical and ideological perspectives. It is our hope that the chapters will raise problems worthy of study for the future. The volume provides insights from local, societal, national, and international levels in understanding cultural industries, technologies, and policies. While political scientists, especially in the US, by and large, ignore cultural industries and technologies, these are prominent in other disciplines. For example, the various ontologies of cultural studies underscore cultural resources and power. Notable exceptions within the social sciences include the culture section of the American Sociological Association and the small interdisciplinary Association of Cultural Economics International. Emphasis on cultural policy at public policy institutes can also be found at the New York University, Princeton, Vanderbilt, and the University of Chicago. Various communication and media programs encompass a few aspects of cultural and media industries but are lacking systematic international or comparative studies of cultural industries and policies.

A predominant reason for the neglect of cultural issues in political science may lie in the legacy of the notions of cultural purity in the first half of the twentieth century and that of the *fin-de-siecle* debates on the "clash of civilizations." These perspectives essentialized or stereotyped grand views of culture and presented them as arenas of conflict (Huntington, 1996). Most political scientists, therefore, shy away from bringing culture back into their research although every now and then there are studies of political culture centered on civil society issues. More recently, there have been attempts to integrate culture more cohesively into the study of political science (Kratochwil, 1991; Katzenstein, 1996) with the constructivist paradigm leading the charge. However, a study of culture as understood in this volume is still missing from these accounts. A smattering of works such as Cummings and Katz (1987), Luke (1989), and Mulcahy and Wyszsomirski (1995), Goff (2007), and Singh (2010) focus specifically on cultural industries and policies, but these are not yet integrated into the broader discipline. While political scientists ignore cultural policy, the subject continues to gain importance in policy, industry, and civil society worldwide. It is therefore time to theorize cultural policies and resources as they become increasingly important in the way that societies and nations view economic and political power at home and abroad.

Cultural industries include the arts and creative sectors that encompass, but are not limited to, fine and performing arts, cultural heritage, publishing, film, television, music, photography, design, and cultural tourism. Information technologies, now more than ever, are considered crucial to the growth of cultural industries. Examples of the prioritization of cultural industries include Latin American telenovelas, China's videogames and films, or India's Bollywood productions and animation. Egypt is a center of Arabic publishing, and Zimbabwe and Mali are centers of music production in Africa. Richard Florida's (2002) book *Rise of the Creative Class* notes that the creative class now includes a third of the US workforce (p. xiv). Estimates of cultural industries vary between 5 and 10 percent of national gross domestic products. An estimate from UNESCO (2005), that did not include tourism, calculated international trade in cultural products to be $59.2 billion in 2002, up from $39.3 billion in 1994 (2005).[1] Hollywood often boasts that it is the biggest export from the US. Vogel (2007, p. xix) notes that entertainment spending globally is nearly $1 trillion, of which Americans spend $280 billion (in 140 billion hours collectively at home and theaters). Tourism is now the biggest industry in the world. World Tourism Organization calculated the international tourism revenues to be $733 billion in 2006, and cultural tourism, an aspect of cultural policy, makes up more than a quarter of the total (UNWTO, 2008; OECD, 2008). None of these figures includes domestic trade in culture products or tourism.

The claims made in this volume regarding the importance of studying cultural industries are situated in the macro socioeconomic trends and academic pursuits outlined above. The next two sections chart the contributions the authors make toward situating the role of cultural industries in thinking about power and governance.

Cultural politics and power

Culture is about group identity. Power is either about effecting or constraining particular outcomes, or about transforming or constituting the identity of the actors and the issues themselves. In the former sense power takes on an instrumental or structural dimension enhancing or constraining particular identities. In the latter transformative sense, this chapter notes the presence of meta-power dimensions (explained later). Chapters 2–6 in this book are about conceptions of power in cultural politics. As resources and identities are highly affected by technologies, the book accords special attention to technologies, especially digital technologies, in the production of cultural artifacts.

Any discussion of power in the realm of cultural politics must start with the context of cultural valuation for individuals and societies. The reasons people value cultural artifacts are strongly related to the role of these products in their lives. The economic valuation of products, rooted in price and incomes, is but one of the ways of estimating this value. This economic valuation of the arts or culture plays an important role in marshaling material support for these endeavors from institutions. However, it does not guide us on the role of these products in people's identities and way of life. Cultural economists, therefore, vary from those like Bruno Frey (2000) who take "price" to be an objective criterion in the measurement of the value of arts, to those like David Throsby who posit various types of value such as religious, aesthetic, spiritual, social, historical, and symbolic value (Throsby, 2001, Chapter 2). Jackson (2008, p. 92) notes: "Art and cultural participation contribute to community conditions in education, economic development, civic engagement, and to stewardship of place." Carole Rosenstein's chapter in this volume (Chapter 2) moves beyond issues of value to note that, first, all politics is cultural and, second, that culture is more appropriately valued as a resource for the sustainability of societies rather than a quality as revealed in a nation, a society, or another form of identity. She highlights the notion of cultural capital as a resource, drawing upon John Dewey's concept of "experience," individuals in interactive social environments, that he later would term "culture." He held these experiences, especially as fostered through arts, to be fundamentally important to democratic governance.

Instrumentally, however, culture can also be viewed as producing docility rather than enabling citizens to exercise agency in due possession of their reason. In this view, informed by progressive and radical analyses that can be traced to Marxian thought, cultural technologies and industries further a false consciousness and thus limit individual or collective agency. Even Plato had warned of the emotional manipulation through arts such as poetry that would take away from good citizenship. Enlightenment-era thought on cultural expressions often assigned them similar rank in thwarting individual reason (Goodwin, 2006).

From a radical perspective, Horkheimer and Adorno (1972) were especially strident in assigning to cultural technologies a central place in furthering a false consciousness. Luke (1989) notes that television screens beguile through entertainment but hardly reveal the forces of production that sustain capitalism behind the screens. Miller and Yúdice (2002) posit a cultural division of labor in which the logic of capitalism allows for core–periphery relations in cultural production and distribution. Miami thus becomes a center of Latin American cultural production in television broadcasting while the US itself organizes its administrative apparatus to regulate, directly through coercion or indirectly through subtler forms of cultural diplomacy, cultural life in Latin America to serve its aims. More recently, Comor (2008; 2002) has parted company with the mode of *production*-dominant Marxian or critical analyses in which production relations determine class conflict and future of capitalism. Instead, Comor points out that capitalism is sustained and deepened through *consumption*, in which shaping cultural choices through commodification of cultural life is important. Luke (Chapter 3) provides an overview of critical theory and then explains the ways in which "cultural technologies and policies enable people to behave in certain ways." Luke harkens the Foucauldian concept of "governmentality" wherein the visible writs of government find their due obedience in the internalized and intersubjective codes produced in the subjects of governance through cultural technologies.

Critical theory's notion of instrumental power reverses the agency of technology; technology itself is the agent embodying forces of domination rather than allowing for agency or empowerment. Oftentimes, this view is taken to be a structural dimension of power. A structural view of power is also apparent in the chapters by Bjarki Valtysson (Chapter 6), Kevin Mulcahy (Chapter 13), and Lauhona Ganguly (Chapter 15).

Power, of course, as noted above, is not just a resource limiting or abetting forms of agency but it is also a process in constituting identities of actors and issues themselves. To understand the transformative aspects of cultural production and policies, we need the concept of meta-power where the constitutive base of both X and Y change (Singh, 2002; 2008a). Liberal and radical political theory concentrate on the instrumental conception: liberal theories view technology as a panacea, and radical theories view technology as a constraining structure. More recently, behavioral and constructivist schools emphasize transformation and change. But, whereas, liberal and radical theories provide an instrumental conceptualization of power, constructivism lacks a particular conceptualization, although it may be argued that constructivism does not lack in its understanding of the process of change. The concept of meta-power supplies the missing link. It deals with the origins and transformation of instruments and thus seeks to supplement, rather than replace, the instrumental understandings. Figure 1.1 illustrates the understanding of instrumental and meta-power developed here in the context of cultural industries and technologies.

Meta-power influences the identity formation of both the actors (X) as well as the issues (Y) in politics (Figure 1.1). Giddens' (1984) distinction between practical and discursive consciousness, although developed in a different context, might be instructive here. Practical consciousness deals with routinized action (instrumental action noted above) whereas discursive consciousness (somewhat like meta-power) helps us name the action and trace its origins. The constructivist ideas of regulative (quotidian) versus constitutive social norms and facts are also relevant (Kratochwil, 1991) in demarcating the lines between what 'is' and 'how' it came into being.

An example illustrating Figure 1.1 might be helpful. Cultural technologies might allow for a circulation of representations on the Internet that might stabilize or destabilize the powers that be or the policies and institutions that support them (the instrumental X and Y). In this sense, they might both empower or disempower a given or new set of actors, but more

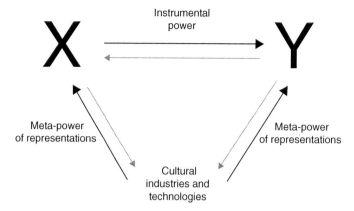

Figure 1.1 Instrumental and meta-power

importantly also suggest new epistemic possibilities or self-understandings to them (the what, who, and how of X). Through interactions, new or hybrid forms of identity might emerge. The meta-power aspects of film, radio, and television in the last century might also be understood as such in this regard. For example, African author-filmmaker Sembene Ousmane gave up novel and fiction writing to take up another narrative form, because to him the African tradition of storytelling was better suited for film media. His film narratives in general cover progressive themes of identity changes in West Africa. Interestingly, Tsitsi Dangarembga, who is quoted at the beginning of this chapter, also gave up fiction writing in favor of screenplays, again examining gender and violence in the hybrid context of historical patriarchy and colonial politics.

The role of technology and new media is especially important for examining meta-power issues. The Hart and Valtysson chapters (Chapters 5 and 6, respectively) both approach a sense of meta-power in positing the transformation of cultural production. Valtysson writes about a "prosumer" who is simultaneously a producer and a consumer, and Hart underscores the transformative shift from analog to digital technologies in noting the differences on cultural production and distribution. Similarly, Sandra Braman (Chapter 4) accords explicit attention to various forms of power inherent in international art treaties that approximate the concept of meta-power noted here.

Interactions, especially those mediated through technology networks, are at the core of identity formation and change in individual and group interests. In a different context, I have argued that international negotiations understood as a set of iterative interactions not only allow for divergent interests to converge, as is instrumentally understood, but also allow for new interests to arise (Singh, 2008a, Chapters 2 and 8). As we speak of networked technologies in our current context, the possibilities for interaction and identity changes are enhanced. In fact, liberal theory lacks a theory of inter-actions, if it supposes the identity of actors and issues to be fixed through these interactions.

Communication theories have long dealt with epistemic possibilities aris-ing from technological interactions. Particular types of interactions facilitated by different media are at the heart of medium theory (Innis, 1950; McLuhan, 1962, 1964/1994). Anderson (1983) details how capitalism and print tech-nologies were ultimately responsible for circulation of representations in lan-guages, other than Latin, that would destabilize the influence of the Roman Catholic Church and lead to the rise of the nation state in Western Europe centered on local languages. Deibert (1997; 2002) delineates how technolo-gies privilege or marginalize particular groups (the distributive impact) while facilitating particular types of collective understandings (the epistemic impact). In general, Braman (2002; 2007) writes of virtual or genetic power as the power of technology to change the information base of identities.

Meta-power in its interactive sense should not be confused with soft-power (Nye, 2002), which deals with persuasion and attraction. Soft-power specifies identities and interests prior to interaction. Soft-power merely allows these interests to converge, a conversion to "our way of thinking" via the instrumentality of public or cultural diplomacy. Cynthia Schneider (Chapter 9) details the soft-power dimension of cultural diplomacy.

Power instrumentally viewed is a *resource*; it is a *process* when attending to meta-power. The process element details the way cultural products, technolo-gies, and industries change identities. Meta-power as a process deals not just with the types of epistemes but the way actors negotiate among the various epistemes. Garcia Canclini (1995/2005) posits hybridity as the result of the process of interventions in cultures as modernity and tradition confront each other. Hannerz (1992; 1996) posits creolization and emphasizes that cultures cannot be understood in territorial terms (1996). Galvan (2004) pos-its syncretism. In general, Appadurai's (1996; 2000) notion of "scapes" and Giddens' (1984) notion of "locales" as sites of interaction allow us to see the process of identity formation in cultures. Dennis Galvan (Chapter 17) speaks to the hybrid and syncretic features of meta-power in this volume. He con-nects cultural production, in his chapter on forms of joking kinship among the Wolof of Senegal, with the macro political economy context of property rights and economic development. Meta-power of cultural production then underlies or provides a window to processes of political economy that extend far beyond creative expressions and industries.

Cultural policies and governance

Processes of governance encompass formal institutions and rules and the intangible shared understandings fostered through various forms of power. Cultural policies in this volume refer to the institutions, rules, and intersubjective understandings that arise in the task of governance. Institutions may be both governmental and non-governmental, and may encompass international organizations such as the World Trade Organization and UNESCO (Chapters 7 and 8), regional organizations such as the European Union (Chapters 10 and 11), businesses (Chapter 12), foreign development agencies (Chapter 14), or film festivals (Chapter 16). International rules involve direct instruments such as trade measures at the international level or UNESCO's capacity building and guidance for cultural industries or heritage. At the national level they may include education policies, subsidies or grants to cultural industries, or measures promoting philanthropic policies or corporate giving. Cultural policies also shape and are shaped by intersubjective understandings. Instances include measures taken globally to thwart Hollywood's dominance, which may be perceived as a threat to local or national cultural identities. Another example is the collective memory and experience of colonialism, which has guided developing countries' quest for identity and voice. In this regard, Kevin Mulcahy (Chapter 13) and Isabelle Brianso (Chapter 14) attend to notions such as *cultural renaissance, recognition, and sustainability* in the context of the developing world.

As with other forms of global governance, international cultural policies reveal a complex landscape of multiple issues and actors intersecting at various levels. In such a shifting landscape, it is hard to isolate policies to a specific region or locality or speak to the efficacy of particular policies. Three broad trends are presented here, with some caution: salience of international cultural issues; institutional and instrumental hybridity in cultural policies; and the importance of cultural voice.

Salience of international cultural issues

Historically policies governing cultural industries and representations have hardly ever tended to gain the kind of national prominence accorded to foreign policy or defense. Cultural policies may still not be at the top of policy makers' agendas, but the importance of their influence on international and national politics is undeniable. Two broad forces, one rooted in political economy of globalization and the other in the latter's identity politics may be identified. Both are related to each other in interesting ways. For example, fears regarding Hollywood's dominance or the euphoria regarding Bollywood's ascendance are to be located in the political economy of globalization and attendant identity politics. This subsection tries to present each separately for analytical reasons.

Braman (Chapter 4) shows that various forms of conventions and treaties have governed cultural products through international and regional organizations. The issue burst forth on the world stage with the so-called audiovisual dispute at the multilateral negotiations of the General Agreements on Tariffs and Trade (GATT, now known as the WTO) at the Uruguay Round

(1986–94). Since then, the issue of cultural products exports, especially from the US, continues to generate prominent international debates. GATT articles had allowed an exception for film protections since 1946, but films as well as other cultural products—audiovisual in GATT/WTO jargon—were being negotiated for market liberalization during the Uruguay Round. The audiovisual negotiations resulted in a stalemate and in 1992–3 almost threatened the success of the Round. While 29 countries committed to market liberalization in audiovisual products, the European Union was allowed a trade exemption, known as a "Most-Favored Nation Exemption," from the agreement. Fearing that the issue was not dead, the Canadians and the French authorities organized an international coalition via UNESCO to institute the Declaration on Cultural Diversity in 2001 and the Universal Convention on the Protection and Promotion of Diversity of Cultural Expressions in 2005, which after being ratified by the requisite number of states, entered into force in 2007. Both UNESCO instruments, while not expressly crafted in political economy terms, seek to provide some international legal backing for protecting national cultural industries, especially films and television. The enforceability powers of UNESCO are weak, but the considerable international attention they have generated testifies to the importance of this issue in global politics. Carol Balassa (Chapter 8) details the US position during these negotiations. Balassa herself served with the US Trade Representative office, which negotiated trade agreements for the country in various capacities. She, therefore, provides an insider's perspective on the US position. Feigenbaum (Chapter 9) specifies an analytical rationale for the disputes located in technology and the US economic organization, and charts the policy space for future cultural options.

The GATT/WTO and the UNESCO debates outlined above are often presented as a battle between culture and commerce. Market liberalization or commerce, led by powerful global corporations, is seen as destroying or weakening local cultures and traditions (Goff, 2007; Miller and Yúdice, 2002; Magder, 2004). Others have pointed out that markets and exchange increase rather than decrease cultural diversity (Cowen, 2002; 1998; Singh, 2007; 2008c) or that there are policy options that preserve both (Voon, 2007; Singh, 2010). Whichever way the debate is parsed, it is hard to deny the importance of cultural identity. Precisely because cultural products touch upon sensitive issues of identity, national elites have often galvanized and marshaled considerable resources and people to protect particular notions of identity, especially national ones (Goff, 2000; Singh, 2010). Thus cultural identity and globalization is an important topic of study. Specific volumes dealing with cultural policy issues include UNESCO (2000) and Anheier and Raj (2008). Several chapters in this volume explore identity issues, but two of them, from the developed-country context, are worthy of mention because of their focus on regional and local levels. Patricia Dewey (Chapter 10) points out the importance of the idea of a European identity to the European Union project in general. In contrast, Jenny Johannisson (Chapter 11) details cultural policies at the municipal and regional levels within Sweden to show their connections with both Swedish and EU cultural policies. Furthermore, all the chapters on the developing world deal with the issue of the evolution of cultural identities upfront. In many ways, while the EU context shows the evolution of identity beyond the national context, the chapters on the developing world problematize the very notion of the "national" in postcolonial and globalization contexts. The subsection below on cultural voice will again return to this point.

Institutional and instrumental hybridity in cultural policies

Cultural policies are currently being enacted by a variety of actors at various levels of governance and present a mélange of measures. Most cultural policies historically grew out of state patronage policies usually enacted for the purposes of projecting national or state power or for national identity or unity. At present state patronage systems are complemented or overlapped by other forms of institutional support. The variety of measures available for support are sophisticated and not altogether that visible, especially in countries such as the US which do not have a ministry of culture.

Cummings and Katz (1987) note that beginning with the early twentieth century, creative workers appeared as a force or a class of workers unto itself. In the European context, the welfare state, that would emerge later, catered to providing for the creative class as a full-fledged member of any economy. Until the nineteenth century, creative work was part-time employment for most producers. In the US context, however, most creative workers survived through market means although government measures directly or indirectly did benefit cultural industries. In the US, direct support for the arts is provided from the National Endowment for the Arts (NEA) at the Federal level and through state and local arts agencies. Cherbo et al. (2008, pp. 18–19) note that in 2007 NEA provided $124 million while the state and local arts agencies provided for $363 million and $817 million respectively. Examples of indirect funding come from tax measures that might encourage corporate or individual philanthropy. Other examples of indirect funding include tax breaks given to industry or enactment of copyright measures.

The chapters that follow in this volume share and provide a few insights at the international level. While they do not offer a comprehensive assessment of the variety of measures in comparative contexts, they do pinpoint the broad forces of change explained here in a set of interrelated points. First, as pointed out earlier, international organizations and global governance mechanisms now offer a supra-national level of cultural policy making. Measures at this level range from trade and international copyright policies to capacity building and support for cultural industries (see Braman, Chapter 4). UNESCO is often derided or praised, depending on the source, as a world ministry of culture. Its programs range from specific conventions on tangible and intangible heritage to normative guidelines on support for cultural industries. Second, what follows from involvement of international organizations or from local governance spheres is considerable levels of intermixing in the same sphere of activity rather than a delineation of activities. Council of Europe provides funding and support for cultural industries at local and national levels (Dewey, Chapter 10), while the Region Västra Götaland and Region Skåne in Sweden formulate their cultural policies with input and support both from Sweden's Arts Council as well as the European Union (Johannisson, Chapter 11). Third, government actors and member-state driven international actors are joined by businesses and civil society involvements in the crafting of cultural policies. Kawashima (Chapter 12) details the role of business support for the arts in Japan, known as *méséna*. Kawashima characterizes *méséna* as playing a "major role in advancing cultural policy." In the case of India, private-sector television programming seeks and provides a cultural policy narrative for a generation of upwardly mobile people (Ganguly, Chapter 15). Fourth, it is becoming increasingly hard to generalize about the efficacy of particular cultural policy measures. As noted above, it is unclear if all international trade measures weaken cultural diversity. Furthermore, market means can step in to make up for the insufficiency of state patronage. Examples include the success of Bollywood films, Colombian publishing industry, or Music from Mali. Fifth, a subtle point made in several chapters is the recognition of new spaces of cultural policy making and new sites of cultural production. Johannisson (Chapter 11) writes of the complex spatial layers of cultural policy making at municipal and regional levels in Sweden. Champenois (Chapter 16) explains the role of the film festival as a platform for marginalized voices.

Finally, several chapters deal directly with the instrumentality of projecting state power or ideologies beyond its own borders. Public diplomacy has experienced a revival since September 11, 2001, rejuvenated after a period of rapid decline and depleting resources, particularly in the US. Cultural diplomacy— the projection of soft-power to persuade people in other countries to appreciate one's cultural values through exhibiting cultural products—is now a major component of cultural diplomacy. Former US Ambassador Cynthia Schneider (Chapter 9) notes that cultural diplomacy humanizes interstate relations and need not be so concerned with involving cultural producers who have a favorable view only of their home country. Schneider cites Dizzy Gillespie, who when briefed for a tour by the State department noted: "I've got three hundred years of briefing. I know what they have done to us and I'm not going to make any excuses."

Cultural diplomacy is an explicit cultural-policy instrument. Other instruments of interstate relations may be more indirect and intangible. UNESCO, for example, crafts norms of cultural production that may reveal the power or preferences of only a few states. Brianso (Chapter 14) notes that the space within which cultural policy for world heritage conservation is conceived is divorced from the actual heritage sites. She especially highlights the role of French cultural officials in creating such cultural heritage from afar. At the level of ideology, Luke (Chapter 3), Valtysson (Chapter 6), Mulcahy (Chapter 13), and Galvan (Chapter 17) caution us about noticing broad structural forces that bind acts of cultural expressions, production, and dissemination. The power of the arts, therefore, works both ways: it may enhance or limit people's possibilities. I turn now to the recognition of the possibilities of finding emancipatory cultural voices.

Importance of the cultural voice

Cultural industries seek to represent cultural conditions, hence their socio-logical importance must be located in what Paulo Freire (1970/2000) termed the "cultural voice," or the ability of people, especially those living under oppression to be able to "perceive the reality of their oppression not as closed world form from which there is no exit, but as a limiting situation they can transform" (p. 49). It is cultural representations that offer new possibilities to a set of people. From the ancient Greek comedy *Lysistrata* to the tragic film *Harvey Milk*, art has provided a window to oppression. Especially in the case of the developing world, cultural expressions and representations reflect on and address past and present oppressive practices.

Freire offers the concept of "dialogic praxis," which entails a combination of thought, action, and transformation. The oppressed can be liberated only through this pedagogy that enables them to find their "cultural voice." Similarly, Appadurai (2004) emphasizes that global networks now allow for global imaginaries that make possible both "politics of recognition" and "capacity to aspire." Culture then becomes "a dialogue between aspirations and sedimented traditions" (p. 84). Separately, I have explored how globalized cultural forms, even when produced through market means, allow for groups to find a cultural voice (Singh, 2007).[2] These cultural forms while resolutely hybrid are also about self-confidence and recognition.

The search for a cultural identity, for example in the European Union, must be distinguished from a cultural voice, which, at least in Freire's sense of the term, is situated in the context of oppression. However, it would be foolhardy to believe that the context is only applicable to the developing world; the appellation of cultural voice in the context of the developing world offers one among many possibilities of its application.

Two themes stand out in the chapters that follow: the location of voice and its hybridity and creolization. Kevin Mulcahy (Chapter 13) begins his chapter with the concept of *coloniality*, "an experience involving dominating influence by a stronger power over a subject state." Given the legacy of coloniality, he then locates the "cultural renaissance" in post-revolution Mexico in 1920 and the current "cultural revivalism" in the Arab and Islamic states. These practices reclaim and reposition cultural identities lost through oppression. Isabelle Brianso provides somewhat of a counterpoint in noting how cultural power from UNESCO and France continues to be exercised in the valorization of particular heritage practices in Morocco and Cambodia. Mulcahy himself is open to such possibilities in his evocation of Edward Said's (1979) concept of Orientalism, which positions the oppressed, in his case the Orient, with inferiority wherein the people are fundamentally incapable of tending to themselves. Cultural authority in the Brianso case belongs to the Occident.

Both Mulcahy and Brianso add an important postscript to the movement started in 1976 by UNESCO—known as the New World Information and Communication Order (NWICO). NWICO advocacy, in parallel with other moves in the United Nations, questioned vociferously for over a decade both the content and the one-way flow of negative news and images from the developing world to the developed world. Studies showed that media corporations from the developed world controlled most media conduits and content from the global South to North, which were empirically calculated and documented (see overview in Pavlic and Hamelink, 1985). In fact, it was NWICO and similar advocacy, in large part supported by USSR and Cold War politics, which prompted the US to leave UNESCO in 1986 (it rejoined in 2004).

Many chapters in this volume address hybridity; the chapter by Galvan contextualizes cultural hybridity within macro practices of political economy and social evolution. Galvan (Chapter 17) also takes relations of power and domineering discourses as its points of entry to examine the evolution of hybrid practices in political economy and everyday life in colonial and postcolonial Senegal. Ending the volume with this chapter is appropriate. Cultural hybridity, and not some notion of an authentic or essentialized cultural value, then offers the possibility of a cultural voice.

Conclusion

This brief introduction notes that a focus on cultural industries and technologies allows us to examine both the instrumental and the transformative or constitutive logic of cultural power and identities. Cultural power and policies are keys to understanding ontologies of global politics that are gaining currency these days. I am referring here to multiperspectival governance (Ruggie, 1993; Rosenau, 2003), multiple identities (Sen, 2006), competition and adaptation to rival epistemes and organizational forms (Keck and Sikkink, 1998; Spruyt, 1996). While the connections between cultural identity and policies inform all the chapters, those detailing policies in the developing world are presented in the context of the possibilities for a "cultural voice." Cultural industries and technologies offer tremendous possibilities for cultural voice, assertions of identities, and economic growth. Nevertheless as with other kinds of politics, governance mechanisms must confront the material resource and ideologies of power holders.

Notes

1. UNESCO relied on customs receipts. If royalty receipts are thrown in, the estimates could quadruple. For example, nearly half the total revenues for the motion picture industry in the US come from foreign sales and exports (Vogel, 2007, pp. 82–3).
2. Here cultural voice arises through commercial and market driven exchanges. I am well aware of Freire's and other scholars' misgivings about capitalism but I assert that there is no proven epistemological reason that a cultural voice cannot be developed through such exchanges (see Singh, 2008b). Garcia Canclini (2000), Appadurai (2000), and many other scholars are reaching similar conclusions, even if with reservations.

Part I Politics, Power, Technologies

2

Cultural Policy and the Political Nature of Culture

Carole Rosenstein

When Obama launched into his story with, "Because I *love* pie," a woman out in that sea of cheering, laughing people shouted back, "*I'll* make you pie, baby!" and to the general hooting laughter the candidate returned, "Oh yeah, you gonna *make* me pie?" Then, after a beat, amid even more raucous laughter, and several other female voices shouting out invitations, "You gonna make me *sweet potato pie?*" More shouts and laughter. "*All* you gonna make me pie?"

"Well you know I love sweet potato pie. And I think what we're going to have to do here"—and the laughter and the shouting rose and as it did his voice rose above it—"what we're going to have to *do* here is have a sweet potato pie *contest* ... That's right. And in this contest, I'm gonna be the *judge.*" The laughter rose and you could hear not only the women but the deep laughter of the men taking delight in the *double entendre* that was not only about the women and their laughing, teasing offers and about their pie that that lanky confident smiling young man knew how to eat and enjoy and judge, but even more now, amazingly, as people came one by one to recognize, about something else. To those people gathered in Vernon Park that bright sun-drenched morning, it was an even more titillating and more pleasurable *double entendre,* for it was most clearly about something they'd never had but hoped and dreamed of having and now had begun to believe they were within the shortest of short distances of finally tasting. "Because you all know," their candidate told them, "that I *know* sweet potato pie."

—Danner (2008, 16)

Politics are cultural, as Barack Obama's campaign and election reminded us again and again. This is true in many and diverse ways. Obama affiliated with and motivated African Americans by selecting from a repertoire of cultural items and styles, by talking not just about pie but about *sweet potato pie*. He displayed his profound cultural skills when creating legible metaphors such as this one Danner parses about—pie as the good life deferred and finally achieved. He also knew how to instantiate and to perform a powerful narrative genre of American culture about the progressive drive to overcome bigotry.

That politics are cultural is evident. Cultural beliefs and values ground ideas about why and to what extent human nature demands governing and what counts as private as opposed to public and legitimately governable. Culture was fundamental to Cicero's ideas about the persuasive power of oratory (see Remer, 1999). Studies of state propaganda, state-sponsored cultural programming and state promotion of heritage and regulation of artistic expression clearly demonstrate the conjoining of culture with power, particularly in totalitarian states. But culture is political as well, and this has perhaps been less well recognized and explored. Relationships between culture and power also can be traced by studying the ways in which individuals and groups employ culture in order to develop "strategies for action" (Swidler, 1986; 1995) that project their voices in the public sphere and propel their priorities in political contests. To understand culture as political in this way, it is necessary to adopt a more sophisticated and nuanced notion of culture than is typically found outside of anthropology, the sociology of culture and cultural studies.

The culture concept is complex. Not only is the concept complex, the phenomena it denotes morph as relations between human groups change. In everyday contexts, culture is taken for granted. In contexts of contact and negotiation, culture loses its transparency. That is why culture has come to prominence during critical shifts in globalization such as past innovations in transportation, the contemporary revolution in digital technologies and the impending climate crisis. But culture also carries enormously powerful folk connotations of autochthony and immutability; it seems organic, inherent, essential and inalterable. You can lose it but you can't change it. This combination of a seemingly inescapable complexity, an almost polar opposition between analytic and popular usage of the term and the kind of fuzzy mysticism surrounding it makes for a blend particularly distasteful to a predictive social science. Avoiding the culture concept, political scientists instead may tend to employ a notion of "nations" or "peoples" to describe groups affiliated with a configuration of traditions, languages and region. These concepts mesh well with the study of states and migrations and draw much more directly on the folk connotations of culture as a given, a factor relatively unhampered by history or government.

However, such notions of culture are inadequate in investigating how culture comes to be embodied in particular objects, texts and practices and how social actors employ such cultural items, styles, metaphors and narratives in ways that manipulate cultural assumptions and affiliations to specific ends. To comprehend culture in this way, it is necessary to see culture less as a quality that is given than as a resource that can be developed.

Cultural resources

Advanced thinking about culture as a resource can be found in theories of cultural capital. In a brief but important essay, economist David Throsby discusses cultural capital as an embodiment of cultural value. He writes:

> An essential element of culture ... is its role as an expression of group or collective aspects of people's behavior, as demonstrated in their activities and belief systems. Thus, in broad terms something can be said to be of cultural value if it contributes to these shared elements of human experience. ... Although there may not be agreement between individuals on the cultural value of specific items, there may be sufficient consensus in particular cases to be able to speak of a "society's" cultural valuation of items of cultural significance for the purposes, for example, of ranking them according to a collective judgment.
>
> (1999, 5)

Throsby's definition of cultural value raises the question of where to look for evidence of such "rankings according to a *collective* judgment" [with emphasis added]. Price is one possible measure. Various forms of contingent valuation study have been tried. While participation data provide the best proxy available, value is reflected not only in what people do, but also in what they believe to be worthy and useful, and even in what they feel socially compelled to claim as being of value. Unfortunately, very little comparable data has been gathered in the US on "public opinion" about cultural activity (Robinson and Filicko, 2000). Further, a whole sociology of culture shows that forms that come to be recognized and legitimized as "art" or "culture" are socially constructed through an immensely complex interplay of markets, institutions and discourses, networks of elites and experts; the status of these forms as collectively valued is deeply unsettled.

Bourdieu shows that rankings of cultural value reflect segmented, typically class-based judgments. In *Distinction* (1984), Bourdieu elaborately sets out the cultural marks through which social agents are identified and self-identify as members of the working, middle or upper class as they engage in social practice: knowledge of opera, a taste for red wine, leisure time spent reading novels or attending soccer matches, keeping a cozy house or a clean house. While all social agents affiliate to such recognized sets of habits and tastes in order to situate themselves in social space and refer to sets of recognized habits and tastes in order to situate others, all *habitu*s and taste regimes do not represent cultural capital for Bourdieu. Upper-class dispositions serve as mechanisms through which upper-class agents can distance themselves from others and define the class positions of others. This ability to enforce social distance and to "make the world" of categories in which others must operate are forms of symbolic violence that both mirror other kinds of power and oppression and underwrite the value of cultural capital. Institutional-structural constraints—a prime example is the education system—curtail the ability of middle- and working-class *habitus* and taste regimes to function as mechanisms of symbolic violence, making them less than viable forms of cultural capital.

What, then, might be *cultural* about cultural value, in the sense of the holistic, collective and shared, public or common values that Throsby stipulates? While Bourdieu sees taste and value as constituted through interactive social practice, he does not allow that values can properly be conceived as *shared* rather than *compelled*. After Bourdieu, it is easy to begin to wonder whether Throsby's concept of cultural capital is viable. If so, it must be developed while continuing to acknowledge the point that cultural capital is unevenly distributed.

A notion of capital (in whatever form) as something that draws its value from truly shared rather than compelled evaluative frameworks can be traced in Robert Putnam's work on social capital (2000; 2003). Social capital, according to Putnam, is an outcome of all sorts of associational activity. Members of country clubs and members of bowling leagues both build social capital. Different associations may result in different economic or social outcomes for individuals and groups. However, in making an argument about the importance of social capital to democracy, Putnam focuses on the aspects of social capital that have positive societal outcomes even when social capital is unevenly distributed. In this optimistic portrayal, associational activity builds *sociability*: the trust, openness, honesty, cooperativeness, tolerance, and respect that enhance civic participation and foster democracy. Sociability is a resource held by both individuals and communities (cf. Portes, 1998). The aspects of social capital that contribute to exclusion and social stratification—both at the individual level through uneven social capital accumulation and at the societal level through the privileging of stasis over change—are by and large left unaccounted by Putnam. At the same time, Putnam's differentiation between the lineaments and outcomes of particular associations and the more abstract notion of sociability as a resource is useful.

John Dewey conceived of cultural resources in ways that resonate with this notion of sociability as a resource. (Dewey's relevance to a full historicization and theorization of social capital has been noted as well, see Farr, 2004.) Dewey focuses on the notion of experience, which he elaborates as the dynamic relation between a human being and the natural and social environment. In some later writings he actually replaced the term "experience" with the term "culture." Dewey's framing of individuals in context reflects his pragmatist philosophy; experience, for Dewey, never inheres in t individual, but rather presupposes and entails a context of interaction, sociability and community. His pragmatist approach to value is similar, holding that value is a function of neither individual preference nor a purely social construct. Rather, value is a quality situated in events. In fact, he is less concerned with instantiated *value* than with processes of *evaluation*.

The kinds of capacities that are built by and through what Dewey calls experience are awareness, reflection and critical judgment, communication, flexibility, commitment to process, recognition of the interdependence and commonalities among diverse elements. The kinds of situations that Dewey identified as maximizing the potential to build these capacities are those focused on arts, learning, and civic participation. And, as he argues in his masterwork *Art as Experience* (1959), first among these are the arts, broadly drawn to encompass and even privilege what Dewey calls the arts of the everyday or commonplace. These contexts are particularly powerful because they enable individuals to confront diversity and conflict and to engage in processes of reintegration and harmonization, processes that are fundamental to aesthetic experience, to education and to democratic governance (Mattern, 1999).

In his essay "The Capacity to Aspire: Culture and the Terms of Recognition," Arjun Appadurai draws on a similar notion of cultural capacity. He notes that while culture has "been viewed as a matter of one or another kind of pastness—the keywords here are habit, custom, heritage, tradition," culture also frames orientations to the future (2004). Appadurai argues that what he calls the cultural "capacity to aspire" is a facility to connect individual wants and needs to cultural norms about what constitutes "the good life, health and happiness" and more broadly to belief systems about "life and death, the nature of worldly possessions, the significance of material assets over social relations, the value of peace or warfare." This facility he describes in terms of narrative and performance. For example, "Gandhi's life, his fasting, his abstinence, his bodily comportment, his ascetical style, his crypto-Hindu use of non-violence and of peaceful resistance were all tremendously successful because they mobilized a local palette of performances and precursors" (2004, 6). Individuals and groups institute change by creating powerful stories that explain, persuade, and address their needs and wants in terms of norms and belief systems. This capacity to aspire, and the hope and confidence it generates, thus, are directly related to economic growth, poverty reduction, and public action.

The arts relate to such cultural skills because art forms can instantiate and condense such cultural principles (Geertz, 1976). Moreover, performances that demonstrate cultural skill by referencing artistic form are a mode of power:

> It is clear that the aesthetics of self-presentation ... often follows principles that are given more formal expression in artistic performance.

If a sheep thief cannot steal with flair, who wants him as an ally? If a politician cannot tell elegant falsehoods that are obviously just that, who would join a party made vulnerable by such weakness? ... To craft a good performance "is to engage in social practice." And to engage in social practice is to commit oneself to a politics of personal value, often translatable into larger idioms of power.

(Herzfeld, 2001, 286)

Like other kinds of resources, cultural resources can be and often are unevenly distributed. Sociologists of culture have tested Bourdieu's theories to find that rather than exhibiting any particular taste regime, US elites exhibit characteristics such as cultural engagement and openness to diversity while lower-status groups in the US exhibit more narrow cultural tastes and interests (see Peterson and Simkus, 1992; Peterson and Kern, 1996; Bryson, 1996). Assessing the value of such cultural resources is an arena of contest and negotiation just as are all other kinds of cultural evaluation. Is it "better" to exhibit tolerance or intolerance? Is openness to new experience preferable or statement of personal preference? The point here is that these characteristics are modes of *social practice* rather than items of cultural form and that understanding culture in this way firmly integrates culture with social and political life.

Policy and the distribution of cultural resources

Policies impact the distribution of cultural resources: policies project and promote certain cultural values and narratives as being shared and public; they shape the ways in which people gain access to places where legitimate and valorized expressions of this shared public culture are created; and they can provide opportunities for people to develop their capabilities to critique and restate such shared and public values in terms that resonate with their own experiences. Policies do this in many and complex ways, some of which are more readily recognizable as resting within the domain of cultural policy and some less so: through arts education agendas; in cultural diplomacy programs; through the development of government-run cultural institutions such as public broadcasters, libraries and museums; through grant-making programs; through censorship; through copyright law; through trade agreements. In the remainder of this chapter, I will elaborate on one example by discussing ways in which policies that regulate access to public space impact the distribution of cultural resources.

Voice in the public sphere depends not only on the capacity to produce compelling and culturally appropriate narratives and performances. It also depends on access to sites where these stories can be seen and heard, that is, the public sphere. Habermas (1989) conceived the public sphere as an open commons for rational discourse and deliberation on key issues of civic concern and topics of enlightened interest. But analysts of cyberspace and mass media have shown that contemporary public spheres are restricted in a variety of ways: by communications and media policy, privatization and consolidation, lack of access to technology and education, dominant linguistic practices, nested networks of participants. Because these restricting policies and forces also affect culture, they have grown central to cultural policy studies. The entire commercial, nonprofit and informal cultural sector—including audiences, artists, museums, performers, presenters, scholars, archives, universities, and presses—is seriously impacted by the regulation of media outlets, the Internet, and digital technologies, and by intellectual property and copyright law (Lessig, 2005; Ivey, 2008).

Policy also impacts culture through regulation of the public sphere in its material as opposed to its virtual manifestations. Cultural studies first began to suggest the ways in which this happens through analyses of institutions of public culture. In her groundbreaking book *Civilizing Rituals: Inside Public Art Museums*, Carol Duncan writes that

> The public museum makes visible the public it claims to serve. It produces the public as a visible entity by literally providing it a defining frame and giving it something to do. ... To control a museum means precisely to control the representation of a community and some of its highest, most authoritative truths. It also means the power to define and rank people, to declare some as having a greater share than others in the community's common heritage—in its very identity. It is they who are best prepared to recognize the history presented by the program and who have most cultivated the skills to produce the particular kind of associations or, as the case may be, the aesthetic attention, implicitly demanded by the museum's isolated objects. In short, those who best understand how to use art in the museum environment are also those on whom the museum ritual confers this greater and better identity.
>
> (1995, 93–102)

Less attention has been given to the public sphere in its physical embodiment in spaces like plazas, town centers, parks, landscapes, and streetscapes. Several forces fundamentally shape the character of these kinds of public spaces. Identified primarily by social theorists interested in the transformation of cities during the period of monopoly capitalism's globalization, these forces include privatization, suburbanization, gentrification, and spectacularization. "The city," writes geographer Edward Soja, "came to be seen not only in terms of its role as a center of production and accumulation, but also as the control point for the reproduction of capitalist society in terms of labor power, exchange, and consumption" (1980, 210). Elaborated by Lefebvre, David Harvey, Manuel Castells and other Marxist analysts of urban space, the city becomes "a consumption machine, transforming luxuries into needs, facilitating suburbanization and its associated privatized consumption ... and working toward the segregation [or] territorial fragmentation of the working class" (Soja, 1980, 216). Since cities are centers for cultural institutions, artists, art worlds, creative industries, and street-life, this transforming role of the city from center of production to center of consumption has important implications for culture (see Deutsch, 1996).

A range of policies that regulate access to public spaces in cities directly impact the ways in which people can develop and employ their cultural resources. Relevant policies include not only obvious ones such as public art programs. They also include policies less obviously related to cultural activity. For example, street performers, parade organizers, neighborhood festivals are regulated by complex and sometimes burdensome licensing and permitting laws and procedures. These artists and organizations depend on public space as a primary performance or distribution venue and so rely on licensing and permitting policies to gain access to their audiences and markets. In Chicago, Red Moon Theater directs a Halloween street performance for which local schools, community organizations and neighbors create puppets, lanterns and choreographed processions. The event has developed into a large-scale public festival, demanding a parade license, and permits for outdoor toilets, street closure, and trash removal. Red Moon Theater's use of themes from the Mexican Day of the Dead became a subject of controversy, prompting some in the Latino community to lobby against the issuance of a license for the event. Fundamentalist Christians have staged a counter-spectacle, prompting a more visible police presence. In New York, where there is a ten-year waiting list for vending licenses, artists have protested the increasingly restrictive enforcement of sidewalk vending regulations. In Boston, grassroots activists have fought for more than 20 years for licensing regulations that would allow street performers and buskers full access to street corners, subway platforms, and central plazas without interference from police. Many permitting and licensing regulations were instituted in the early nineteenth century to control begging and public drunkenness, and are governed by public servants from outside the cultural sector. They are typically administered by people who have little experience adjudicating conflicts over free speech.

The role of police in implementing policy presents a particular challenge. During the late 1990s, police in San Francisco were hassling audiences at outdoor dance concerts and those leaving clubs in the early-morning hours, raiding late-night clubs, and arresting local DJs and club-owners to an unprecedented extent. A coalition was formed to act as a liaison between police, neighborhood associations, and the late-night community. They successfully advocated for legislation that removed responsibility for the late-night permitting process from the police department to a separate agency, the San Francisco Entertainment Commission. In the US, police have the power to disrupt the use of public space for political and cultural expression for reasons such as excessive noise, suspicion of drug use or drug dealing, suspicion of the presence of illicit firearms, traffic violations, disorderly conduct, and other unspecified nuisance. Elsewhere, these regulations are harsher and more consolidated; in the UK, for example, the notorious Criminal Justice and Public Order Act of 1994 gave police the power to arrest citizens suspected of preparing to attend a rave. In the period after the World Trade Organization protests in Seattle in 1999, artists and cultural organizations known to have participated in the public demonstrations and protests were subject to police intimidation through harassment, surveillance, and unnecessary police visits. In an important case, the studios of Spiral Q Puppet Theater were declared a fire hazard in an attempt by Philadelphia police to prevent them from participating in demonstrations at the 2000 Republican National Convention.

Lack of regulation or lax enforcement also can impact access to public space. In Houston, Texas, the city's lack of zoning has meant that large studios and alternative venues were relatively easy to site within both central parts of the city and residential neighborhoods. Lack of enforcement of existing regulations has enabled them to stay even when, for example, performance venues exceed allowable capacity or when studios are used for large-scale construction or as artists' illegal live/work space. Similar situations can be found in other cities where vibrant cultural centers had grown in districts where zoning regulations were ambiguous or enforcement negligible. While lack of enforcement is characteristic of many poorer neighborhoods and deindustrializing districts, as these areas increase in real estate value, enforcement increases apace. Around the US, previously unenforced zoning regulations have been used to displace artists and cultural organizations from redevelopment districts and gentrifying neighborhoods. In Boston's Fort Point District of old shipping depots and warehouses, for example, the city's redevelopment of the waterfront displaced a thriving community of large studio workshops and a range of alternative arts venues that had developed in a past environment of permissive zoning enforcement.

These examples were gathered as part of a 2001–2 study of culture workers conducted by the Urban Institute (see Rosenstein, 2004). Data from that study indicate that artists and organizations that depend on public space as a primary performance or distribution venue feel the impacts of policies regulating public space with the greatest force. These are not large arts institutions and the "professional" artists employed in them but rather tend to be smaller organizations, alternative organizations, avant-garde and ethnic arts organizations, political artists, folk and immigrant artists, and artists of color. These asymmetries are reinforced by other policy mechanisms such as tax exemption laws that promote nonprofits to invest in capital development and the tendency for government funds to be used for capital expenditures. Those mechanisms mean that larger, institutionalized cultural activities grow increasingly "built" while smaller organizations are increasingly pushed out of central urban areas. The regulation of public space, therefore, has important implications for cultural democracy. As a vibrant civic culture depends on maintaining the public sphere as a commons, a vibrant public culture depends on free, fair, and liberal representation in and access to the public sphere.

As this example illustrates, one thing that is valuable about the study of how cultural expressions are produced, distributed, promoted and regulated is the light such study can shine on culture as constituted—as opposed to given—within social arenas where expressions and their meanings and values are contested and negotiated. Even though cultural policy studies can show how culture is shaped by politics, they don't always do so. For example, in the US, cultural policy study has given considerable—sometimes seemingly exclusive—attention to the value of the arts to public life. The arts have been promoted as having inherent value. The economic impacts of the arts have been measured and the arts promoted as development tools. And the contributions of the arts to social capital have been articulated and documented. What is striking about this terrain is that while the aesthetic, economic and social dimensions are accounted for, the dimension of culture is curiously lacking. That is to say, almost completely absent from this set of approaches to evaluating the arts as public goods is the analytic domain within which to consider the contributions the arts make to dispositions, systematic models for explaining difference, structures of value and belief. A large part of the difficulty here is an implicit assumption operating in cultural policy study that arts are simply direct indicators or examples such dispositions, values and beliefs, that is, of culture. Perhaps a more developed dialogue between cultural policy studies and political science would provoke the abandonment of such depoliticized notions of culture. If so, it is only for the better.

3

The Arts, Culture, and Civil Society: Power Stations in the Grids of Governance

Timothy W. Luke

In a time of rampant economic crisis and technological disruption, why should one care about the play of cultural industries and policies as political forces? The discipline of political science in the US has often given these topics short shrift, but that response is not attuned to the important roles played by culture industries today in the workings of power. This brief set of thoughts, then, constitutes a serious call to revisit such theoretical and practical engagements to highlight the always-crucial significance of culture in politics.

The idea of culture industries as discrete formations securely nestled in economy and society as the forces of production was introduced into wider currency by Max Horkheimer and Theodor W. Adorno (1976). Seeking answers for the relative quiescence of the working class in their acceptance of both commercial exploitation and fascist rule everywhere in Germany during the 1930s, and then finding what they regarded as comparable phenomena embedded all across the US while in exile during the 1940s, Adorno and Horkheimer approached the sustained production and active circulation of cultural goods and services as advanced means for accommodating otherwise restive groups within the reproduction of advanced capitalism.

While others had toyed with comparable ideas before Adorno and Horkheimer, whether it was Antonio Gramsci (2008), Leo Lowenthal (1961) or Thorsten Veblen (1998), more recent critics, such as Roland Barthes (1972), Jean Baudrillard (1996), or Marshall McLuhan (2005), make parallel claims in their intellectual projects about culture and the economy. Yet, Pierre Bourdieu (1984; 1988; 1999; 1993) has conducted many quite remarkably wide-ranging studies of culture as a normalizing industrial formation. Whether writing about art, television, education or decorative goods, Bourdieu's understanding of culture as a new framework for capital, industry, and labor provides a crucial contribution to any study of this critical research thematic.

Today in the US, a planned build-up of cultural industries is frequently touted as the new royal road to global supremacy, national power, and local growth. To some, it appears as "soft power" (Nye, 2004); for others, it morphs into "public" art, culture, or science (Appadurai, 2000; Latour, 2004; Jameson, 1992); and for still others, it is the basis for the "classy creativity" needed to forestall the flight of "the creative class" (Florida, 2002) from collapsing rustbelt cities. As ageless wisdom is rehabbed to serve as output for "knowledge industries," and treasured knowledge is continuously reprocessed in data mining, product semantics or meme design, cultural policies clearly have become a fulcrum for neoliberal collaborative governance experts to leverage complex transnational job-creation alliances to compete more effectively in global markets (Harvey, 1989). These are but a few concrete instances of why political scientists should care about culture now, but such issues also are the contemporary manifestations of more enduring political questions about the interplay of art, culture, and civil society with government (Lyotard, 1984; Ong, 1999; Robertson, 1992; Jameson, 1992; Hardt and Negri, 2000; Virilio, 1995).

By and large, American political scientists, however, have tended to ignore cultural industries, science communities, and new technologies. Consequently, truly sustained scholarly attention to these formations have been given far more prominence in other disciplines, like geography, cultural studies, sociology, international relations, communications, social informatics, and anthropology (Cassierer, 1955/57; McLuhan, 1962; Foucault, 1970; Lefebvre, 1984; Bourdieu, 1993; Rabinow, 1996; Kittler, 1999). Still a few experts in political studies have not ignored cultural industries (Marcuse, 1964; Agger, 1990; Baudrillard, 1996; Deibert, 1997) and some of my work focuses on the conjunction of art, culture and civil society as a concern for politics (Luke, 2002; 1992; 1989; 1985; 1983). If one pulls together all of this research, one key finding emerges from these analyses, namely, that the arts, culture, and civil society are power stations in the grids of governance. In turn, they merit attention as epistemic, ethical, and experimental structures for communicative, discursive or informational interactions that police both thought and action. Indeed, when exploring the linkages between cultural policy and national power, one could consider cultural industries, technologies, and policies as "base load" power stations for sustaining governance and its grids of control through images, values, and beliefs.

In his "*Omnes et Singulatim*: Towards a Criticism of 'Political Reason,'" Michel Foucault advances an analysis of self-identity and collective organization rooted in styles of "individualizing power," which cannot be divorced from culture and technics. Against "the hard power" of the state with its administration and bureaucracy, he explores some contours in soft power by probing various "techniques oriented towards individuals and intended to rule them in a continuous and permanent way" (1979, 227). Foucault identifies them, first, as pastoral, and, then later, as political power in different modes of governance. This yearning to reorganize the pastoral relations of soft power more politically gained new creative expression in modernity as aristocratic rulers and their magistrates began differentiating between

the "reason of state" and the "theory of police." Contemporary
the "police state" rooted in the history of Nazi Germany, the Soviet Unic..
or Communist China truly rankle many political scientists when Foucault
asserts this point. His sense of "policing," however, draws from the early
modern distinction between *die Polizei* and *die Politik*. Here, *Politik* "is basically a negative task. It consists of the state's fighting against its internal and
external enemies. The *Polizei*, however, always serve at a positive task: it has
to foster both citizen's lives and the state's strength" (Foucault, 1979, 252).

As King (1972) records, Turguet de Mayenne argues in his odd cameralist
text, *Aristo-Democratic Monarchy*, that the police should be regarded as the
best magistrates of soft power, cultural policy, and technological life itself.
Policing, in fact, for Turget, "branches out into all of the people's conditions,
everything they do or undertake," because, like culture, "the police includes
everything" (Foucault, 1979, 248). Cultural industry and policy are essentially at their core "policing practices." As Foucault suggests,

> What are the aims pursued? They fall into two categories. First, the police
> has to do with everything providing the city with adornment, form, and
> splendour. Splendour denotes not only the beauty of a state ordered to
> perfection; but also its strength, its vigour. Second, the police's other
> purpose is to foster working and trading relations between men, as well
> as aid and mutual help. There again, the word Turquet uses is important:
> the police must ensure "communication" among men, in the broad sense
> of the word. Otherwise, men wouldn't be able to live; or their lives would
> be precarious, poverty-stricken, and perpetually threatened.
>
> And here, we can make out what is, I think, and important idea. As
> a form of rational intervention wielding political power over men, the
> role of the police is to supply them with a little extra life; and by so
> doing, supply the state with a little extra strength. This is done by con-
> trolling "communication", i.e., the common activities of individuals
> (work, production, exchange, accommodation).
>
> (Foucault, 1979, 248)

Here art and culture can appear as both splendorous adornment and
communicative interaction: these practices are "cybernetic moments" of
governance via informational/semiotic/aesthetic mediations to foster bio-
political capacities (Foucault, 1980). Without such policies, governance leaves
humans to endure lives that are precarious, impoverished, and threatened.

In a world where many see only *The Clash of Civilizations* (Huntington,
1996), political science should neither forget these insights from Foucault
about government nor neglect the role of culture industries, technologies, or
policies in governance. Seeing global alignments between nations changing
from those denominated in the register of competing secular ideologies to
ones defined by conflicting cultures, Huntington concocts a vision for world

order which strangely has projected—unconsciously or consciously—many prevailing prejudiced views of many—both inside and outside of the US. In fact, for those devoted to waging culture wars in the US, contemporary political crises dressed up by Huntington as "a clash of civilizations" have proven to be rich rhetorical resources for many different bands of culture warriors over the past decade. In this guise, the policing qualities of culture are cast, ironically, fostering greater development of the state's citizens and building greater strength for the state.

Samuel Huntington's more recent work, *Who are We?* (2004), for example, raises this question amidst what he sees as clashing civilizations caught up in the conflict of cultures. On this contested terrain, cultural industries in the everyday life of each society's collective consciousness cannot be ignored (Bhabha, 1994). At least since the eighteenth century, culture industries have been, in fact, producing many different answers in response to Huntington's question. It is from industrialized cultural practices and beliefs that individuals and groups learn who "we" are, how we "are" as we are, and whom the "who" in question as well as who "they" are, how "they" became "them," and whom defined "them" for "us." Yet, the better answers to such queries come from those who turn culture industries against themselves. Those moves undercut the pat acceptance of the clash of civilizations thesis and then embrace the often-civilizing influences found in clashing new technologies as they clatter through cultural policies, practices, and projects.

If culture operates—in accord with Foucault's claim—as a *Polizeimacht* without *Polizeibeamter*, then cultural practices, movements or structures essentially work more elusively in "plain-clothes" or, even better, "undercover." Metaphorically, they are always presences, effects or programs branching out to observe, control or assess all peoples' conditions in everything they undertake. Cameralist culture, following de Mayenne, must provision the polity with adornment, form and splendor to assure its vigor, strength, and perfection. And, under these same canopies of control, popular and elite culture today carries communicative interactions necessary for work, trade, and aid. The discriminant functions of "we-ness," "who-ness" or "are-ness" in Huntington's existential self-examination always must be initialized, and then finalized, around culture as clusters of comity and/or enmity.

For some, culture comes as pure white cubes in which truth is already regarded, as Latour (2004) would have it, as a closed black box with no holes, no doubts, and no contraries. For others, like Brown (1998), Dosse (1999) or Greenfeld (2001), culture rises as thick gray mists. Almost by its nature, culture cannot ever be captured inside any finally closed blackened boxes (Bourdieu, 1984). Instead of choosing "either/or," one must accept "both/and," because new cultural developments foster and fuel, in part, the civilizing qualities of continuing clashes between the powerful and the powerless (Berger and Luckmann, 1966).

These formulae for culture are important for Huntington, who asserts everyone requires, and mostly already holds "some sort of simplified map of reality, some theory, concept, model paradigm" simply in order to "to think seriously about the world, and act effectively in it" (1996, 29). Of course, he aims his arguments at policy audiences working in the fields of diplomacy, international politics or foreign affairs, but this ideologically charged vision of a "reality map" basically is "culture." And cultural industries plainly are generating many plots and ploys out of such definitive epistemic first-principles. "For in the back of our minds," Huntington believes, "are hidden assumptions, biases, and prejudices that determine how we perceive reality, what facts we look at it, and how we judge their importance and merits" (1996, 30). Without saying so, and with little consciousness of what his claims imply, Huntington illustrates the importance of the culture industry in contemporary global affairs. In any society, as Cassierer (2000) argues, the technologies of cultural industry and policy constantly shape individual and collective subjectivity.

While they are not the only institutions involved in such epistemic and ethical engineering, cultural products and policies provide explicit or implicit models that enable individuals and groups to:

1 order and generalize about reality;
2 understand causal relationships among phenomena;
3 anticipate and, if we are lucky predict future developments;
4 distinguish what is important from what is unimportant; and,
5 show us what paths we should take to achieve our goals.

(Huntington, 1996, 30)

Cultural formations, as Huntington's analysis suggests, are enduring concrete totalities in which "the overall way of life of a people" streams into technology and policy as "a culture writ large" (1996, 30), defining politics by setting out imperative epistemic categories, ontological first principles, evaluative criteria, institutional strata, and personal identities (Hannerz, 1996; Habermas, 1987; Harvey, 2006).

Such precepts about shared common understandings of reality, temporality, fortune, worth, and strategy are, for Foucault, "power-at-work." The governmentality of culture is busy here individualizing its codes of conduct as well as conducting its codes through collectivizing clusters for "overall ways of life." For the many and the one, culture individualizes power; but, once so powered up, empowered, or power-ridden, such power formations flow out and around cultural collectives (Giedion, 1948; Jacobs, 2004). Culture is never lost, but it must always be found, and then reestablished again and again in each move of distinction and evaluation, anticipation and prediction, ordering and understanding (De Certeau, 1984; Hacking, 1999; Appadurai, 2000).

Culture industries and policies should not be separated from Huntington's clash of civilizations arguments, because they are important zones where the overall ways of life of a people are writ large as part of local, national, global culture (Luke, 2002). Huntington's quite polemical book *Who Are We?* (2004), openly agonizes about how America possibly is losing its "core culture" and "identity" as a nation. This turn follows from Americans allegedly facing dangerous new threats from "deconstructive criticism," "Mexican immigration," and "globalization" (2004, 17–27). Political science has often ignored such cultural anxieties as social, political, and cultural realities, but it is no surprise that such cultural frictions have become a new conceptual conjuncture for the analysis of political conflict, dissent, and struggle. Nonetheless this should not always be viewed as a negative development; instead, it can be quite positive. All of these relations unfold, at the same time, through everyday life's materialized narratives and routinized practices, which convey normative codes of conduct through culture industries producing commodified artifacts, corporate products, essential goods, technological devices, and art works for enjoyment in everyday lives (De Certeau, 1984; Mattelart, 2003; Mumford, 1971; Schiller, 2000).

Hence, culture and its industrial expressions are indeed key articulations of power (Virilio, 1995). As Foucault indicates, power is not a mysterious substance, a strange property, or an occult origin for authority. On the contrary, like culture,

Power is only a certain type of relation between individuals. Such relations are specific, that is, they have nothing to do with exchange, production, communication, even though they combine with them. The characteristics feature of power is that some men can more or less entirely determine other men's conduct—but never exhaustively or coercively. A man who is chained up and beaten is subject to force being exerted over him. Not power. But if he can be induced to speak, when his ultimate recourse could have been to hold his tongue, preferring death, then he has been caused to behave in a certain way. His freedom has been subjected to power. He has been submitted to government. If an individual can remain free, however little his freedom may be, power can subject him to government. There is no power without potential refusal or revolt.

(Foucault, 1979, 253)

Culture, therefore, cannot be disentangled from either enforcing governance or mounting resistance to government.

Cultural technologies and policies enable people to behave in certain ways, concretizing the conduct of conduct in governmentality, while at the same time providing a freedom to potentially refuse or revolt by misbehaving in other unknown ways. In one way or another, then, culture is always deployed in "police posts," cultural institutions are "police stations," and cultural expertise is "police authority" to ensure "everything is included" in the workings of power on these grids of governance. No attempt to assess "power reconsidered" can ignore these material realities in any of the high technologies or social policies tied to today's culture industries.

Approaching culture as power, generated in grids of governance, and civil society as service zones of these grids, grounded in the arts and culture, both become tight turns on the trails cut by these concepts that few political scientists are willing to track down. As a result, the trained incapacity that disciplinary rigor engenders within its mainstream deflects scholarly attention from some of the most decisive conjunctures of conflict, community, crisis, and continuity in today's systems for governance. Because it is rooted in cultural products and processes, "soft power" is largely neglected beyond being noted. Yet, in a time when "hard power" and its overextended and ill-considered use in the war on terror, is causing more harm than good, the base capacity of soft power either must keep much of the world comparatively harmless or diffuse some of the worst effects of hard power. These missions cannot be underestimated. When violence is followed by the healing effects of ethical care, moral regard or collective concern, usually carried by culture, to lessen the precarious, poverty-stricken, and threatened qualities of life behind "all of the people's conditions," then the grids of governance are definitely up and running to distribute the generated capacity of culture industries. In turn, art itself then can help each individual and group prosper as this ordering serves a greater perfection of the community at large through the arts, culture, and civil society.

Power enables subjectivities to develop, individual identities to unfold, collective values to coalesce. Arts, culture, and tradition in civil society cannot be easily divided from such power, and they underpin the community, identity, and subjectivity made possible within the crackle of these grids for governance. Culture industries are power stations, and their energies must be better assessed, gauged or mapped to understand how personal identities develop, popular subjectivity thrives, and persistent communities prosper.

Note

An earlier version of this chapter was originally prepared for APSA Short Course No. 20, "Culture Industries, Technologies, and Policies," at annual meeting of the American Political Science Association, Philadelphia, PA on August 30, 2006. Parts of it are drawn from my chapter in *Museum Philosophy for the Twenty-First Century*, ed. H. Genoways, Lanham, MD: AltaMira Press, 2006.

4

Art–State Relations: Art and Power through the Lens of International Treaties

Sandra Braman

As one manifestation of the rising salience of information-policy issues that has been observable since the late 1980s, art is now of central interest to political scientists and practicing policymakers. Wallerstein's (1990) theoretical argument—"culture is the battleground of the world system"—has been operationalized in developments as diverse as research method innovations that investigate visual art in order to identify significant conflict variables (Smith, 2004) and the use of electronic game design for political purposes (Bogost, 2006). Several features of art become visible from the perspective of its functions in an information production chain that includes a variety of types of information creation, production, flows, and use, several of which are of particular importance for art-state relations. Many information industries specialize in one type of informational activity, but information can be simultaneously collected, generated, and created de novo in the course of producing artworks. Multiple forms of information processing may take place during a single art production process. Artistic production processes often emphasize non-linear rather than linear planning approaches, make outcomes less predictable statistically. And, increasingly, artworks should be treated as both goods and services.

From the perspective of those involved with the arts, this shift in the nature of art–state relations joins other transformations of the functions of art in society, resulting from informatization, that include its growing importance from an economic perspective (Braman, 1996a), contributions to phase transitions of the state as a complex adaptive system (Braman, 1996b), and new types of both threats to the right to create (Braman, 1998) and policies to promote or shape art (Braman, 1994). From the perspective of the informational state—the successor to the bureaucratic welfare state (Braman, 2007)—this is one among the many renegotiations of relations between the state and information industries (see, e.g., Braman (2000) on higher education–state relations and Braman (2008b) on library–state relations). From the perspective of the evolution of the law itself, these trends are among the laws in which legal globalization is taking place (Braman, 2009), as international treaties are being used to force harmonization across states that historically differed significantly regarding the treatment of art (Grover, 1992). And from the perspective of international relations, this work can be read in conjunction with research on information policy in arms control treaties (Braman, 1991) and international trade agreements (Braman, 1990).

Data gathered from *The Art Newspaper* for a study on the impact of international treaties on art as an information industry since 1990 (Braman, 2008) are revisited here for the exemplars they provide of the ways in which states are using art in the exercise of power. The chapter opens with a discussion of the literature on art and treaties; goes on, in the following sections, to explore the diverse ways in which art is being used by states as a tool of instrumental, structural, symbolic, and informational power; and concludes with some thoughts regarding the impact of the use of art on the relative importance of power in its potential, actual, and virtual phases.[1] As is always the case with analyses of power, the effects of uses of art as a form of power are rarely quantifiable, and multiple forms of power may be exercised in any single instance, process, phenomenon, or event. The work is intended to be suggestive rather than comprehensive, using this limited set of cases to inductively build a framework for and raise questions to be addressed in future research.

Art and treaties

The literature on art and treaties to date falls into three categories of pertinent substance, and one of pleasure.[2] Research in the first category includes discussion of agreements that specifically focus on the arts and culture (e.g., UNESCO's World Heritage Convention); general agreements that include some provisions dealing with art and/or culture, such as the Maastricht Treaty; and agreements without any explicit provisions dealing with art or culture, but which have significant direct or indirect effects on the arts, such as the Treaty of Rome. The literature that is a source of at least personal pleasure involves ways in which artists themselves deal with treaties, from depiction of agreements and the effects of agreements all the way to the making of treaties themselves.

Culture-specific agreements

The literature dealing with culture-specific international agreements addresses a variety of types of questions. Beaudreau (2006), for example, examines the likely effectiveness of the UNESCO Convention on the Protection and Promotion of the Diversity of Cultural Perspectives from the perspective of relationships between consumer behavior and identity; it is rare for any discussions of other treaties to involve specific reference to the arts. Economists analyze the impact of UNESCO's World Heritage Convention (e.g., Gilley, 2001), suggest incentives for reporting newly discovered antiquities (Villanueva, 1995), and make policy recommendations intended to counter the extent to which network externalities in the consumption of cultural goods can lead to under-production of diverse types of art in smaller countries (Rauch and Trindade, 2005). UNESCO's Convention on the Protection of the Underwater Cultural Heritage—which affects how artworks unearthed in the course of salvaging shipwrecks—has provoked discussion in marine policy circles (e.g., Fletcher-Tomenius and Forrest, 2000). The problem of how to protect works of art during periods of war is of growing interest (Toman, 1996). Works dealing with policy developments at the national level in response to such international agreements are rife; examples include analyses of legal developments after the 1970 UNESCO Convention on Cultural Property in the UK (Gaimster, 2004) and US (Edelson, 1984).

General agreements with cultural provisions

A number of international treaties and conventions contain provisions that pertain to the arts even though the entire agreements are not devoted to the subject. For example, the cultural impact of international trade agreements at the level of General Agreements on Tariffs and Trade (GATT) has been discussed since the 1980s (Braman, 1989; Singh, 2008), and analysis has more recently expanded to include regional trade agreements both in general (Galperin, 1999) and as they affect specific countries (Crean, 2000). The Hague Convention of 1954, which includes provisions relating to treatment of cultural property, is receiving renewed attention because it is intended to protect artworks during times of war (Anglim, 2004; Sandholtz, 2005). The Maastricht Treaty, of course, has stimulated a great deal of discussion about the interactions between national and regional law and policy for the arts in Europe, including critiques of what Barnett (2001) refers to as the resulting "governmentalization" of culture at the EC level, recognition of art and other cultural forms as sources of resistance to the European community (Cunningham, 2001), and an analysis of case law treatment of cultural matters in the European Court of Justice (Chechi, 2004). The list of agreements with pertinent provisions is surprisingly long, including such treaties as the Organization of African Unity (OAU) Convention on the Prevention and Combating of Terrorism, the Protocol on Strategic Environmental Assessment to the Convention on Environmental Impact Assessment in a Transboundary Context, and the Protocol on Water and Health to the 1992 Convention on the Protection and Use of Transboundary Watercourses and International Lakes.

General agreements without culture-specific provisions

Studies of the impact on art of non-culture-specific treaties are more rare. Human rights treaties have raised two types of issues: there is the possibility that the universalism inherent in human rights treaties may be abusive of cultural and religious practices in ways that may have implications for the arts (Zechenter, 1997). And there is a danger that extreme art practices, such as Santiago Sierra's practice of paying very poor individuals with cash or drugs to serve as a medium for his work (Mariño, 2006) may themselves be in abrogation of human rights treaties. Myers (2004) argues that issues important to subordinate cultures which are at a remove from those signing treaties but are affected by them should be taken into account in both developing and analyzing these political instruments. The same impact at a remove can be seen in the impact of treaties on arts-related sectors to which the legal instruments themselves do not directly apply, as Littoz-Monnet (2005) points out has happened with the book publishing industry in Europe. There are numerous instances, many discussed below, in which general commercial law such as the Treaty of Rome affects artists and arts institutions.

Treaties as subject and medium of art

Recent developments in the other direction—artistic depiction of or engagement with treaties—have been particularly interesting. There is a long history of artworks *depicting the signing of treaties* that receives attention from art critics; the painting of William Penn signing a treaty with tribal groups in the US—again for sale a decade ago (*The Art Newspaper*, 1973)—receives continuous attention (see, e.g., Palumbo, 1995; Rigal, 2000; Tobin, 2007). Sometimes such depictions are self-reflexive, as the image of a treaty that facilitated an art exchange between the King of Siam and Louix XIV on a medallion, identification of the role of Ramesses II of Egypt in negotiating the first peace treaty in recorded history (with the Hittites) as among the reasons the public should be interested in an exhibition of objects from his tomb at the Louvre, or exhibitions and/or catalogs organized around efforts to recuperate art transmitted between nations as a result of treaties in the past. New artworks are still being commissioned to celebrate treaties, as when New Zealand commissioned a new museum to celebrate the hundred and fiftieth anniversary celebrations of the Treaty of Waitangi between the British and the Maori that served as the founding document of modern New Zealand.

Over the last decade, however, artists have also gone further. There is work *depicting the effects of treaties*, such as massive migrations of asylum seekers responding to the consequences of treaties and the shifting of national borders (Faulkner, 2003). *Artwork by treaty negotiators* has also appeared: *The Art Newspaper* reported on doodles by President John F. Kennedy, who drew a sailboat with the words "Blockade Cuba," "NATO," and "Fidel Castro" during the Cuban Missile Crisis in October of 1962, and sketched a large mushroom cloud with the word "bomb" during the 1963 Nuclear Test Ban Treaty period (*The Art Newspaper*, 1999). Short stories written by Singapore's Foreign Minister before he took office have been analyzed as sources of insight regarding the types of international arrangements he might favor (Holden, 2006). Artists have begun to use *treaties as an art medium*. NATOarts, for example, is a conceptual art group that presents itself as the cultural arm of NATO, governed by a board of directors with representation from each of the NATO member states. Its works include a project to prove that the Danube is actually pollution-free, an international competition to design a uniform for NATO, and a CD of ambient music called "Distant Early Warning," described as the first record ever to be funded by NATO (Dannatt, 2000). The Yes Men similarly present themselves as representatives of the World Trade Organization (WTO) and set up a website on the GATT, the international treaty dealing with trade (Dzuverovic-Russell, 2003).

Finally, there are instances in which work presents *artists as diplomats* themselves, as in an exhibition of work by Venetian painter Gentile Bellini from the period in which he served as a diplomat as well as a court artist in Istanbul (1479–80) following the signing of a peace treaty between Venice and Turkey. Perhaps most striking of all are the creation of *artists' treaties*, modeled in 1988 by Palestinian and Israeli artists who wished to further exchanges between the two communities, stimulate political treaty-making, and enable collaborative work (Seikaly, 1989).

Instrumental power

The exercise of instrumental power shapes, constrains, and directs behavior through control over the material world. We are most accustomed to thinking about instrumental power in the form of weaponry, but art can be used in the exercise of this form of power in ways that include the use of force and as a limit to the use of force. We can include some types of interactions between art and capital in this category, as well, for fundamentally the concept of capital refers to the capacity to make things happen (in the material world) in future.

Art and force

In relation to international treaties, art becomes involved with physical force when artworks are treated as prisoners of war, when concern over the treatment of art under international treaties stimulates physical resistance, and when the consequences of treaties yield disruptions of the material environment in pursuit of art. Interactions between art and force that are beyond the scope of this chapter include funding for art as a means of support for the military (the US Army marching band receives more funds than the National Endowment for the Arts), and relatively new uses of electronic media to take advantage of the ability of information to act as an agent on its own.

Prisoners of war

Parker (2005) describes artworks as prisoners of war when they are captured during wartime and not returned to their rightful owners or their heirs afterwards. Following the most massive taking of such prisoners in history during World War II, legal and political battles over the return of such prisoners—"restitution"—continues into the first decade of the twenty-first century and is likely to go on for decades more in processes that involve not only the signing of treaties, but also their ratification, and subsequent internal harmonization of national laws with treaty terms once agreed to.

The struggle is so complex because these artworks involve intricate interactions between national heritage, human rights, diverse economic concerns, and the survival needs of the artworks themselves. Because so many artworks are involved, neither comprehensively listing the items nor quantifying their value is an easily accomplishable task; the issue of restitution has stimulated the development of cultural policy itself through a turn from specific works to general concepts of cultural property (Monten, 2004). When restitution works, the return of artworks taken during time of war to the source country offers high moments in political life. In Berlin, for example, the reuniting of paintings from the former East Germany with those of West Germany was deemed worthy of a national celebration. There are times, however, when the problems raised by restitution appear to be irresolvable. The Austrian government, for example, simply refused to pay the market price in order to return paintings by Gustav Klimt to their rightful immigrant American owner, and Istrian artworks were never returned to the former Yugoslavia because the treaties mandating restitution were never formally signed.

Physical resistance

Restitution issues that used to be a matter only of interest to the cognoscenti are now becoming the subjects of popular culture, getting such wide coverage in tabloids and televised investigative reporting that it can stimulate crowds to physical action. A vivid example is provided by the growth of popular interest in the return of a fourth-century Ethiopian obelisk taken by Mussolini in the 1930s from the Italians, an artwork specifically mentioned in the 1947 peace treaty between the two countries. Decades of demands and alternative proposals—such as the building of a hospital in Ethiopia instead—led nowhere. By the early 1990s, however, interest in the matter had risen to such a feverish pint that 40,000 soccer fans chanting "Let It Return" carried posters with their demands during a match that was broadcast on television. (It was only after the work was damaged by natural causes, however, that Italy agreed to return the work.)

Impact on the material environment

Perhaps one of the most counter-intuitive ways in which the implementation of international treaties reveals the impact of art as a tool of instrumental power is treaty facilitation of massive amounts of physical activity that changes the natural environment itself. In one example of growing importance, the activity of salvaging the thousands of shipwrecks that litter the ocean floor must abide by international treaties dealing with protection of "underwater cultural heritage." And in a particularly dismaying but revealing example, the digging up of landmines in Cambodia following the 1996 peace treaty between the Khmer Rouge and the Cambodian government was followed by illicit excavations all over the country by people seeking artifacts to sell on the international art market.

Art and limits to force

Art is being used in the exercise of instrumental power as a limit to force as well. This occurs when agreements to protect artworks are put in place to set the limits to war, and when artworks are treated as a fundamental element of human rights.

Limits to war

The first suggestions that cultural property should be protected during war appeared during the Renaissance, but it was not until the nineteenth century that specific provisions were developed to protect works of art during wartime (Merryman, 1986). The Lieber Code of 1863, which bound the Union forces during the US Civil War, required soldiers to move works of art rather than harm them, if necessary. The Lieber Code influenced a number of subsequent nineteenth- and twentieth-century agreements including, recently, treaties between the Czech and Slovak republics regarding ownership of works of art, the division of cultural property, and the care of cultural objects and monuments that could not be moved prior to the dissolution of Czechoslovakia in 1994 (Cook, 1993).

The Nuremberg Trials, however, marked a turning point in holding states accountable to such agreements by treating damage to artworks as a matter of human rights (Gottlieb, 2005). Since then, the problem of how to protect works of art during periods of war has been of growing interest (Toman, 1996). The Hague Convention of 1954, for example, is playing an important role because its provisions relating to treatment of cultural property are intended to provide such protections (Anglim, 2004; Sandholtz, 2005). These international treaties must, in turn, be translated into law at the national level, as exemplified in legal developments after the 1970 UNESCO Convention on Cultural Property in the UK (Gaimster, 2004) and US (Edelson, 1984).

Art and human rights

Over the last couple of centuries, debate over issues involving the transfer of artworks across borders have increasingly come to be viewed as a matter of human rights. The polity first appeared in state considerations regarding how artwork would be handled under treaties in 1815 at the Paris Conference. A request for the return of artwork Napoleon had taken from Italy to France was rejected because, it was argued, doing so would disperse the objects involved with the result that they would become unavailable to the public. It was only when the promise was made that the artworks involved would be made accessible in a public gallery that the negotiators supported the return of the works of art from France to their places of origin (Jayme, 2005).

The concept of universal human rights was embedded in the World Heritage Treaty, which was set up in 1972 after a major rescue operation was mounted to save the temples of Upper Egypt by UNESCO in 1960 (Haywood, 1995). This is one of UNESCO's most prestigious and visible programs; even when the UK and the US were not members of UNESCO, they continued to adhere to this treaty. Unfortunately, this link with human rights has not prevented governments from using the treaty for political purposes: China refused to add Tibetan sites it occupied since the 1950s until very recently, Turkey refuses to put forward any proposals relating to Armenian culture, Chile was very slow to move on Easter Island, and Syria chooses to ignore sites that are reminders of the Crusaders' presence during the Middle Ages. For sites that are designated as world heritage under the treaty, however, there is an additional feature that serves the public interest—no polluting facilities can be built near world heritage sites.

On the model of the Nuremberg Trials, successful prosecutions of military commanding officers before the International Criminal Tribunal for ex-Yugoslavia were important landmarks for legal protection of cultural property. Similar issues have been raised in discussions of the conduct of the second Iraqi War. Concern about public access to works as a human right continues to be voiced in a number of contemporary cases involving restitution. At times, however, the notion of a right to individual access to works becomes blended with the concept of competitor access to markets or services. Thus international tours, museums, art fairs, and international exhibitions are all now being discussed in terms of the equity and fairness with which dealers or gallery owners may have access.

Claims of universal human rights also support arguments that universalistic claims are actually repressive of particular cultural and religious practices (Zechenter, 1997). And there is the danger that extreme art practices, such Santiago Sierra's practice of paying very poor individuals with cash or drugs to serve as a medium for his work (Mariño, 2006) may themselves be in abrogation of human rights treaties.

Art and capital

We can treat uses of art as a means of accumulating capital as a matter of instrumental power because, as mentioned above, capital is essentially the capacity to make things happen in the future. Analyses of art and other cultural property under international treaties has been the subject of a rapidly growing literature since the 1980s, when international flows of information became the focus of international trade negotiations.

International trade

This large and growing literature on cultural property and international trade includes both discussion of art, and the impact of treaties on art, in the international environment (Singh, 2006; Braman, 1990; Galperin, 1999; Lewis and Miller, 2002) and within specific countries (e.g., Crean, 2000). With the establishment of the WTO, the concept of cultural trade itself needed definition. Distinctions were drawn between cultural goods and services, core cultural tradeables and tradeables related to culture, and cultural hardware and cultural software (Grasstek, 2005). WTO agreements require specific commitments, by sector and mode, for each of the four different ways a cultural good or service can be exported: when *cross border supply* takes place, services by a supplier in one country are provided to a consumer in another country (direct broadcasting services [DBS] is an example). When *consumption takes place abroad*, a consumer travels to the point of delivery (tourism provides multiple examples). With *commercial presence*, there is temporary or permanent establishment abroad of a supplier through investment (film co-production, for example). And with the *presence of natural persons*, people move to a foreign country on a non-permanent basis to supply a service (e.g., a foreign cameraman is hired to work on a particular film). Illegal exports introduce another set of categorical distinctions, among goods that may have been stolen prior to being smuggled out of a country, goods that are smuggled out by their rightful owner with the purpose of being sold abroad, goods that are legally purchased within a country and then smuggled out, and objects that are not returned at the end of a lawful temporary export.

Tariffs

Recent developments under the World Trade Organization (WTO) set up in the 1990s rest upon a long history of differential design of tariffs (taxes applied when goods cross borders) specific to art (Fishman, 1977). Often these were set lower than tariffs on other kinds of goods to encourage cross-border flows of art. In a premiere example of interactions among diverse forms of power, such tariffs involve informational power as well as instrumental power because they rest upon establishing definitions of art as a distinct type of information creation, processing, flows, and use. The problem, of course, re-emerges with each new artistic genre, medium, or school of art. The representational test historically used by US Customs, for example, became problematic with the appearance of abstract art. In a famous court case, *Brancusi v. the United States* (1928), photographer Edward Steichen finally won the right to import a sculpture by Constantin Brancusi as an artwork for free (rather than as an object of manufactured metal to be taxed at 40 percent of its value)—but only after a 12-year battle. It took 30 more years before changes to the Tariff Act removed substantially all barriers to the free entry of modern and abstract works.

Export controls

International trade agreements exercise structural power, as discussed below, but they also can exercise instrumental power when they forbid the movement of artworks across borders. Article 30 of the Treaty Establishing the European Community, for example, contains exceptions to the prohibition on cross-border trade restrictions between states when it comes to art defined as "national cultural property" (Jayme, 2005). The European Community took up the problem of defining just what that is in 1968, when the European Court of Justice determined that works of art were "goods" for the purpose of the EC treaty (Goyder, 1997). In 1992, the EC began the process of distinguishing among categories of art. In a related vein, it is up to European Court of Justice to even decide whether or not a particular activity—such as curatorial practice—involves a profession for purposes of application of EC rules regarding free movement of persons throughout Europe. Curators and art historians are not necessarily allowed the free movement through Europe for work purposes that is available to others when states desire to restrict such movements to protect their national cultural property.

Structural power

Structural power stimulates, shapes, and constrains behavior through control over the rules and institutions within which people operate. Pierre Bourdieu's (1993) work on cultural capital provides a theoretical way of understanding the importance of art to structural power for the state. While the concept of cultural capital has been further developed to refer to a variety of ways in which mastery of cultural practices and knowledge of cultural forms serve individuals and groups as they position themselves within society, Bourdieu's theory begins with the recognition that "certification" of certain genres and works as "high" art is accomplished by institutions that themselves have received the imprimatur of the state. In turn, involvement with these arts institutions and knowledge of the works they produce and exhibit is key to the process by which specific individuals and families build and retain their roles in the socio-political power structure. DiMaggio (1991) builds on this work to specifically explore the role played by art in the development of the bureaucratic state. In order for cultural capital to be possible, both the state and arts institutions must have capacities that are widely recognized; there must be a common focus for public life; forms of culture must be differentiated from each other; and distinctions among forms of culture must be hierarchically organized in ways that have ritual potency. The structures of the art industry serve not only agents and institutions of the artistic field, but also those of the larger social field (Lash, 1993). The specific forms in which art appears are the combined results of historical economic and political—as well as creative—processes (Amariglio, 1988;

Smith, 1990). The influential work of Benedict Anderson (1983), and that of researchers in the industry Anderson spawned, on the role of the arts in creating the "imagined community" of the state, provides theoretical and empirical detail for how these processes unfold across societies and as they include popular culture in addition to high art.

Earlier work (Braman, 2008) explores interactions between the art industry and the state in one direction, ways in which international treaties to which states adhere shape the structures of the art industry. Here, we look at the reverse, ways in which art activities under international treaties affect the nature of government and provide structural limits to the treaties themselves.

The evolution of government

Treatment of art under international treaties has effects on government structure, the passage and interpretation of laws, the nature of the legal process, and approaches to jurisdictional and other problems raised by globalization.

Government structure

During the period studied, international treaties involving art stimulated the development of new decision-making entities specific to art in two countries reported upon by *The Art Newspaper*. France took advantage of the Treaty of Rome to set up a new regulatory body for art auctions that enabled the state to assert monopoly control. Since these auction houses deal with many kinds of art that cannot legitimately be considered important cultural heritage, however, there was an intense struggle over liberalization of this regulation; ultimately non-French auction houses such as Sotheby's and Christie's were allowed to operate in France (and within just a few years completely dominated the French art auction market).

In the US, there was conflict over whether statutes specific to cultural property or general criminal law should govern in cases involving contested importation of cultural goods into the country. This debate had structural implications because the statute specific to cultural property gave a great deal of power over decision-making to a committee tasked with evaluating such criteria as the cultural significance of the specific objects involved; the applicant's efforts at conservation, preservation, and site protection; the applicant's record of granting museum loans and export permits; whether other significant market nations have imposed similar restrictions; and whether current looting in the source country has reached crisis proportions. Under criminal law, determinant questions involving whether or not theft had taken place and whether or not there was knowledge of such theft are resolvable in typical judicial fashion. Though critics argued that the decision-making committee had an undue amount of power and had opportunities for abuse, ultimately it was determined that the law specific to cultural property should govern.

Change in laws

Often to the surprise of those who entered into such agreements, interactional treaties involving art often subsequently require new laws at the state level in order to comply. In China, for example, bureaucrats involved in the signing of a bilateral treaty with the US to restrict the smuggling of cultural relics were so focused on the possibility of increasing Chinese stature in global cultural affairs that they failed to realize that treaty provisions required changing domestic law in such a way that a number of key stakeholders were undermined and relationships among various facets of the art sector then needed reorganization. In Cambodia, uncertainty regarding who has the legal right to give permission to remove artifacts of cultural importance from the country almost prevented a major exhibition of Khmer art scheduled for Paris and Washington from taking place at all.

The need for changes in domestic law can delay the signing of treaties for long periods; it was for this reason that Switzerland was only able to sign on to the 1970 UNESCO Convention on Movement of Cultural Property in 2003, and Japan was able to sign the same convention only in 2002.

Change in legal process

The logistics of implementing treaties related to cultural heritage have resulted in some very interesting procedural developments. According to the 1995 Unidroit Convention on Stolen and Illegally Exported Cultural Objects, a requesting nation desirous of recovering cultural property must prove that loss or removal impairs the physical preservation of the object or its context, the integrity of a complex object, the preservation of information, the traditional or ritual use of the object by an indigenous community, or is of significant cultural importance for the requesting state. Evidence to support such claims can include documentation of the influence of the piece in art, uniqueness, the extent to which the work introduces introduction new techniques or iconography, and the religious significance of the work.

This Unidroit convention also affected the nature and extent of confidentiality between art dealers and their clients. Until this agreement was put into effect, cultural property had been the last valuable asset which could be traded without full disclosure of title, and it was the only one for which concealment of provenance had been defended. Both of these features contributed to the attractiveness of the international art trade for those who sought to use it as a means of laundering money gained during other illegal activities, such as those involving drugs.

Treaties can serve as enforcement mechanisms even when it is not their own provisions being enforced. States can, for example, use the potential for treaties as justification for action, as when Canadian police asked Interpol to extricate individuals in a Canadian art fraud case from Anguila, a country with which Canada did not have an extradition treaty. The request for help was based on the justification that Canada *could* have such a treaty, and therefore it was legitimate to ask Interpol to intervene. In a similar way, the existence of the UNESCO and Unidroit treaties was used to support an opinion in a Swiss court involving the return of a stolen painting, even though Switzerland itself is not a signatory to those treaties.

Globalization

The impact of globalization on the art industry has been large. Art theft is now a multi-billion dollar business estimated to be second in size only to drug trafficking as the most profitable form of illegal trade. Appreciation of the profits to be made has brought drug rings and others involved in organized crime into the art trade, increasing the violence and sophistication of techniques used. The lack of harmonization of national laws makes it easier for those involved in the illegal art market to operate, for they can locate various activities and transactions in those jurisdictions with the most favorable laws.

Techniques used to reinforce—or enable—the export of works considered important to national cultural heritage are quite various. This opens up space for strategy when choosing which jurisdiction should govern in international situations involving multiple possible choices of jurisdiction. When German artist Joseph Beuys sold works in London, for example, the transaction was not subject to German law even though the works had to be shipped to London for the sale and the deal setting up the sale was made in Germany, because no legal nexus with Germany was identified (Jayme, 2005). Recognition of a jurisdiction can itself be a tool; the 1922 Treaty of Rapallo was critical to the sell-off of Russian art that Stalin began in 1928, for example, because the agreement permitted Germany to recognize the Soviet government and, thus, the legitimacy of its nationalization—and subsequent sale—of private art collections. Granting and withholding export licenses provides a third example of the diversity of techniques that can be used to force or prevent movement of cultural heritage items across borders. In response to the concerns of owners of important works who fear they may lose profits if they are not able to sell on the international market, for example, the UK defers export licenses in order to buy time to allow domestic buyers to meet prices offered by collectors or museums outside of a country.

Limits to treaties

Treaties creating the European Union, from the Maastricht Treaty through the Treaty of Amsterdam have stimulated a great deal of discussion about the interactions between national and regional law and policy for the arts in Europe, including critiques of what Barnett (2001) refers to the as the resulting "governmentalization" of culture at the EC level, recognition of art and other cultural forms as sources of resistance to the European community

(Cunningham, 2001), and legal struggles generated by tensions between state and EC laws as applied to art (Chechi, 2004). In sum, art and artists are often treated as exceptions in international treaties in ways the art world sometimes finds problematic, and sometimes prefers. In Europe, artworks do not participate in the same type of free market put in place for other types of goods. Nor can artists and curators count on being able to travel freely for work in the way that those involved in other industries can, whether that is because their low income is not sufficient for a residence permit, there are residency requirements for jobs or grants from public bodies that exclude foreign nationals, or there may be restrictions regarding personnel involved in cultural heritage work.

There are times, however, when art is *not* treated as an exception under international treaties, but those involved in the industry wish that it were. The 2001 UNESCO Convention on the Protection of Underwater Cultural Heritage, which applies to items salvaged from shipwrecks in international waters, is of concern to those in the art world because it does not acknowledge the artistic value of archeological finds even though many items recovered from shipwrecks are of deep interest in the art world, are commoditized as artworks, and wind up in art collections or museums. In addition, the convention protects only works that are at least 100-years old, though important artworks created more recently are also involved in shipwrecks.

Symbolic power

Symbolic power shapes, promotes, and constrains behavior through the effects of communications on how people perceive and understand the world. The role of symbolic power in shaping and sustaining the identity of the state has been extensively examined, including the use of art for this function. Art also exercises symbolic power when it is used for diplomatic purposes, and when international treaties themselves are used as rhetorical devices.

John Dewey offered a theoretical explanation for the symbolic power of art in such functions in his exploration of art as the most effective form of communication. He believed that it provides a means through which people can develop the sense of commonality that is fundamental to community (Mattern, 1999)—a conclusion supported by empirical research (Burton and Ruppert, 1999). Thus, in general, as Alderson et al. (1993) argue, cultural policy is important because artists are inherently engaged in envisioning a larger civility, and political economy is of particular use in studying policy that pertains to the arts (Cameron and Becker, 1993). In particular, Jayme (2005) points out, treaties will be more successful than efforts to use state law extraterritorially when resolving litigation over artworks that involves states. We begin here by looking at the familiar and important issue of role of art in the formation and sustenance of state identity, and go on to look briefly at diplomatic functions and the rhetorical power of treaties themselves as additional ways in which art is used as an instrument of symbolic power through the medium of international treaties.

Art and state identity

Explicit and deliberate use of art in the formation and sustenance of identity by the modern state goes back at least to the early nineteenth century, when nations such as Germany and France—longing for unification—commissioned artworks specifically to express nationality. A large proportion of media discussion about international treaties and the arts involves state identity via attention to the movement of works across borders, whether for the purpose of restitution (the return of works removed during time of war) or sale of objects potentially or undeniably a part of a country's national cultural heritage. The habit of commissioning artists to celebrate political leaders and events if of course ancient, but the first recorded intervention into what we refer to as the fine art market for the explicit purpose of protecting state identity occurred in the seventeenth century, when Pope Urban VIII ordered an Italian painter to send a copy of a painting commissioned by the Queen of England[3] rather than the original in order to prevent Italy from being deprived of the piece. By the early nineteenth century, artworks were commonly being created in a self-conscious effort to articulate state identity in cultural forms such as the sculpture in Florence of a person mourning at the tomb of the national poet (Jayme, 2005).

A number of questions come up, however, when trying to reach agreement regarding just what constitutes cultural objects important to a particular nation's identity. It is even not consensually clear what should be defined as the country of origin of a particular work. The UNESCO Convention on the Means of Prohibiting and Preventing the Illicit Import, Export, and Transfer of Ownership of Cultural Property (1970) offers several categories that can be used for this purpose, including work created by the "individual or collective genius of nationals of the State concerned" and "cultural property of importance to the state concerned created within the territory of that State by foreign nationals or stateless persons resident within such territory." The multiplicity of possible relations between the creators of an artwork and the state claiming that work as critical for its identity means that more than one country could claim rights to the same work; in one case involving a silver collection, for example, three different countries claimed the same items as their own national treasures. The International Council of Museums (ICOM) speaks of "those objects and documents which are indispensable to people in understanding their origin and culture," and the drafters of the Unidroit agreement took the position that every country has a right to at least an adequate representative collection of its own national cultural heritage (Prott, 1997). The US government has discussed requiring every government with which it deals to develop itemized lists of every object that would fall into this category; as further discussed below, since this is a clearly impossible task, going this route would effectively eviscerate laws and regulations intended to protect cultural heritage. Part of the difficulty is that just as there is no one trait that distinguishes all ethnic groups from each other (some use food, some use dress, etc.), or is used for cultural differentiation by the same group in all contexts (e.g., the Romany people use dress in some places and language in others) (Greenfeld, 1992), so while every country in the world treats at least some aspect of its domestic cultural life as a public good, there is enormous variance in what that is (Grasstek, 2005). French reluctance to let go of government control of the art auction business suggests the sense that the marketing of art itself should be added to the list of things that might be defined as part of national heritage. For Singapore, it is important to emphasize that works important to cultural heritage may not necessarily be old, and that heritage is important even for those countries that have not played in role in building the ancient cultural heritage of humankind (Lee, 2004).

Defining artwork as of national importance can pit private and public interests against each other when owners of those works find they cannot sell them outside of the country even though doing so would significantly increase profit. The desire to build and protect national identity must also be balanced against other needs. Geopolitical developments can affect the extent to which a given government is concerned about art and its national identity, and the ways in which this concern is expressed. When negotiations opened in 1987 regarding the possible entrance of Turkey into the European Union, for example, the Danish minister of cultural affairs was moved for the first time to develop materials depicting key Danish cultural treasures and distributed them to every citizen, arguing that "We must know why we are and how we are" (quoted in Jayme, 2005, p. 933). Eastern European analysts explicitly link closely related restitution issues to changes in the nature of the state, reflecting recent regional in which claims by the state to guarantee a distant future lost ground to an interest in responding to contemporary social needs (Lufkin, 2006b).

There are times when governments prefer *not* to identify particular items as critical to state identity even though the cultural heritage link is strong. The British, for example, did not include all scheduled heritage sites and objects on the list of things to be protected during wartime because there are so many that, it was feared, enemies could legitimately argue they needed to ignore them all. Australia has dawdled on the question of identifying cultural heritage sites because of the resource demands of the environmental protections that must then be applied. Personal passions may intervene, as happened when President Eisenhower was deeply reluctant to let go of a painting he loved (Manet's *Winter Garden*) when the call for restitution came.

example

Art and diplomacy

The link between artworks and state identity joins access to art as a universal human right to explain why artworks are often treated as diplomats deserving of safe conduct protections when they travel. In "public diplomacy" programs that send artists and artworks abroad as "soft" forms of political persuasion, art is explicitly being used to serve diplomatic functions in pursuit of foreign policy goals (see Schneider chapter in this volume). Because calls for restitution are by definition the result of changing interstate relations, they involve not only redress, but also another form of art service to present and future foreign policy objectives.

Treaties as rhetorical devices

In international relations, "unequal treaties" are treaties between states that are vastly different in relative negotiating power. Interestingly—and perhaps evidence of the growing salience of treaties for those in the arts—the same language is now being used to refer to agreements between arts institutions of different states, level of resources, and relative importance to the global art world. Thus the Japanese described the arrangement between the Boston Museum of Fine Arts and Nagoya Museum as the result of an unequal treaty because the Boston institution refused to take into account Japanese input when designing what should have been collaborative projects, and the Chinese used the phrase in its opposition to a Guggenheim Museum proposal for a branch in China because it was felt the terms offered were like those of an unfair treaty imposed on a defeated country.

Informational power

Informational power involves both new forms of power that were not historically available (such as data mining across types and scales of data) and transformations of power in its instrumental, structural, and symbolic forms through interventions into their informational foundations. The theoretical links between art and informational power are multiple, including art as a form of knowledge both for its creators and for those who engage with the work (Barney, 2000), artistic production as a means of cultural action (CAE, 2001), and art as artificial intelligence (Dewdney, 1998). Because the use of informational power can include structural features of institutions and societies as manipulable media, the common use of artworks in boundary formations (Cawelti, 1978) is also a dimension of its use as informational power. In the information society, it is increasingly the idea, not the phenomenon, that is of value (Greaves, 1994), and art often has economic value as an informational service rather than as objects or events (Braman, 1996). Specific examples of uses of art in the service of informational power already evident in the language and impact of treaties can be seen in the areas of data about art and surveillance. Current activities such as those in the tactical media movement—an alternative media movement focused on manipulations of technological media, rather than the content communicated through such technologies, for political purposes—are likely to yield further examples of art as informational power dealt with by treaties in future.

Art and data

Art and data are linked in the exercise of informational power in two ways. Artworks can be understood as data in themselves. And data about art are generated as tools of power. There are, of course, interactions between the two.

Treatment of art as data—and data as a medium for art—developed during the eighteenth-century encyclopedia movement, when the elaboration of complete taxonomic series came to be perceived as aesthetic objects themselves (Clifford, 1988). This development was translated into social science research methods by the highly influential sociologist Emile Durkheim, for whom works of art were, like statistics, records of taste of scientific value (Smelser, 1976).

Exercises in developing data about art during and after World War II in response to the demands of international treaties, or in preparation for such treaties, triggered an extremely interesting set of developments in the area of cultural policy. Munten (2004) provides a detailed report of how this unfolded from the Soviet side. In 1942, Soviets began preparing lists of what the Nazis were taking so that they could be compensated with artwork from enemy museums that was comparable. When it was discovered that this was difficult to manage, and that the number of works involved was hard to quantify, the Soviets switched their attention from a numeric evaluation to one based on cultural capital, listing just those items considered masterpieces in enemy museums. The process of collecting data about these artworks stimulated the concept of a super museum. Ultimately, the focus shifted from replacing specific items that had been lost to reactive removal of cultural objects as a penalty. Over the course of just a few years, then—in direct response to the effort to collect data about stolen artworks—the Soviets moved through several stages of cultural policy that can be summarized in this way:

Stage 1: It is the number of artworks that matters.
Stage 2: It is the value of artworks in terms of cultural capital that matters.
Stage 3: It is having a comprehensive/universal collection across types of items with high cultural capital that matters.
Stage 4: It is the process of building and holding cultural capital that matters.

Recent developments in US law add a fifth stage. The Convention on Cultural Property Implementation Act requires countries that wish to protect their cultural heritage to specifically list all of those items that they don't want exported. Because this is an impossible task, from the cultural policy perspective this is, then:

Stage 5: Demands for quantification of cultural capital as a tool to justify limits on treaty compliance.

Art and surveillance

Surveillance mechanisms made possible by today's digital technologies have both affected the ability to ensure treaty compliance and changed the use of art in the exercise of instrumental, structural, and symbolic power. The phrase "confidence- and security-building measures" (CSBMs) came into use following the establishment of the Conference on Security and Co-operation in Europe (CSCE) in 1975 to refer to mandated flows of information and communication among states as a way of reducing international tensions and building peace (Braman, 1991). This same set of policy tools is now being applied to art. The use of satellite surveillance to track illegal movement of artworks, the exchange of information among national policing units, and the establishment of databases identifying all artworks of interest are examples of this trend. As has been the case with environmental information collection, this raises the research and policy question of the extent to which information collection and distribution for purposes related to the arts and culture contribute to information-gathering for military and other purposes, and vice versa.

Current practices in the art world include establishing channels for the rapid exchange of information on matters relating to the smuggling of antiquities, including the development of publicly accessible websites to report on and help track illicit trading. There is discussion of embedding electronic tracking chips into important artworks to make such tracking easier. International agreements putting in place common language to describe artworks as they move across borders is another form of informational power involving art that assists in the surveillance process.

In the early 1990s, the EC began discussing asking every cultural artifact that would need protection to be accompanied by an identity certificate— a requirement now embedded in US law. This requirement shifts the burden of proof from the buying country to the source country, and from rule-driven identification of goods to item-by-item identification and certification. In the US, accompanying provisions include requiring evidence that particular objects were in danger of pillage rather than evidence of a history of abuse, and labor-intensive annual reviews of all import restrictions. Perhaps most controversially, there has been discussion of requiring public disclosure of details of foreign nations' requests for relief, including a full description of the sites at which looting was a concern. As critics of such proposals point out, providing this type of detail would offer a road map for future looters and actually encourage theft.

Conclusions

This secondary analysis of data gathered for a study of the impact of international treaties on the international art world has provided an opportunity to inductively explore the varieties of ways in which art is being used as a tool for the exercise of power in its instrumental, structural, symbolic, and informational forms by the informational state. As has long been important for our understanding of journalism, and is now important for other information industries given the particular features of the informational state, this exercise has utility as a contribution to a theory of art–state relations.

There was unfortunately not room in this piece for additional exploration of the relative importance of art as a tool for the exercise of power in its various phases: actual (in use), potential (available but not currently in use), and virtual (not currently in existence but could be brought into existence using existing knowledge and resources). Given the functions of art in boundary and phase transactions and as attractors during the transformations of complex adaptive systems—including those of politics—and given the growing use of tactical media practices and other means of using hardware and software as artistic media, this topic, too, is worthy of future exploration.

Notes

1. The theoretical framework for this piece is explicated most comprehensively in *Change of State: Information, Policy, and Power* (Braman, 2007). Space constraints in this book chapter preclude presentation of full citations for all of the information sources used in this earlier study. Readers are referred to that study both for more detail on the cases discussed and for full reference information on those materials.
2. Conventions, which serve many of the same functions as treaties though they are slightly less formal in nature, are included in this literature review and analysis.
3. The painting was *Nozze di Bacco e Arianna*.

5
Toward a Political Economy of Digital Culture: From Organized Mass Consumption to Attention Rivalry

Jeffrey A. Hart

Introduction

According to the editor of this volume, the term "cultural industries" includes "the arts and creative sectors that encompass, but are not limited to, publishing, film, music, photography, design, and tourism."[1] Because of the development of digital technologies in computers and telecommunications equipment, more and more cultural artifacts are being produced, stored, and delivered digitally. The increased speed of digital devices and innovations in computer networks and digital compression technologies make it both easier and less expensive to deliver words, music, symbols, and images (in fact, anything that can be digitized) to consumers around the world.

One of the key consequences is that the cultural industries, which used to depend solely on analog technologies, have had to adjust their business models and strategies to deal with the new digital technologies. Some firms have done this successfully, others have not. Also, cultural industries catering to mass audiences tended to use one-way distribution systems (e.g. television and radio broadcasting) and stored media like CDs and DVDs to deliver their services to consumers. The interactivity of digital technologies and file sharing of large digital files via the Internet is making business models premised on one-way distribution and the sale of content on stored media increasingly obsolete.

The ability of information and communication technologies (ICTs) to facilitate interactive exchanges among those connected to networks also makes it more difficult to differentiate consumers and producers as "consumers" share their writings, images, and music with others. The Valtysson chapter in this volume refers to this phenomenon in the context of the "prosumer" who combines production and consumption functions. One important example of this is the recent rapid growth of the "blogosphere" which is widely interpreted as competing with the mainstream news media.[2] A blog is a web page with topical items which is regularly updated in reverse chronological order.

The blogosphere is the collective community of all blogs. By 2008 there were over 70 million blogs.[3] Most of these are not competitors to the mainstream news media but a small minority, such as The Drudge Report, Salon, Daily Kos, The Huffington Post, and Politico, are. The mainstream media have become increasingly dependent on the more widely viewed blogs to identify what is newsworthy and what is not, as a result.

Another example of the importance of interactivity is the growing popularity of social networking sites such as Facebook and MySpace. As of September 2008, Facebook had 39 million unique visitors while MySpace had 59 million.[4] On both sites, users network with others and share photos, videos, and URLs.

The profusion of cultural material available via the Internet means that old producers have to compete with a wide variety of new producers for the attention of audiences, which is what I call "attention rivalry." To be more specific, Table 5.1 below lists the old and new players in a variety of cultural industries to show how the competition for ears and eyeballs has increased.

Some of the new players are owned or controlled by the old players. For example, Hulu.com is owned by NBC, and BMG (a major recording studio) owns Napster. There have also been mergers and acquisitions within and across the two groups. For example, Google recently purchased YouTube, News Corporation bought MySpace, and Disney purchased ABC and Pixar. The large media companies are still looking for the right combination of analog and digital channels.

The ease with which anything digital can be copied, transmitted, and stored forces the distributors of content to look at new business models. A good example is Apple's creation of iTunes as an alternative to the distribution of music via recorded media such as audio CDs.[5] The recording industry reported that aggregate sales of CDs and other recorded media dropped precipitously after the introduction of file-sharing software and digital audio players. The retail value of the sales of RIAA member firms declined from a high of $14.6 billion in 1999 to $8.0 billion in 2007.[6]

Table 5.1   Old and new players in the cultural industries

Industry	Old analog players	New digital players
Television	ABC, NBC, CBS, Fox, HBO, other cable channels and networks	HDNet, YouTube, Yahoo, Google, Hulu, Joost, Vimeo
Movies	Major Hollywood Studios	Dreamworks, Lucasfilm, Pixar, BitTorrent file-sharing software
Music	Major recording studios	iTunes, Napster, Rhapsody, Amazon
Books	Traditional publishers	Google, eBooks, Amazon
Journalism	Newspapers and TV news	Slate, Politico, Blogs, CNN.com

In record stores near wired college campuses, sales frequently dropped to zero.[7] Even though some of these lost revenues were recovered in the form of payments for legal downloading of digital files, consumers would not go back to purchasing albums that included songs that they really did not want to buy.

In book publishing and other print media, the shift to digital distribution has begun, but portable high-resolution digital readers are still not widely available. Two impressive recent entries in the market for digital readers are Amazon's Kindle and Sony's Digital Reader. Still, it is unlikely that books, magazines and newspapers will be as strongly affected by file sharing as audio and video recordings, at least until these and other digital readers come down in price and go up in quality.

More important for print media is the attention rivalry from other media that may be driving people away from reading. According to recent studies of media usage, increased time spent viewing websites on the Internet is cutting into the time spent reading newspapers and listening to the radio while TV viewing is so far relatively unaffected. When asked where they get their news, people are reporting that they turn to the Internet increasingly and decreasingly to newspapers (see Figure 5.1). Declining circulations and the loss of newspaper advertising revenues to online services like Craigslist is putting many local newspapers out of business (Patterson, 2007).

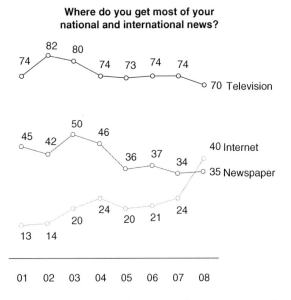

Figure 5.1   Where do respondents get their national and international news?
Sources: Pew Internet and American Life Surveys.

In addition, the average price of all but mass-market paperback books is rising rapidly. Textbook and academic journal prices are rising much faster than the rate of inflation.[8] Libraries are acquiring fewer books and journals and dealing with gaps in their collections via interlibrary, so academic books that are not textbooks are now less economically viable than previously. This is a major problem for young scholars in fields where scholarly book publication is the main criterion for promotion and tenure.

The content of mass media is shifting in response to increasing levels of attention rivalry. TV shows are trying to mimic the interactivity of social networking sites and new radio stations are copying the eclectic musical programming of iPod and MP3 player owners.[9] Internet delivery currently favors short formats over long ones, but that is probably only a function of current computing and network transmission speeds (Hart, 2009). People are demanding that their consumer electronic devices be capable of dealing with multiple channels, so car radios now permit users to easily plug in their iPods or MP3 players, some game consoles can play DVDs and let users access the Internet, and TVs can be connected to devices that let users play video clips from YouTube. The next generation of consumer electronic devices will let users share media with others on a variety of players and platforms.

Infotainment, edutainment, and attention rivalry

One of the consequences of the transition to digital technologies is that the boundaries between previously separate cultural industries are becoming fuzzier. There was already some movement in this direction under analog technologies. In television, for example, the distinction between entertainment programming and news programming eroded as networks increasingly focused on ratings and advertising revenues. With the ability to package audio and video information in both analog and digital formats and to combine them with the interactive capabilities of the Internet came new possibilities for convergence.

Infotainment refers to the combination of information and entertainment, while edutainment refers to the combination of education and entertainment. We are experiencing, for example, a considerable trend toward infotainment and edutainment in higher education. Professors are expected to entertain classes just as news anchors are expected to entertain their television news audiences.[10] The enhanced use of graphic aids in the classroom via PowerPoint and other types of presentation software is part of this trend. As students, and just about everyone else in society, like to "time-shift," professors find themselves uploading their digital presentations to the web so that students can view them at their leisure. In order to keep classroom attendance up, many resort to making attendance part of a student's grade.

No one denies that the transition to digital production, storage, and delivery of entertainment, information, and education has the potential of having a positive impact on society, but there are obviously many downsides as well. Attention rivalry leads to a more distracted public, always looking for ways to filter out unwanted information. Consider, for example, the problem of cleaning out the spam from one's email inbox. Spam filtering software is easily defeated by dedicated spammers, but people buy it anyway in an effort to reduce time wasted doing the filtering by hand.

More importantly, people who used to get their political information from print and electronic media that, because of their need to attract broad audiences, include multiple viewpoints so that readers can decide for themselves about different issues, now can get access to news that is aimed at smaller audiences with a particular slant on public affairs. As a result, people will be less exposed to views that are in opposition to their own.

Another potential downside is that people will get used to and actually enjoy being presented with too much information, a phenomenon that most of us have observed in our children's so-called multi-tasking. The child who plays a networked computer game on a laptop while listening to music, watching television, and chatting with friends online is becoming a common sight in many US households. In university classrooms, we find students instant messaging on their laptops or texting on their cell phones.[11] We used to talk about the benefits of multimedia presentation of information, but the object was to do this with a coherent set of ideas so as to improve learning outcomes for children with different learning styles. How much learning is going on in homes and classrooms when there are no restrictions on multitasking?

The role of government

Political institutions can influence the way in which digital technology is introduced and deployed in a variety of ways. Laws regarding distribution systems can obviously influence the ability of consumers to access digital content. The government gets involved in the building of new telecommunications network infrastructure, either directly or via authorization/subsidy of private efforts. So far the US government has favored relying on the telephone companies and cable TV providers to build out the broadband network. The consequence is that broadband in the US has become dependent on the ability of those two types of firms to find ways to extract additional revenues from households for Internet access and pay TV services. The US is far behind countries like Korea and Denmark on the percentage of citizens who have access to broadband as a result.

The transition to digital television requires administrative and legislative authorization and new forms of regulation. Governments can put an official stamp of approval on new technical standards and can use government procurement policies to support one form or another of digital technology (Hart, 2004; Galperin, 2004; Starks, 2007).

Governments willing to employ industrial policies can subsidize the development of new digital technologies and related industries, as was clearly done in the case of the broadband policies of East Asian countries like Taiwan and Korea—copying the earlier success of Japan (Noland and Pack, 2003). But this is only one method; there are many others: for example, rapid depreciation rules for business taxation, R&D tax credits, negotiation of new digital standards, reforming capital markets to make it easier for digital startups to get access to venture capital, etc. So far the US has decided not to employ these methods to shape or speed the deployment of digital technologies.

The introduction of digital technologies creates pressures for political and policy change. The movie and recording industries, for example, want protection from the potential negative effects of file-sharing by making it more difficult or even illegal for individuals to share copyrighted material. In the late 1990s, they engaged in a massive campaign to educate the public about the evils of digital "piracy" and lobbied governments intensively to enforce intellectual property rights. In the US, this effort culminated in the passage of the Digital Millennium Copyright Act (DMCA) of 1998.[12] The industry's lobbying effort continues with ongoing debates over the so-called Broadcast flag[13] and digital rights management (DRM).[14] The success of the industry's congressional lobbying efforts has spawned a countermovement led by legal scholars like Lawrence Lessig (2005) and Tim Wu.

Toward a political economy of digital culture

Digital information and communications technologies are clearly transforming what Arjun Appadurai (1996) called the "mediascapes" of modern societies. Especially in the US, where the media are controlled by private firms, media creators, packagers, and deliverers have had to revise their business models to deal with the need to compete effectively with other media in a crowded media environment. There are still plenty of non-digital ways to participate in the cultural aspects of society, but the digital media are making major inroads against the analog alternatives especially in mass or popular culture. Power shifts accompany these changes in the mediascape. We saw in the 2008 presidential election campaign, for example, how one candidate gained an important advantage over others by utilizing digital media effectively.

Developing a political economy of digital culture will allow us to look not just at the net outcomes for society as the digital transition goes forward, but also to predict who within society will win or lose. The potential losses of old players in the culture industries and the potential gains of new ones are likely to play a key role in political systems across the globe. We should examine carefully the claims of those pushing the digital transition so that citizens will be empowered by access to computers and high-speed networks, especially if there are only a few providers of that access and citizens have little control over the rules and architecture of the system. We should remain equally skeptical about claims that the digital transition will result in "surveillance states."[15] As social scientists, we can inform public debates over these and related issues by applying the methods and theories of political economy and political science to this dynamic new area.

Notes

Prepared originally for a short course on Culture Industries, Technologies, and Policies, at the annual meeting of the American Political Science Association, Philadelphia, August 30, 2006.

1. J. P. Singh, "APSA Short Course on Culture Industries, Technologies, and Policies," August 20, 2006, available at http://www3.georgetown.edu/grad/cct/10344.html (accessed December 1, 2008).
2. "Blogosphere," *Wikipedia*, available at http://en.wikipedia.org/wiki/Blogosphere (accessed December 1, 2008).
3. Technorati, *State of the Blogosphere 2008*, available at http://technorati.com/blogging/state-of-the-blogosphere/ (accessed December 1, 2008).
4. "Twitter Grows Fastest, MySpace Still the Social King," *Nielsen News*, October 23, 2008, available at http://blog.nielsen.com/nielsenwire/online_mobile/leading-social-networking-sites-still-growing/ (accessed December 1, 2008).
5. "iTunes," *Wikipedia*, available at http://en.wikipedia.org/wiki/ITunes (accessed December 1, 2008).
6. Recording Industry Association of America, *2007 Year-End Shipment Statistics*, available at http://76.74.24.142/81128FFD-028F-282E-1CE5-FDBF16A46388.pdf (accessed December 1, 2008).
7. "New Twist on CD Sales," *p2pnet.net news*, April 10, 2004, available at http://p2pnet.net/story/1187 (accessed December 1, 2008); and Felix Oberholzer-Gee and Koleman Strumpf; "The Effect of File Sharing on Record Sales: An Empirical Analysis," June 2005, available at http://www.unc.edu/~cigar/papers/FileSharing_June2005_final.pdf (accessed December 1, 2008).
8. Margaret Webb Pressler, "Textbook Prices on the Rise," *Washington Post*, September 18, 2004, p. E01.
9. Dave Demerjian, "Imitation iPod' Invades Radio," *Wired*, July 13, 2006, available at http://www.wired.com/culture/lifestyle/news/2006/07/71362 (accessed December 1, 2008).
10. This idea appeared first and most convincingly in Postman (1985).
11. "Law Professor Bans Laptops in Class, Over Student Protest," *USA Today*, March 21, 2006, available at http://www.usatoday.com/tech/news/2006-03-21-professor-laptop-ban_x.htm?POE=TECISVA (accessed December 1, 2008).
12. US Copyright Office, The Digital Millennium Copyright Act of 1998: U.S. Copyright Office Summary, December 1998, available at http://www.copyright.gov/legislation/dmca.pdf (accessed December 1, 2008).
13. Electronic Frontier Foundation, "Broadcast Flag," available at http://www.eff.org/IP/broadcastflag/ (accessed December 1, 2008).
14. "Digital Rights Management," *Wikipedia*, available at http://en.wikipedia.org/wiki/Digital_rights_management (accessed December 1, 2008).
15. For example of works in the surveillance school, see Gandy (1993); Lyon (2001); Marx (forthcoming). The recent revelations about the Bush administration's massive mining of telephone and SWIFT data ostensibly to prevent terrorism gives these claims more credibility than they had before.

6
Playing with Power: The Cultural Impact of Prosumers

Bjarki Valtysson

Introduction

Cultural policy is a fascinating construction. It is fascinating in its endeavors to control, and up to a certain extent tame the concept of *culture*, which Raymond Williams famously referred to as being "one of the two or three most complicated words in the English language" (Williams, 1976: 76). Williams is, of course, right in his assessment regarding the complexity of the concept, but in order to narrow its scope a bit I find it quite useful to refer to the *circuit of culture* model, which exemplifies the multidimensional use that makers of cultural policy can apply to the concept. The model is composed of the five different, but interrelated dimensions of *representation, identity, production, consumption* and *regulation* (du Gay et al., 1997). This still might not be particularly clear; the reason for this is that it is extremely hard to get around the complexity inherent in culture. Indeed, Stuart Hall refers to it at another occasion as representing a system of "shared meanings" (Hall 1997: 1). The important task for makers of cultural policy is to detect and affect the processes of representation, production, consumption, regulation, and how these processes affect the identity formations of people, and for what purposes.

Even though this might sound as an impossible task, makers of cultural policy on local, regional, national and supra-national levels have taken on the challenge and constructed policies that use culture to obtain certain goals. This is true of the cultural policy of different cities, such as Copenhagen, Berlin and New York; the cultural policy of different nation-states, such as Denmark, Germany and the US; and of constellations that are meant to serve global interests, such as the European Union, the Council of Europe, and the United Nations. These cultural policies differ greatly as they ascribe to different legal platforms, different traditions of governance and different political systems, and to make things even more complex and vague, they also differ internally, as a given cultural policy is obviously very much dependent on the political climate that dominates at any given time. What cultural policies do share,

63

however, is the fact that they are human constructions that are supposed to serve certain interests and take on certain specific roles. And this is what I mean by a *fascinating construction*. They are fascinating as they aim for the impossible, and they are constructions as they are meant to prioritize certain discursive formations, at the cost of others.

And it is here that the notion of *power* becomes essential. Cultural policies are no innocent constructions as they are meant to realize certain objectives, and in this context power becomes decisive. Indeed, in my view, all policies are grossly induced by power, as they are formulated to reach certain objectives. No matter how noble these objectives might be, there will always be other objectives that are at odds with the ones being pressed forward, and this creates a venue of conflict. In the case of cultural policy, this venue of conflict acquires particular importance as the concept of culture is extremely charged with meaning, and is commonly applied on different levels of policy making, be it on foreign affairs, industrial development, tourism or education. Nevertheless the final aim is always the same, namely to construct discourses that privilege certain kind of cultural knowledge, or shared meanings, and this happens at the cost of alternative versions of this cultural knowledge and shared meanings.

The main objective of this short chapter is to account for a certain paradigm shift in controlling these discursive formations concomitant with the advent of Web 2.0 and the cultural production, participation and distribution that takes place on the various digital platforms such as YouTube, MySpace, Flickr and Facebook. It is important to note that these discrepancies do not revolutionize the field of cultural policy, but rather play on the lively and productive characteristics of power. There are no evident signs that indicate the end of macro-power structures, as large-scale economical and political actors in the cultural field still exceed great influence on the outcomes of reigning cultural knowledge and shared meanings. There are, however, many signs that indicate that the transformational characteristics of power, or what sometimes is referred to as *meta-power*,[1] have gained new means to manifest itself on the various Web 2.0 platforms. The self-publishing nature of these platforms diversifies the scope of modern cultural policy, as well as challenging some of the basic conceptual frameworks that cultural policy is accustomed to work with. These include the notion of authorship, copyright, aesthetics and cultural governance. What follows is a further speculation on the nature of the cultural interventions made by the "new" cultural users, which have been termed *prosumers* (Stalder, 2001), indicating the changed relationship between cultural *production* and cultural *consumption*, in particular from the viewpoint of power and cultural governance.

Cultural policy and power

As I stated in the introduction, cultural policy has many roles, depending on the context in which it is applied. In overarching terms, cultural policy could be said to consist of complex interactions between various stakeholders of the cultural field. The more notable actors of such field are the various nation-states, regional authorities, the market, the cultural industries, the mass media, large-scale cultural producers and private corporations, and large international bodies. These actors could be said to belong to the macro structures, thereby inducing macro streams of power. However, in its versatility, the cultural venue is also composed of grassroots movements, smaller cultural actors and institutions belonging to civil society, artists, amateurs and of course the widespread consumers. These actors do not usually have the same financial means or networked power as do, for instance, major culture and media conglomerates within the cultural industries and major movements within the political structure, but their contribution is pivotal to the circulation of power within the field of cultural policy.

This is at least the case when Michel Foucault's definition of power is applied, but according to him power has a networked and productive nature. This means that streams of power do not just travel from one station to the next, where typically macro-power exerts some kind of acts of colonization towards micro-power streams, but on the contrary, the various micro manifestations of power are of resistant nature. This basically means that in the long run, emancipative micro manifestations are capable of changing the course of its macro counterpart, thereby causing unpredictable outcomes that do no necessarily correspond to the main objectives of a given cultural policy.

In Foucault's view, the interaction between power and knowledge operates within the so-called *discursive formations*. By this, Foucault means certain conceptual frameworks pave the way for some specific modes of thought, thereby denying, or at least downplaying, other alternative modes of thought. These formations work within a body of both written and unwritten rules which decide what is allowed to be spoken, thought, created and done within different fields and during certain periods of time. We do of course live in a world of immensely heterogeneous mass of discourses and so-called valid statements, but what Foucault is really referring to, through his idea of discursive formations, is the man-made overarching system of thought, which follows, despite its immense versatility, certain system of regularity, ethical conduct and moral values. In his work *Archaeology of Knowledge*, Foucault describes the notion of a discursive formation in following terms: "Whenever one can describe, between a number of statements, such a system of dispersion, whenever, between objects, types of statement, concepts, or thematic choices, one can define a regularity (an order, correlations, positions and functionings, transformations), we will say, for the sake of convenience, that we are dealing with a *discursive formation*" (Foucault, 2002a: 41; italics in the original).

Therefore, Foucault's discursive formations, which are actually clusters of various related discourses, could be said to be the means by which as institutions exercise their power through a complicated process of definition, difference and exclusion, and thereby construct a given topic or, in the perspective of this chapter, a given cultural policy. From the viewpoint of state cultural policy, Foucault's notion of *governmentality* (Foucault, 2002b) applies to such institutional processes, where a privileged cultural knowledge and shared meanings are meant to construct citizens that obey these processes. The British cultural theorist Stuart Hall adds yet another important dimension to the notion of Foucault's discourse, as the following lines from his work *Representation* demonstrate: "It defines and produces the objects of our knowledge. It governs the way that a topic can be meaningfully talked about and reasoned about. It also influences how ideas are put into practice and used to regulate the conduct of others" (Hall, 1997: 44).

This is an extremely important point as in Foucault's terms it is discourse that produces knowledge. But discourse is not a fast-frozen, rational entity incapable of change and transformation, but on the contrary a complex mixture of the effects of language and practice which defines, produces, rules and governs, along with power, the object of our knowledge. Foucault underlines these interrelations between power, discourse and knowledge explicitly when he maintains that "in a society such as ours, but basically in any society, there are manifold relations of power which permeate, characterize and constitute the social body, and these relations of power cannot themselves be established, consolidated nor implemented without the production, accumulation, circulation and functioning of a discourse" (Foucault, 1980: 93).

To put it in slightly simpler terms, discourse, power and knowledge are all interrelated and merge into those discursive formations which combine various discourses that refer to the same object and share the same style, support a certain strategy and belong to a certain institutional, administrative and political drift during a specific epoch.

When Foucault's concept of power and discursive formations is transmitted to the field of cultural policy, it becomes better known what I mean by my former statement that cultural policy is not an innocent construction. Cultural policy is indeed responsible for setting quantitative demands and constructing qualitative taste hierarchies. On a national plan, it governs, constructs and reconstructs the cultural heritage, thereby directly stimulating regional and national identity in a certain direction. Furthermore, if a given cultural policy wishes to respond to modern multicultural societal formations, it has to include dimensions, which Tony Bennett refers to as sub- or multinationalist, autochthonous, diasporic and indigenous approaches (Bennett, 2001).

Cultural policy also tries to meet, serve and develop the aesthetic experiences and knowledge of the general public, as well as creating suitable working conditions for professional artists and cultural institutions. But to add yet to the multiple and somewhat paradoxical role of cultural policy, it also encourages amateurs and social and educational sectors to participate in the making and enjoying of arts and culture. Finally, just like the state and the various non-commercial and non-governmental organizations and institutions in civil society, the market and the cultural industries also have cultural policies. Their aim typically is to use culture to gain financially or to use it for branding purposes, often to soften the image of a given corporation. In his work on corporate cultural politics, Mark W. Rectanus takes, for instance, the example of the cultural policy of Philip Morris, and how many corporations use the value of aesthetics and design very strategically in marketing and in their public-relations work, where they participate eagerly in the mediation of contemporary culture and in forming lifestyles (Rectanus, 2002).

Having said that, it should be quite clear that cultural policies have many different roles and serve very different purposes depending on the state's, the market's, civil society's, citizen's and supra-state's influence on a given policy. But there is of course also differentiation between these categories as well. Different nation-states adopt different policies during different times, depending very much on the privileged discursive formations. In the case of the Nordic nations, Peter Duelund has traced various transitions since Second World War, starting with the treatment of cultural policy as a legitimate governmental tool to counteract the standardization of culture and the arts by the cultural industries. According to such discursive formations, the aim was to govern in a top-down fashion, typically by applying a highly selective humanistic version of high culture. A bottom-up, decentralized approach followed the earlier onewhere the anthropological view of culture replaced the elitism of the humanistic one, resulting in discursive formations that privileged the stimulation of local cultural activities through state reimbursement programs. The aim of such discursive formations was to increase cultural participation by the general public, instead of aiming for artistic excellence. Finally, Peter Duelund points towards a development that had already started in the 1980s; cultural policy increasingly followed the mantra of neoliberalism and was noted mainly for its commercial potential. The state acknowledged the fact that culture can indeed make money and encouraged a symbiosis between culture and businesses, for instance by introducing tax reforms and legislation on funding the arts, with the intention of increasing the involvement of private patrons and companies in sponsor and buy art (Duelund, 2003).

What has been happening in the Nordic countries is therefore a transition from looking upon cultural policy as means to privilege the "high arts", to privileging the cultural participation of the general public, and finally to privileging increased intervention of the market forces. In another recent study, Annabelle Littoz-Monnet refers to cultural-policy models as being divided into *liberal*, *dirigiste* and *federal* approaches (Littoz-Monnet, 2007), depending on the overall aims, the degree of decentralization, and the adaptation of direct means of governmental interference such as arm's length cultural agencies, result-based contracts, tax exemptions, and such.

It should therefore be quite clear that cultural policies serve different purposes and have different aims depending on the context to which they are applied and the discursive formations they serve. Here, the notion of power plays a crucial role as it is the main generator of the knowledge that is being produced within a given discursive formation. The power to distribute and govern cultural political resources is spreading across more actors such as international organizations and strong financial bodies belonging to the market sphere, thereby creating new fields of power relations and diversifying the scope of modern cultural policy (Kangas, 2003). This is of course not a totally new development as cultural cooperation has existed between nation-states and global organizations for a long time. However, concomitant to the rise of the network society, with its networked global flow of digital cultural information, there has been yet another change in the possible manifestation of the different paradigms of cultural policy, and this calls for a certain reconceptualization of the field, in particular from the viewpoint of networked streams of micro-power.

Micro-power and the prosumer

What has been said so far about cultural policy and power still applies. Cultural policy is always put to use with a certain purpose in mind. In some parts of the world, the urge to use it for financial growth and active participation in the experience economy (Pine and Gilmore, 1999) might be the strongest one, while in other contexts the main objective might be to generate increased cultural participation of the general public. It really depends on the reigning discursive formations of a given place, during a given period of time.

The network society, or the information society, is without doubt one of the most significant manifestation and description of contemporary life. Informationalism, as the "technological paradigm that constitutes the material basis of early twenty-first century societies" (Castells, 2004: 8) has therefore added yet another dimension to the multifaceted role of cultural policy. The term informationalism is frequently used by Manuel Castells in his attempts to describe the paradigm that is the most prevalent nowadays, and according to him, computers and digital communications are the most direct expressions of such a paradigm. Castells detects three main distinctive features of these technologies, namely, their self-expanding processing and communicating capacity, in particular in terms of volume, complexity and speed; their capacity to recombine because of their digitized, recurrent communication; and finally their distributing flexibility which comes about because of their interactive, digitized networking (Castells, 2004: 9).

These three features have had a major impact on the cultural production and cultural consumption of the general public for the last ten years or so, where digital cultural material is being downloaded, mixed, remixed, uploaded, distributed and redistributed in colossal volume and with great speed, thereby adding another dimension to the field of cultural policy. I find it very important to refer to the paradigm of informationalism as an *add-on* to the diversified tasks of cultural policy, since the older ones have not disappeared. Therefore, it would be a big mistake to get all enthusiastic over the potentials of emancipation that certainly go along with the digital add-on, or to follow the other extreme, focusing only on the colonizing panoptical dimensions that is certainly one characteristic of digital communication, and our use of the Internet. The important thing is not to take sides, but rather to acknowledge that this online cultural participation and production adds a very challenging dimension to cultural policy, where key concepts such as authorship, cultural production, cultural consumption, copyright, and of course governance, are scrambled.

The immense self-expanding processing, communicating capacity, the recombining features and the distributive flexibility of the Internet have exploded with Web 2.0. Even though the actual notion of Web 2.0 is extremely vague, I refer to it on similar terms as David Hesmondhalgh does in his work on the cultural industries, where its user-generated characteristics are emphasized, along with the creation of networks and production and consumption and remixing of digital material. Hesmondhalgh is wary of the emancipative potentials that these decentralized platforms offer and even if they have enabled new means of communications between people, he still refers to their productions as "huge amounts of small-scale cultural activity" (Hesmondhalgh, 2007: 261). Even though these kind of cultural productions may represent forms of subversion and insubordination, Hesmondhalgh points to the fact that these subversions do not dismantle the enormous concentration of power inherent in the cultural industries, but rather represent a *disturbance* to their structure.

And it is here that Michel Foucault becomes interesting again. This disturbance represents quite well in my view the multifaceted nature that Foucault ascribes to power; it is not only totalitarian and oppressive, but also creative, playful and productive. Hence, in order for power to thrive and develop, there has to be some kind of productive resistance, and this can best be described with terms like macro-power and micro-power; or as Foucault would have it: "A power relationship, on the other hand, can only be articulated on the basis of two elements that are indispensable if it is really to be a power relationship: that 'the other' (the one over whom power is exercised) is recognized and maintained to the very end as a subject who acts; and that, faced with a relationship of power, a whole field of responses, reactions, results, and possible inventions may open up" (Foucault, 2002b: 340).

Even though the techniques of power force the subject into certain positions, molding its opinions according to ruling discursive formations, power still has an ambivalent nature. Indeed, power is a set of actions upon other actions, resulting in a critical minority that keeps society from developing into a static and homogenous system. This critical minority, composed of alternative discourse or counter-publics, resists adapting to the subject positions that have been constructed by a given society, and by doing that, it opens up for emancipative flow of micro-power.

I do generally agree with David Hesmondhalgh in his verdict that the cultural productions taking place on the Internet and in particular on Web 2.0 have not revolutionized the cultural industries, or the field of cultural policy for that matter. But it would in my view be very unwise for the makers of future cultural policy to totally ignore this so-called *disturbance*. The reason for this is twofold. First, when looked upon from the viewpoint of demand, the colossal *volume* of cultural production taking place on YouTube, MySpace, Flickr and Facebook (to mention only four of the extreme variety of Web 2.0 platforms on the Internet) is on such scale that it easily overcomes other productions that cultural policy typically has supported, at least in terms of volume.

Second, the very *nature* of this cultural production and consumption taking place on Web 2.0 is different from what cultural policy is accustomed to. Here, I am mainly pointing towards the disturbances that a culture of digital remixability poses to key concepts of cultural policy, in particular the notion of authorship, copyright, distribution, production and consumption. Indeed, as I already stated, the last two have been commingled into the term *prosumer*, that is, the *consumer* is also a *producer* (Stalder, 2001). When looked upon from the viewpoint of reception studies, this might not represent anything new as we can be said to be constantly *prosuming* the signs surroundings us, as they first start to make sense when we interact with them in a cognitive, as well as creative manner. The difference, however, lies in the easy-facilitating of manipulating digital data, and the fact that people, or prosumers, are doing it in a volume that is unheard of.

The reason why so many prosumers are participating in, producing, consuming, and distributing digital products is the user-friendly interface that most of the Web 2.0 platforms offer. It is very simple to create and operate a blog, to submit videos and pictures on Facebook and YouTube, to participate in a chat and participate in expanding networks that concentrate on specific topics. It is likewise very easy to operate standardized video and sound editors that are included in most computers, thereby making the act of digital mixing and remixing a commonplace affair. The great volume of digital material circulating the nodes of the global network of new media is a blatant manifestation of digital cultural processes. I would therefore conclude that even though this *prosumption* might be looked upon as a disturbance, at least from the viewpoint of the macro-power that the cultural industries are capable of inducing, the multiple forms of micro-power that this kind of cultural exchange induces gives rise to a different way of engaging with culture, and this alters the power balance within the field of cultural policy.

Indeed, as Felix Stalder notes, this kind of culture is moving the barriers further from what he refers to as *object-oriented culture*, to that of *exchange-oriented culture* (Stalder, 2005). The former looks upon culture as made of discrete objects, while the latter looks upon culture as continuous processes. The exchange-oriented culture corresponds nicely to Manuel Castells' view of this kind of culture as consisting not of *content*, but of *processes*. Indeed, according to him, the kind of culture that certainly is flourishing on Web 2.0 platforms "is an open-ended network of cultural meanings that can not only coexist, but also interact and modify each other on the basis of this exchange" (Castells, 2004: 40).

I do think it is far too simplistic to talk about a definite shift from object-oriented culture to that of exchange-oriented culture, as the two do not exclude each other. In fact, as I said earlier, the digital dimension with its most blatant manifestation on Web 2.0 is an add-on. Because of its decentralized nature, this add-on will have a hard time generating streams of macro-power to the same extent as powerful nation-states and conglomerates are capable of, but its strength lies in empowering different prosumers with a voice of their own – a voice which can be heard immediately, on many different platforms, in many different versions, distributing either original cultural material, or remixes, through the manifold platforms that the typical Web 2.0 user is confronted with every day.

This kind of prosumption does, however, inflict numerous challenges to the field of cultural policy, thereby upsetting the streams of power and the dominant discursive formations. Felix Stalder summarizes many of these challenges as: "Ranging from the de-centering of authorship, which moves away from individuals to groups, networks or communities, to the blurring of the line between artists and their audiences, the organization of cultural industries, the adaptation of intellectual property law, the future development of technology, and the status of a work of art itself" (Stalder, 2005: 7). Seen from the perspective of cultural policy, these are some serious challenges.

Can it be controlled?

The multidimensional view that Michel Foucault ascribes to power underlines its oppressive and playful, destructive and productive nature. In the case of cultural policy, the norms, regularities, positions, the order and correlation of dominant discursive formations channel streams of power that define and construct the object of prioritized knowledge. As I briefly mentioned, this dominance changes during different epochs, precisely because power is not static, but on a constant move. The streams of macro-power, that are generated mostly within the field of cultural policy nowadays, seem to prioritize economic norms, where the aim is first and foremost to use culture to soften the image of corporations and brand them as being socially responsible, and of course to enhance financial growth.

This is at least the case when a further look is taken at the changes of discursive formations that have occurred in the Nordic cultural model in the last 50 years or so. In the case of the Nordic countries, the state has traditionally possessed a dominant position within the field of cultural policy and for the last two decades, there has been a clear tendency to facilitate the dominance of such 'liberal' discursive formations. Cultural institutions financed by the state are increasingly demanded to act as private companies, following instructions that prioritize new public management techniques, result-based contracts and quantitative data, both in terms of finances, as well as in terms of attendance figures (Duelund, 2003). But as my brief overview of shifting paradigms within the field of cultural policy indicates, this has not always been the case. And this is so because of the playful, productive characteristics of power, as treated by Foucault.

In my view, this playfulness of power is acquiring an interesting microdimension concomitant to the cultural prosumption that takes place on the various Web 2.0 platforms. What this basically means for makers of cultural policy is that it is going to be a lot harder to tame and control the concept of culture, as the traditional tools of cultural policy prove to be ineffective in the online cultural landscape created by prosumers. From the viewpoint of the different cultural policies of nation-states, it is much more difficult to politically construct discursive formations that are favorable to and encourage the ideals of certain national identities. And the same goes of course for regions and municipalities. It is much more difficult to construct a system that ensures financial allocations to artists, artist organizations, library taxes, etc., as the cultural landscape in which prosumers operate is global. Furthermore, as the prime medium of prosumption, the Internet, is highly decentralized; it is much harder to control, than say, the cultural policy which a given Ministry of Culture on a national stage wishes its cultural institutions to follow.

These challenges, which the cultural policies of nation-states all over the world are confronting, can also be transmitted to the corporate cultural policies of diverse corporations. In case of the global cultural industries, the route to financial growth has traditionally been to keep the source of the code as tight to you as possible. But the micro-power streams generated by the remixable culture of prosumers thrive and grow on opposite terms. Indeed, it is pivotal to their growth to have access to the codes of cultural production and distribution, as without them, the prosumption of digital cultural items becomes a lot harder.

When a quick look is taken at, for instance, the videos that are being uploaded on YouTube, there is no question that despite the cultural industries' attempts to close the code, the code seems to be alive and well. What this means is that people are boycotting the laws, uploading, mixing and remixing material that is guarded by copyright. Much of the prosumption taking place on the Internet is therefore illegal. This brings me to the conclusion that the remixable culture of prosumers cannot be controlled, at least not with the traditional methods that cultural policy has grown accustomed to in the "analogue" world. The streams of micro-power that are being generated from this kind of exchange-oriented culture are indeed affecting the regularities, positions, the order and correlation of the dominant discursive formations within the field of cultural policy. Whether it is correct to talk about these micro-power streams in terms of disturbances is up to debate, but cultural policy is in my view forced to rethink some of its strategies and find ways of channeling these productions in a creative, and most importantly, legal manner. This demands a shift in mentality, especially from the makers of future cultural policy, where it has to be acknowledged that this kind of digital add-ons cannot and should not be controlled to the same degree as for instance culture political decisions concerning tax deductions, the implementation of the arm's length principle, which project to finance, and which not, etc. The important thing is to acknowledge the playfulness of power and adjust the tools of cultural policy accordingly.

This could for instance be done by focusing on providing meta-frameworks or digital databases where legality is ensured (for instance by applying the Creative Commons license) in a manner similar to what the open source movement has been doing for quite some time. This demands a shift in looking upon authorship as something final, as prosumers are quite accustomed to look upon their efforts as being collaborative. This demands a shift in aesthetic perceptions, as the cultural products made by prosumers cannot be said to belong to the realm of high culture, but follow rather the culture political bottom-up approach of privileging the cultural participation of the general public. This demands a shift from looking upon the artwork as a fast-frozen object to seeing it in terms of fluid exchange. This demands a shift from looking upon copyright as a fixed construction to looking upon it in terms of variable choices, where it is in fact the individual prosumer who decides the terms. And finally, and perhaps most importantly, this demands a shift in terms of governance, where makers of cultural policy have to break up some of the streams of macro-power, thereby creating discursive formations that do not have the same calculated outcomes and cannot be controlled as easily as their predecessors.

Conclusion: Channeling the collective intelligence of prosumers

As a concluding remark, I want to emphasize the fact that the remixable culture of prosumers is a digital add-on to the field of cultural policy, and a highly specific one. Other aspectcs of cultural policy will not vanish and indeed, they should not. The cultural production and consumption finding place on Web 2.0 does not eliminate other kinds of cultural productions and consumption. It does, however, upset the kind of cultural governance that most cultural policies have grown accustomed to. And it does so because of the sheer volume of prosumptions, enabled by information technologies and digital communication, and it does so in terms of the exchange-oriented nature of such prosumption.

In my view, cultural policy will still be a fascinating construction where streams of macro-power will be generated to serve the interests and objectives of ruling discursive formations in society. This kind of power will still be relatively centralized on few hands, be it powerful nation-states, or powerful media and culture conglomerates, and perhaps David Hesmondhalgh is indeed right in his verdict of looking upon the cultural activities taking place on the Internet, and particularly on Web 2.0, as disturbances. These disturbances, generated by micro-power, could however escalate, particularly in the light of the Internet's recombined, flexible volume, and this is a challenge which cultural policy has to adapt to.

The role of future cultural policy is therefore not to tame and control the accepted discursive formations of the culture political field, as it lies in the very nature of power to circulate, and constantly defer such absolute control. The role of future cultural policy is in my view more realistically described from the functioning of the playful aspects of power, and this basically infers a certain change in paradigm, where the aim is not to control, but to design circumstance where power will be channeled productively and playfully. Otherwise, cultural policy will not succeed in channeling the collective intelligence of prosumers in a creative and legal manner.

Note

1. See J. P. Singh's introduction to this volume.

Part II Cultural Policies: US, EU, Japan

7
The Political Economy of Cultural Diversity in Film and Television

Harvey Feigenbaum

Two related global trends have had a serious impact on the world's cultural diversity. These trends are—first, the gradual but relentless reduction in barriers to international trade and second, the increasing popularity of neoliberal economic policies in much of both the developed and developing worlds. When combined with new innovations in technology, the fears that many countries expressed in the 2005 UNESCO Convention on the Protection and Promotion of the Diversity of Cultural Expressions are well on their way to being realized.

The first of these trends, known by the shorthand term of globalization, has led to the increasing integration of world markets and the parceling out of different stages of the production process to those areas with the most obvious competitive advantages (On the concept of *competitive advantage*, see Porter, 1990: pp. 29–30). Advocates of integration stress the benefits of increased efficiency and the gradual spread effects on world development, especially as several of the newly industrialized countries have taken advantage of these developments to expand their export markets and attract inward investment, thus experiencing a rise in incomes. By and large, the advent of globalization has been received positively, and in some quarters—especially those populated by neoclassical economists—enthusiastically.

The cultural aspects of globalization have been less warmly received. The US dominates world markets for film and television programs. This is not news. Most films exhibited in most countries are Hollywood films, that is, they are produced and often distributed by companies that are based in southern California. The companies, primarily the major studios that were founded at the dawn of the twentieth century, are no longer—necessarily—American, at least in terms of their ownership. Some, like Sony Pictures Entertainment (originally, Columbia Pictures) are part of well-known international firms. Some have changed hands repeatedly: Universal Studios was owned by Matsushita (Japan), Seagrams (Canada), Vivendi (France), and General Electric (US) in rapid succession. Sometimes the prize was so big that it was the new stockholder who changed citizenship, rather than the corporation—as was the case with Twentieth Century Fox and the formerly Australian Rupert Murdoch with his News Corp holding company.

While the nationalities of these entertainment producers are ambiguous, the implications of Hollywood's pervasive presence are less so. They are, however, controversial. In October of 2005 UNESCO produced its Convention on Cultural Diversity. The Convention was mostly the outcome of energetic negotiations led by the representatives of Canada and France, two countries where cultural issues are especially salient and where the leadership has often identified American films and television shows as unduly pervasive. However, while it is true that behind the scenes both countries offered carrots and sticks to bring especially the developing countries into line, this can hardly be the entire reason (see Balassa, 2008). The only countries to vote against the Convention were the US and Israel. There seemed to be an overwhelming majority of countries who feared, or were at least concerned about, the damaging effects to their cultures if trade in entertainment products remained one-sided.

Cultural diversity

If the concept of globalization is relatively straightforward, at least in economic terms, what one means by cultural diversity is not. The UNESCO (2005) convention, formally entitled "Convention on the Protection and Promotion of the Diversity of Cultural Expressions" provides a somewhat unhelpful definition:

> "Cultural diversity" refers to the manifold ways in which the cultures of groups and societies find expression. These expressions are passed on within and among groups and societies.

> Cultural diversity is made manifest not only through the varied ways in which the cultural heritage of humanity is expressed, augmented and transmitted through the variety of cultural expressions, but also through diverse modes of artistic creation, production, dissemination, distribution and enjoyment, whatever the means and technologies used.

Tyler Cowan (2002) has rightly pointed out that the term is ambiguous. One can imagine a world where no form of exchange takes place, but collectively constitutes a great variety of cultures. Conversely, one can imagine a world of great exchange where each country benefits from more and more cultural choices as a result of trade and technology, but where the world collectively consists of countries increasingly similar to each other in the cultural choices they offer (Cowan, 2002). The issue is further muddled by the use of *cultural diversity* as code for cultural protectionism, which implies diversity more in Cowan's first sense of the word, and not the latter sense. In this regard France and Canada seem to be favoring a world of culturally unique societies. They do not seem to want a world where all countries offer an array of choices, but where the options are roughly the same in each country.

If we are to stay at a level of understanding cultural diversity as an abstraction, my own take on this is to borrow from Talcott Parsons' definition of culture as an "ordered system of symbols" and to consider cultural diversity as the variety of symbols to which people attach meaning (Beer, 1973: p. 24). In political terms this means a diversity of frameworks "for interpreting the actions and motives of others" (Ross, 1997: p. 44).

Of course, when one leaves the world of the abstract and rejoins the real world, the main issue for the champions of cultural diversity is to avoid an asymmetric exchange where America dominates and where all countries begin to look more and more American. It is my contention that the economics of film and television tend toward this outcome, and that this Americanization has political consequences. In my view, these consequences justify a measure of political interference in the market.

Political ramifications

American dominance in the market for audiovisual goods and services has political ramifications. Work done in both communications theory and cognitive science suggests that the impact of America's dominance of popular culture crowd out what Habermas called the "public sphere," the metaphorical space (presumably isolated from the influence of market relations) where people may freely gather and discuss society's problems. Furthermore, I believe American cultural dominance may even pose a threat to creativity and innovation (Habermas, 1989).

To the extent that television screens and movie theaters play American products, they take the place of local products. They become part of the discourse, and provide many of the symbols of everyday speech. Moreover, symbols are the shorthand of politics and imported categories can constrain thought (Dallmayr, 1984). The symbolic and semantic aspects of politics are hardly trivial. They trigger emotions and are used to both persuade and to manipulate. Much of the efforts in political campaigns are devoted to how arguments are framed, with each side doing its symbolic best to evoke images favorable to its side (Lakoff and Johnson, 2003). Innocent and apparently apolitical reference points, such as "the family" or "the police," become symbolic cues which redirect political discourse. Moreover, access to popular images approaches the very root of human thought. A wealth of literature from the fields of psychology and cognitive science documents the widespread view (well known to advertisers and political campaigners) that people think in metaphors and that metaphors have consequences (Dallmayr, 1984; Fiumiara, 1995). That which is familiar often becomes translated into a sense of comfort and identity. Countries on the receiving end of American culture fear losing their very own identities, the essence of who they are. Not to put too fine a point on it, they fear losing their souls.

as a threat

The dominance of American films and television shows has been reinforced by the application of neoliberal policies in many of the UN member states. Privatization policies in the audiovisual industries outside the US have been a disaster for those countries worried about protecting their cultures from Americanization. The proliferation of private television networks financed by advertising, added to a flood of new media options provided by cable and satellites, has led to a Hobbesian competition for market share amid an overall audience that has barely expanded. Simple arithmetic has meant that fewer and fewer people are watching any given show or movie. Private networks, now the majority in most countries, are thus increasingly cost-sensitive, and have evoked a strong preference for importing cheap American products over locally produced television shows, despite near universal preferences of audiences to see their own cultures on television.[1] The film industry is somewhat different, but virtually all non-American film industries survive by virtue of subsidy programs or favorable tax treatment, often added to protectionist measures on film exhibition. Neoliberal policies which undermine preferential treatment of national film and television companies are a threat to these measures as well.

Technology as a threat

For the reasons outlined above, many countries have adopted policies which establish minimum quotas for local content on their national airwaves, and occasionally in movie theaters as well (Feigenbaum, 2003). Two important technologies, direct broadcasting by satellite (DBS) and digital compression, undermine national efforts to reserve a part of primetime for non-American products. Widely available for over a decade, DBS allows consumers to put up a satellite dish not much larger than a dinner plate, and to receive programming from a number of private companies. The companies offering these options to European and Asian subscribers are often based in countries different from that of their customers. They offer a mix of programming, with much of it, due to price, coming from Hollywood. The European Commission permits national enforcement of quotas which have been legitimized by its "Television without Borders" Directive, (recently renewed as the Audiovisual Media Services Directive), and European courts have extended the reach of national quota legislation to satellites, but the reality is different. It is the nature of its "footprint" that makes the satellite broadcast inherently international for all but continent-sized countries. Companies profit from the cross-border satellite coverage to extend the reach of their shows despite national quotas. Companies like TNT or the Cartoon Network take advantage of the broad sweep of the satellite and run their programs with multiple soundtracks, allowing broadcasts in several languages (McPherson, 2000). There is very little a country can do to prevent DBS transmissions that do not respect quotas. Technically this would probably require jamming, and employing such a technique would immediately associate those jamming the signal with a practices associated with nondemocratic governments. Just in case international opprobrium for jamming were not enough, the European Court of Justice ruled that EU states, at least, could not take "excessive measures" to block transborder reception (ibid.: p. 101).

The other technology that favors Hollywood and subverts national quotas is digital compression. The latter, similar to a "zip file," is based on the engineering insight that not all elements of a television picture move. If one broadcasts only the information for pixels that are required to change, this greatly reduces the amount of information that needs to be carried and expands the capacity of the spectrum many hundreds of times. What this makes possible is "video-on-demand." Video-on-demand allows viewers to choose a program or film from a library and to be able to see it at anytime. Viewers are unlikely to be especially sensitive to the national quota legislation when weighed against their entertainment whim of the moment. Under such conditions, national quotas will become meaningless.

Countervailing technologies[2]

Of course, not all technologies undermine cultural diversity. Cable television, for example, did make it possible for small communities to diffuse local content at costs that would have been prohibitive in the earlier age of terrestrial broadcasting. Digital video cameras have made moviemaking extremely inexpensive and allows even the smallest countries to produce their own movies. New software has made it possible for elaborate special effects to be produced on a desktop computer (Feigenbaum, 2003). Other digital innovations, such as nonlinear editing and digital projection reduce expenses, although the latter requires high initial outlays. These new digital light projectors eliminate the need for costly prints and elaborate distribution. Finally and famously, the Internet's invention of narrow casting and digital stream allow the distribution of cultural content from even the smallest community.

Unfortunately technologies which reduce costs for small countries also do so for the dominant power. As a former CEO of the Australian Film Commission noted, "Digital distribution and internet streaming just make it easier to deliver American product" (K. Dalton, personal correspondence, 2001).

Impact of current trends

The combined impact of economic incentives, inappropriate policies and the widespread application of new technologies poses a threat to cultural diversity. However, it is worthwhile to see exactly what is threatened. That is, what are the advantages to cultural diversity. Besides the fact that every country thinks its own culture is intrinsically valuable, it can be argued that cultural diversity is a collective good which benefits everyone.

It is my argument that cultural diversity stimulates creativity and often leads to economic innovation as well. First, it should be noted that cultural diversity is a boon to Hollywood. Part of the reason that American films are successful in world markets is that the domestic American audience is already culturally diverse. To succeed in the US market, films must appeal to a wide variety of people, from jaded urbanites to rural teenagers. They must be able to attract Jews, Latinos, Blacks, Whites, women, men, workers and professionals. Not all films attract everyone, but it is the accumulated experience of understanding the diversity of the American market that gives Americans studios a leg up on international markets. Second, Hollywood attracts and uses talent from all over the world. "American" films are frequently made by Australians, Germans, Chinese and a host of other immigrants, each bringing a particular sensibility acquired outside the US.

More generally, exposure to the exotic can stimulate the mundane. Cowan quite correctly reminds us that all cultures are really hybrids (Cowan, 2002), so it is not a huge leap to consider a micro-level version such hybridization. Starbucks is a useful illustration. Howard Schultz, the entrepreneur behind this phenomenal success, visited Italy and decided that combining Italian coffee culture with an American sweet tooth could make a lot of money. It did. Similarly, the visit of an American postmaster general to Europe in the 1960s led to adoption of US zip codes, vastly improving the efficiency of the American delivery system.

There is, of course, a special place for the role of diversity in the arts. Arts lobbies in the US have tried to make economic arguments to justify spending on culture (see for example, Tepper, 2002). These tend to be of two types: first, that arts spending creates spread effects.

Spending on the arts generates small businesses with employment consequences such as restaurants around an art museum or as is the case with film, spending on film infrastructure attracts investment (from movie producers) and generates high paying jobs (electricians, technicians etc.) in an industry that does not pollute. A second kind of argument focuses on the changing of the economy, with prosperity being most likely in countries that foster the creative sectors. Analysts such as Richard Florida (2004) have argued that public spending on the arts improves the local quality of life and thus attracts the creative types who bring the most value-added to the economy.

Like most economic arguments, these are controversial. More than likely, some arts spending generates spread effects beyond the initial investment, while other spending does not. Nor can anyone doubt that some creative people are responsible for generating an awful lot of money. From highly paid movie stars to brilliant software engineers, this is a truism. However, that is not to say that all creativity is lucrative, nor that most creative people pay for themselves. The poor, starving artist is not a cliché for nothing.

However, while economic appeals for cultural policy do not always fall on sympathetic ears, there can be little doubt that much of the impetus behind spending on local film and television production is motivated by high-minded nationalism and by low-minded pandering to the imprecations of lobbies.[3]

Conclusion

Reasons for America's domination of entertainment markets would necessarily make the length of this paper unwieldy, but to summarize, American films dominate the world for essentially three reasons: 1) the huge internal market allows for lavish spending on production values which make US films attractive to audiences looking for entertainment and escape; 2) US film companies are the only ones with a capacity for world-wide distribution (Farhi and Greenfield, 1998); and 3) The need to appeal to a multicultural domestic market has guided the evolution of American films toward stories that are broadly appealing and good candidates for international sales.[4]

Thus, there are convincing reasons for countries to wish to promote their cultures by protecting and subsidizing their native film and television industries. However, as with most policies, some work better than others. Moreover, as the international environment evolves for reasons owing to both changes in technology and developments in the world economy, it is worth considering a host of ideas to protect cultural diversity. However, the first step is to recognize the problem. This has been done thanks to the actions of UNESCO and especially its Universal Convention voted in October of 2005.

Notes

1. In a comparison of the most watched television shows in Australia, France, Italy, Sweden and the US, only in Australia was the most watched show an import. Curiously, once Australia is excluded only France had an American production in the top ten: the movie *Star Wars*. See, "Television: Most-watched Programs," *International Herald Tribune*, May 23, 2005: 10. Since Nielson ratings are proprietary, it is hard to extend this argument systematically. However, my reading of television program sales at the annual MIPCOM market in Cannes, France, shows the American producers outsell Europeans most of the time.
2. This section borrows heavily from my article, "Is technology the enemy of culture?," *International Journal of Cultural Policy*, 10 (3), 251–63.
3. One conservative French official told me that politicians were simply afraid of being labeled anti-intellectual, a statement it would be hard to imagine hearing from an American politician.
4. I develop these arguments in an upcoming article, "Hollywood: From Flexible Specialization to Globalized Production," in *Economia della Cultura*, 2/2005 (in Italian) and in "Hollywood: The Bottom Line" *Le Monde Diplomatique (English Edition)*, (originally published in French as "Hollywood à l'ère de la production globalisée,") August, 2005.

8

An "Economic" Approach Toward the Trade and Culture Debate: The US Position

Carol Balassa

Introduction: The trade and culture debate—a debate over applying trade rules to motion pictures

Negotiation of the Cultural Diversity Convention has been portrayed as but "the latest chapter in the longstanding debate over the relationship between trade and culture," a debate that pits two radically opposing views of cultural products against each other: "One approach sees cultural products as entertainment products that are similar, in commercial terms, to any other products and therefore completely subject to the rules of international trade. The other view is that cultural products are essential instruments of social communications which convey values, ideas and meaning, and thus contribute to fashioning the cultural identity. As such, they should be excluded from the reach of international trade agreements" (Bernier, 2005).

Left undefined in the above description of the trade and culture debate is the term "cultural products." Is the term intended to encompass those artistic endeavors which, by their nature require the presence of an audience at a given site at a given time, are we talking about a broadly disseminated creative undertaking which can be easily replicated at relatively little or no cost to a global audience, or are we talking about both simultaneously?

Given the language used above to describe the parameters of the trade and culture debate, it appears unlikely that "cultural products" refer to painting, sculpture, theater or opera, whose value, to a greater or lesser degree, lies in its limited availability to audiences. Rather, in the context of trade negotiations, "cultural products" refer to motion pictures, video discs, television programs, and sound recordings, the grouping of services which in the Uruguay Round were included under the heading of "audiovisual services," and which, as is to be demonstrated in the discussion to follow, have been the focal point of the trade and culture debate in both the World Trade Organization (WTO) and the United Nations Educational, Scientific and Cultural Organization (UNESCO). In this context, the US position in the trade and culture debate will be examined from the perspective of its most contentious, and most widely discussed facet—trade in motion pictures.

It is the thesis of this chapter that the US position on applying trade rules to motion pictures is today a complex and evolving balance of economic and cultural components which the US has, for reasons that span both sides of the debate, been unable to realize in either the General Agreement on Tariffs and Trade (GATT), later reformulated as the WTO, or UNESCO. Despite the relative isolation of the US on the issue, however, the fact that WTO trade disciplines apply to audiovisual services, as to virtually all services sectors, is of significant importance to the international trading system.

The first four sections of the chapter trace evolution of the US position in the trade and culture debate as follows: (1) Preparations to negotiate trade in services (1980–5); (2) The Uruguay Round (1986–91); (3) The Doha Development Round (2000–8); and (4) The UNESCO Cultural Diversity Convention (2003–5). The chapter concludes by focusing on (5) Assessment of the foundations and influence of the US position in the trade and culture debate.

Preparations to negotiate trade in services (1980–5)

Background: US report on trade in motion pictures

In the early 1980s, in preparation for upcoming negotiations of an agreement on trade in services in the Geneva-based GATT, the Office of the US Trade Representative (USTR) drafted reports for 12 different service sectors[1] to determine whether GATT trade principles—such as most favored nation (MFN), national treatment, market access, and transparency—would effectively address the problems that US service providers encountered in their foreign operations. The reports were also intended to determine whether GATT trade principles could be systematically applied across a broad range of different services sectors. The report on the US motion-picture sector "Trade in Motion Picture Services," (Motion Picture Report: Balassa, 1981)[2] provides a preliminary view of the US position on applying international trade disciplines to motion pictures.

The starting point for the Motion Picture Report is the dual nature of motion pictures. Pointing out that motion pictures is the only service sector to be covered by the GATT, the report explains that, as a tangible product, the feature film has been made subject to most GATT rules, but because the sector at the same time embodies a nation's cultural identity, it has been accorded special treatment. Article IV of the GATT, "Special Provisions Relating to Cinematographic Film," acknowledges, for example, that "government protection of a domestic film industry for cultural purposes is a legitimate social objective" (Balassa, 1981, p. 29). For this reason, the difficulty domestic film producers faced in finding screen time to exhibit their films in the immediate post-World War II period was taken into account while drafting GATT Article IV, which permits countries to retain existing screen-time quotas as long as they do not introduce new MFN discrimination. Article IV is the sole exception in the GATT to the principle of national treatment (WTO, 1990, p. 1).

The trade argument

The Motion Picture Report makes the case that motion pictures are widely traded and face problems similar to those encountered by other traded goods and services. Linking the absence of trade barriers to the economic viability of the industry, the report points out that motion pictures, like other traded goods and services, benefit significantly from international trade. In what came to be the economic cornerstone for the US position on trade in motion pictures, the paper explains that

> The technology of the motion picture industry is such that nearly all the cost of making a film goes into the production of the first print. Once the original is completed, the cost of making additional prints is relatively small as compared to the initial cost of production, though rapidly rising copying and advertising costs are somewhat changing the picture. Nonetheless it is to the producer's interest to seek the widest possible market – both domestic and foreign – in order to maximize the return on his investment. Moreover, because the investment required to produce a feature film is substantial – $10 million on the average in the United States today [1980][3]—the motion picture industry is dependent on its export markets.
>
> (Balassa, 1981, p. 18)

The US motion-picture industry has often been accused of adopting a "siege mentality" in international negotiations, taking a position that, regardless of market size, any trade barrier is a threat to the entire industry. Addressing this position, the report explains that

> The realities of the motion picture business are such that, except in cases of blockbusters, the margin of profit on a film is often small. Consequently the loss of even a relatively small market may mean the difference between profits and loss which gives one company the edge over its competitor and provides the overall profit for a production. Such profits, in turn, permit the individual producer, engaged in both a commercial and artistic undertaking, to train talent, experiment, and undertake the risks intrinsic to his profession. Measures that reduce the producer's profits are therefore regarded as a threat to the very features that are basic to a successful motion picture industry.
>
> (Balassa, 1981, p. 19)

Expanding its discussion to include the benefits of trade to smaller economies, the report notes that, for the local movie industry, experience has shown that contact with imported films serves to stimulate rather than to retard the production of high quality films. Countries with the healthiest film industries are the ones to have the least restrictive trade policies, for they understand the artistic stimulus and technical education that comes from contact with imported films.

Importation of high quality films also benefits the local industry, the report continues, by helping to develop a movie-going public whose increased attendance at cinemas will provide an assured market and the stable conditions necessary to secure the investment for producing feature films. Conversely, a restriction which delays importation of a film may prevent it from being shown during peak exploitation periods, creating uncertainty that aggravates the financing problems of an industry that requires large investment and faces difficulties in obtaining financing at home (Balassa, 1981, pp. 21–7).

Given the importance of trade to the US motion-picture industry, it is not surprising that the US was a leader in urging creation of a multilateral discipline for trade in services that would include motion pictures. Moreover, because the motion-picture sector was the only sector to be covered by GATT trade disciplines and at the same time share characteristics with service sectors, the US regarded the motion-picture sector as a model for application of services trade rules.

The culture argument

The Motion Picture Report balances discussion of trade benefits for the motion-picture sector with recognition that governments often undertake restrictive trade measures "to foster a local film industry as a means to express a nation's cultural identity." Turning its attention to the Organization of European Cooperation and Development (OECD) as well as the GATT, the report notes that in the GATT and the OECD, "protection of a local film [with screen time quotas] for cultural reasons is recognized as a legitimate social objective" while in the OECD subsidies are permitted as well (Balassa, 1981, p. 24).

Outlining a position it would largely abandon in the heat of the Uruguay Round negotiations (cf. discussion in section 8.2 below), the Motion Picture Report acknowledges that screen-time quotas and subsidies "permit governments to pursue legitimate social objectives without unnecessarily distorting international trade." Citing industry sources, the paper states that "reasonable screen time quotas are a relatively straightforward and acceptable means of protecting a domestic film industry; subsidies, when paid for from general revenue (and not from box office receipts) have little impact on trade patterns" (Balassa, 1981, p. 35).

multilateral trade negotiation

The Uruguay Round (1986–94)

Background: Confrontation with the EU

In the Uruguay Round, motion pictures came to be classified as part of the audiovisual services sector, which, as noted above, also included videotapes, television programs, and sound recordings. Negotiations over audiovisual services in the Uruguay Round became a bitterly contentious issue between the US and the EU that came near to derailing the entire negotiation. The confrontation, often cast as a more general debate over "culture," centered essentially around two major issues.

First, arguing that audiovisual services were conveyors of a nation's unique cultural identity and so differed from other traded goods and services, the EU wanted to remove the audiovisual sector entirely from the framework of the General Agreement on Trade in Services (GATS) so that the new trade rules for services would not apply to the audiovisual sector. This was the "cultural exception" argument that the EU had taken up at France's insistence (Balassa, 1998, pp. 25–31). Second, the EU did not want to cap or remove its Television Without Frontier Directive [TWF Directive][4] regarding the amount of foreign programming material that could be broadcast. It also did not agree to US requests that it administer its generous system of film subsidies on a national treatment basis.

By contrast, the US wanted the new GATS framework to include all service sectors and wanted the EU to make a specific commitment for audiovisual services that would remove the foreign content restrictions of the TWF Directive. The US also sought to have the EU either cap its screen production subsidies or administer those subsidies, financed from box office taxes and blank tape levies imposed largely on US content, on a national treatment basis.[5]

Focus on economic issues

Convinced that the EU's aggressive stance on audiovisual issues in the Uruguay Round had little to do with protecting a nation's cultural identity, but much to do with protecting its domestic industry, the US refuted efforts to make the case for a cultural exception, responding that there is "nothing economically special about these products ... as justifying a repudiation of free trade premises" (Sauve and Steinfatt). The position of US trade negotiators was reinforced by the president of the Motion Picture Association of America (MPAA) Jack Valenti, who, convinced that the EU's content quotas and cultural exception efforts posed serious threats to his members, warned:

> I don't want there to be any ambiguity. If those quotas exist, this is Armageddon time. In the United States, I'm on the Hill in a New York

minute bringing out every Patriot missile, every F-16 in our armory, leading whatever legions we can find opposing this agreement … Any GATT accord that allows the TV quota to stay in place would be totally unacceptable to us. I would fight it to the death.

(Quoted in Stokes, 1991, pp. 434 and 438)

To press its case against the content quotas of the TWF Directive, the US underscored that in the promising new areas of cable networks and direct satellite broadcasting services, the quotas were as counterproductive for the EU as for the US: restricting content for these new services, said one US negotiator, will have a "devastating" impact within the EU on development of the new services which require an ample supply of films from all sources to attract viewers. Implying that the content quotas placed the government in the position of determining viewers' choice of content, the US negotiator asked rhetorically, "Do you really expect your consumers to pay for programming they don't want to see?"[6]

Elsewhere, to obtain support from EU broadcasters, US negotiators pointed out that the low cost of US programming would help broadcasters overcome the hurdle of relatively high start-up costs: once established with the help of budget-priced American programs, so the US argument went, EU broadcasters could then devote their limited resources to development of local programming.

US objections to a cultural carve out from trade rules extended beyond concerns for audiovisual services. While seriously concerned about the impact of a cultural carve out on one of its most "lucrative areas of export," the US was also concerned that, if an exception from WTO trade disciplines were granted to one sector considered "sensitive" by some, a precedent would be established for other countries to demand exceptions for sectors that they, too, considered "sensitive" (Acheson and Maule, 1998, p. 12). The result would be an unraveling of a services trade agreement whose economic benefits depended importantly on covering trade in virtually all service sectors.

Outcome of the Uruguay Round

The Uruguay Round confrontation between the US and the EU ended essentially in what was viewed at the time as a "draw." The GATS agreement did not result in an EU commitment to modify the TWF Directive nor to cap the 51 percent quota on non-European content programming as the US had hoped. At the same time, however, the final GATS text did not contain language that provided a "cultural exception," as the EU had desired.

As a result, no legal distinction was drawn between audiovisual services and any other service sectors—the general rules of the GATS applied to the audiovisual sector as to all service sectors (with the exception of civil aviation). Relatively few countries scheduled commitments for audiovisual services however, and those commitments that were scheduled were, for the most part, seriously circumscribed. This meant that while general obligations of the GATS, such as most favored nation (MFN) and transparency, applied in principle to the audiovisual sector, only 13 countries undertook specific-market access and national-treatment obligations for the sector. Moreover, a number of countries took an MFN exception for audiovisual services, in large part to cover co-production agreements, further limiting the impact of the general MFN obligation (WTO, 1998, p. 8).

Despite the apparent balancing of wins and losses in the audiovisual services negotiation, the bitterness and disappointment left by the negotiation was all too evident. Jack Valenti, for example, "express[ed] his frustration at the end of the GATT negotiations by declaring that culture was the European word for protectionism" while President Mitterand had, a few months earlier, publicly asked "who could be blind today to the threat of a world gradually invaded by Anglo-Saxon culture, under the cover of economic liberalism" (Veron, 1999).

In retrospect, the US came to realize that although the Uruguay Round may have ended in a draw between the US and the EU, the US hard-line position on audiovisual services had antagonized a number of countries, making future liberalization of the sector more difficult. Further, some of the US industry's strongest demands—especially those relating to current and future application of the content quotas of the TWF Directive, proved to be exaggerated. USTR reported in its 1998 *Foreign Trade Barriers Report*, for example, that "by the time an agreement was reached on a revised directive [in 1997], the divisive issue of strengthening European content quotas had fallen by the wayside despite the Parliament's protectionist line" (USTR 1998).

The Doha Development Round (2000–8)

Background: The US Audiovisual Objectives Paper of 2000

To prepare for the upcoming Doha Development Agenda round of trade negotiations (Doha Round), the WTO Group on Negotiating Services (GNS) invited WTO members to table papers in December 2000 outlining their negotiating objectives for specific services sectors. In response to this invitation, the US included a number of sector-specific papers, including one for audiovisual services, "Communication from the United States: Audiovisual and Related Services" (Objectives Paper) (WTO, 2000).

The Objectives Paper for audiovisual services that the US tabled at the WTO in 2000 represents a significant change in both tone and substance from the earlier US position on audiovisual services. The change indicates serious concern on the part of the US Government and its motion-picture industry that its Uruguay Round position on content quotas and subsidies had hardened opposition to future liberalization commitments for the sector.

The US was also mindful, this time, of ongoing discussions led by Canada and the EU to create a new international instrument to address cultural issues in UNESCO. The threat of having the audiovisual sector removed entirely from multilateral trade rules was not taken lightly, either by the US Government or its motion-picture industry, and, in an effort to thwart such an eventuality, the US set about to improve its image vis-à-vis the issue.

Change in tone

Signaling that the US wanted to give a fresh start to audiovisual services negotiations, the US Objectives Paper sets out to place the forthcoming Doha Round negotiations of audiovisual services in a new light: The paper begins by noting that "The audiovisual sector in 2000 is significantly different from the audiovisual sector of the Uruguay Round period when negotiations focused primarily on film production, film distribution, and terrestrial broadcasting of audiovisual goods and services" (p. 1).

Directly addressing the trade and culture debate that had characterized so much of the Uruguay Round discussion on the issue, the paper refutes the notion that the debate over the audiovisual sector in the WTO is an "'all-or-nothing' game" in which "the only available options were to exclude culture from the WTO or to liberalize completely all aspects of audiovisual and related services." Instead, in an effort to lay the groundwork for a constructive negotiation, the US paper, recognizes "public concern for the preservation and promotion of cultural values and identity," and outlines a proposal where preservation of national identity and liberalization of trade in audiovisual services may in fact reinforce each other (Objectives Paper, p. 3).

To establish the link between trade and culture, the Objectives Paper emphasizes that "The ability to make and distribute audiovisual products both to domestic and foreign audiences is not independent of business and regulatory considerations." Pointing to the costly and uncertain nature of the audiovisual sector, the paper points out that there is, "of necessity a commercial aspect to this artistic activity that will affect both the production and distribution of audiovisual product, which is widely traded internationally."

The developmental objectives of the Doha Round are also served by liberalizing trade in motion pictures, the US Objectives Paper points out. "As part of the explosion in information technology that has taken place in the past decade ... Audiovisual services, too, play their role in fostering a nation's economic development, both through the spread of information and ideas and by fostering investment in a nation's advanced communications infrastructure" (p. 1).

Change in substance

Turning to specific negotiating suggestions, the Objectives Paper responds to criticisms that trade rules are too inflexible to address the "special cultural qualities" of audiovisual services. As examples of WTO flexibility on cultural issues, the paper points to the GATT national treatment exception for cinematic films and the flexibility that WTO rules offer countries in scheduling commitments for audiovisual, or any other, services sector "so long as the regulation is not administered in a way that represents an unexpected trade barrier" (pp. 1–3).

In a most notable shift away from its Uruguay Round stance, in its Objectives Paper the US revised its position on subsidies. The subsidies issue was a dividing line between the US, which had no history of direct federal subsidies to its profit-making arts sector, and most of its trading partners, whose arts programs, including those for motion pictures, were heavily dependent on government funding (WTO, 1998, p. 6). Concern that WTO trade rules could restrict a government's ability to fund motion-picture production and distribution was a key factor in isolating the US in WTO and in UNESCO Cultural Diversity Convention negotiations (Balassa, 2008, p. 20).

Acknowledging that government funding of audiovisual services is "a sensitive issue for many Members where local theatrical film production is dependent on government support," the US Objectives Paper states that "The US delegation is of the view that development of trade disciplines for the audiovisual sector need not necessarily restrict government subsidies for domestic film production and distribution, as long as subsidies are not derived from discriminatory practices." The paper concludes discussion of the issue with the suggestion that "Members may also want to consider developing an understanding on subsidies that will respect each nation's need to foster its cultural identity by creating an environment to nurture local culture." Negotiation of a subsidies code for motion picture was made contingent, however, on "negotiated commitments for audiovisual services" (Objective Paper, p. 3).

Impact

The negotiating tone for audiovisual services was far less confrontational in the Doha Round than in the Uruguay Round. While the conciliatory tone of the US Objectives Paper contributed somewhat to the improved negotiating atmosphere, it is far more likely that other factors, both positive and negative, were responsible for the change in negotiating dynamics.

On the positive side, in the Doha Round the US was no longer totally isolated on the audiovisual issue as it had been in the Uruguay Round. Five other countries with significant motion-picture export interests—Japan, Chinese Taipei, Hong Kong China, Singapore and Mexico—now came forward to join the US in forming a Friends Group for Audiovisual Services (a.k.a. the Film Fans Club).[7]

On the negative side, the absence of conflict over audiovisual services reflected not consensus, but unwillingness on the part of a number of countries, especially potential EU members, to discuss the issue in WTO bilateral request-offer negotiations. The EU, for example, made clear to prospective EU members that their membership in the EU would be compromised if they made any commitments for audiovisual services. Influenced in part by EU intransigence on audiovisual services, other countries justified their refusal to discuss audiovisual services by referring to the ongoing UNESCO negotiation of the Cultural Diversity Convention.

The UNESCO Cultural Diversity Convention (2003–5)

Background: A disguised trade negotiation

In the post-Uruguay Round period, beginning in 2001, France and Canada renewed their efforts to achieve the cultural exception they had unsuccessfully fought for in the Uruguay Round by establishing a new international instrument, which came to be known as The UNESCO Convention for the Promotion and Protection of Diversity of Cultural Expressions (Cultural Diversity Convention). The chosen forum for negotiating the new instrument was the Paris-based UNESCO.

To help coalesce support for the Convention, France and Canada played on the dominant role of US motion-picture exports worldwide, viewed by many as responsible for the problems that domestic film industries encountered in their local and regional markets. Exports of US motion pictures in 2003, for example, accounted for 73 percent of box-office revenues in Europe (Hanson and Xiang, 2007).

Though the US originally attempted to support the broad objectives of the Convention, subject to specific requests for language changes, its position gradually hardened in reaction to ever more troublesome language inserted into the Convention's text without consensus.[8] In the two-year period from October 2003 to October 2005, which overlapped with the ongoing WTO Doha Round of negotiations, the US focused primarily on the Convention's implications for current and future multilateral and bilateral trade negotiations (Balassa, 2008, p. 19). Relatively little attention was paid to the cultural issues that attracted broad support from many UNESCO delegations.

Trade implications of the convention

As expressed in various statements by US officials, US concerns over the Convention's possible impact on trade centered on the Convention's broad and vaguely defined scope, sweeping operational mandates, and ambiguous provisions outlining the relationship between the Convention and other international agreements (US Department of State, 2005).

US officials recognized that supporters of the Convention were motivated in large part by the dominant position of American motion-picture exports in most markets. The US was concerned, however, that because the scope of the Convention was broad and ill-defined, its provisions could be interpreted to extend far beyond motion pictures, touching on any service, good, or agricultural product that might be viewed as being related to cultural expression.

Concerns over the broad and undefined scope of the Convention were heightened by the Convention's sweeping provisions concerning implementation. Paragraph 1 of the Convention's Article 6, "Right of parties at the national level," reads that "each Party may adopt measures aimed at protecting and promoting the diversity of cultural expressions within its territory."[9] So broadly cast was this language, some argued, that it could be misread as providing countries with broad authorization to impose an unlimited range of restrictive trade measures in the name of "protecting" cultural diversity.

In addition to the broad and undefined scope of the Convention, US negotiators were seriously concerned by the so-called Saving's Clause of the Convention (Article 20),[10] a section that conveyed mixed signals about the relationship of the Convention to other international agreements (Voon, 2006, p. 2).

Article 20 first provides that the Convention should not be interpreted as modifying rights and obligations under any other treaties. Confusing the situation, however, Article 20 also states that the Convention is not subordinated to those other treaties and must be taken into account when interpreting and applying the provisions of other treaties. So unclear was Article 20 that the interpretation of the section "was disputed even among EU members, with the UK saying the provision 'did not permit the exclusion of cultural goods and services' and France saying that it did" (Petit, 2005, p. 1). According to statements by US officials, Article 20's message on the relationship between the Convention and other international agreements could "be misinterpreted as support for ... major world markets to shut out goods and services from developing and other markets" (US Department of State Bureau of International Information Programs, 2005). Further, the ambiguity of Article 20 could "impair rights and obligations under other international agreements [including the WTO] and adversely impact prospects for successful completion of the ongoing Doha Development Round of negotiations" (ibid.).

Finally, US trade officials also expressed concerns about Article 21 of the Convention, which obligates parties to "promote the principles and objectives of this Convention in other international forums." By making "consultation and coordination 'with other international forums' a key element in the application of Article 20," the US argued, the article could be widely misunderstood as further justification for parties to block or limit progress in future trade talks on any matters bearing on cultural goods and services (Mattelart, 2005).

Human rights implications of the convention

In addition to its concerns over the Convention's possible trade implications, the US focused on the possibility that the Convention's vague language could easily justify government-imposed restrictions on freedom of expression, including censorship and limitations on press freedom, and suppression of minority rights. If the Convention were, for example, to be used to restrict access to foreign or minority views in the name of protecting cultural diversity, then, the US pointed out, the Convention could undermine UNESCO's constitutional obligation "to promote the free flow of ideas by word and image." (US Department of State, Bureau of International Information Programs, 2005, pp. 3–4).

Underlying US comments on the Convention's human rights implications was the message that the Convention was, in fact, more likely to restrict cultural diversity than to promote it (US Mission to UNESCO, 2005). The US also linked the Convention's potential for human rights abuses to the Convention's unstated trade agenda. In her address to the General Conference Plenary, Ambassador Louise Oliver referred to "disturbing statements by some government leaders who have indicated a clear intention to use this Convention to control—not facilitate—the flow of goods, services, and ideas". By attempting "to block the import of agricultural and other products from the developing world and others," said Ambassador Oliver, "those leaders would extend the Convention's reach into trade matters, for which there is no justification ... The goal of the United States is to ensure the free flow of diversity in all its forms—cultural, informational, and trade." (US Department of State, Office of International Program, 2005).

Outcome of the negotiation

The US faced multiple challenges in attempting to build support to oppose or delay adoption of the Convention—the US arrived late to a negotiation that had started on an informal basis several years earlier; its return to UNESCO after a 19-year absence was greeted with suspicion by a number of delegations, the UNESCO process was marred by serious procedural irregularities, and efforts to transmit concerns by some WTO delegations over the relationship between UNESCO and the WTO encountered serious procedural obstacles.[11]

With few delegations won over to its trade and human rights objections to the Convention, the US found itself virtually isolated when adoption of the Convention was put to a final vote. On October 20, 2005, the UNESCO General Conference adopted the Convention on the Protection and Promotion of the Diversity of Cultural Expressions by a vote of 148 to 2. In a strongly worded statement of opposition, the US, joined only by

Israel, voted to oppose the Convention. Australia, Nicaragua, Honduras and Liberia abstained (US Department of State, October 2005).

Assessment of the US position in the trade and culture debate

Foundations of the US position

Throughout the 25-year negotiating period involving motion-picture trade issues discussed above, we have seen that the US has consistently argued that motion pictures, along with video tapes, television programs and sound recordings, should be subject to the same trade disciplines imposed on other goods and services that enter into international trade. To characterize this position, as is often the case, as that of a "military and economic behemoth" (Cowan, 2006, p. 3) that sacrifices cultural values or beauty to crass commercialism is, however, a misreading of the US position as expressed in recent negotiations and the historical forces that have shaped it.

First, while it is indeed correct that economic objectives are fundamental to the US position, this is only a partial picture of the US position on the issue. As the US Objectives Paper stated, there is no inconsistency in applying trade disciplines to motion pictures to attain cultural, as well as, economic objectives, and indeed, the two goals may reinforce each other. Second, reliance on trade and trade disciplines for the motion-picture sector, as for other goods and services, reflects a core belief in the social and political, as well as the economic, benefits of trade, unfettered by government-imposed trade barriers.

Fundamental to the US position in the trade and culture debate is long-standing suspicion of government involvement in the arts and in the production of content viewed by its citizens. In the US, for example, the federal government has virtually no specific role in the production or distribution of cinematic motion pictures. There is no Ministry of Culture devoted to the development of the US film sector, and there are no direct US government subsidies to motion pictures made for commercial distribution.[12] Further, with the exception of obscenity, the federal government does not regulate or limit films imported into the US and it is not in the business of distributing or exhibiting cinematic films (Balassa, 1998, p. 25). This policy is in part based on US adherence to free trade principles. It is also based on the First Amendment guarantee of free speech that, holding that diversity of viewpoints and programming is valuable, extends to films and television programs. From a constitutional point of view, it appears unlikely that the federal government could limit the viewing choice of its citizens by restricting their access to programming based on its country of origin.

Disagreement over subsidies to the motion-picture industry has been one of the most divisive issues in both WTO trade and UNESCO Cultural

Diversity Convention negotiations, reflecting profound political and social differences between the US and Europe in the way that the arts, and especially motion pictures, are funded (WTO, 2005, p. 12). The difference is explained in part by historical tradition,[13] in part by reluctance to have the government become the arbiter of which arts projects should receive federal government funding.[14]

Unlike arts policy in Europe, which is based largely on direct subsidies, in the US arts policy is financed largely though indirect subsidies – such as tax deductions for contributions and bequests to nonprofits, and public support of universities that in turn foster the arts. "Commonly a German, French or Italian theater, museum, or orchestra will receive 80 percent or more of its budget directly from government", Tyler Cowan explains, pointing out that, by contrast, in the US, direct US government support accounts for no more than 5 percent of the total budget of nonprofit arts organizations (Cowan, 2006, p. 32).

Elaborating on the distinction between direct and indirect subsidies which underlies US–EU differences in arts funding, Cowan further explains that the US approach permits individual donors, and not the State, to decide which institution receive the funding. The neutrality of the tax deductions means that policy does not target any specific destination for the donation, and, in keeping with suspicion of government intervention in the arts, keeps the government out of the business of determining which arts are worth supporting (Ivey, 2008, pp. 39–41).

Impact of the US position on international negotiations

This review of the US position in trade and culture debates is striking in that, despite the fact that US trading partners in general recognize the benefits of applying trade rules to goods and services, and the flexibility for audiovisual services that the US signaled in its Objectives Paper of 2000, so few countries have come to support the US position on applying trade disciplines to the audiovisual sector.

In the WTO, for example, to date only 29 WTO members have made commitments for audiovisual services out of a total membership of 153.[15] Of those 29 commitments, many of which are severely circumscribed, 13 were made at the conclusion of the Uruguay Round. Most of the remainder have been made by acceding WTO members, who, in order to meet US demands for accession, were required to include some audiovisual service commitment in their accession schedule.[16] In the Doha Round, of members making new or revised services offers, only seven included new or improved commitments for audiovisual services.[17]

Challenges that the US has encountered in attempting to gain support for its position in the trade and culture debate are both self-inflicted and systemic. The dominant position of the US motion-picture industry worldwide has created suspicion that US economic arguments in favor of trade rules is self-serving and intended only to assure the US sector's continued global supremacy. Frustrations encountered by foreign film producers attempting to enter the US market have reinforced this position (Balassa, 2008, p. 4), as did US audiovisual demands for rollback of quotas and national treatment access to subsidies in the Uruguay Round.

Against this background of hostility and resentment, US efforts to change the negotiating climate for audiovisual services in its Objectives Paper of 2000 met with little success, as did US efforts to press its trade case during negotiation of the Cultural Diversity Convention in UNESCO. Perhaps most importantly, as the above discussion on subsidies illustrates, the trade and culture debate reflects a historic divide between the US and most other countries on the issue of the government's role in cultural activities.

Resolving such fundamental differences in a trade negotiation is difficult, though creative solutions might be considered to help bridge this gap, for example, develop a film distribution program to address the frustration of many countries whose film producers lack the technical skills to distribute their films locally or regionally; negotiate a special subsidies code for motion pictures as suggested by the US in its Objectives Paper; develop an Audiovisual Services Annex that addresses in a trade forum the culture issues surrounding trade in motion pictures; develop a mechanism by which the US. Government enters into co-production agreements with its trading partners.

Despite the challenges the US has encountered in the trade and culture debate, the US has been successful in the critical issue of preventing a cultural carve out for audiovisual services from WTO disciplines, a not-insignificant victory with the following consequences for current and future international negotiations:

1 Supporting application of trade disciplines to all services sectors has strengthened the WTO's institutional mandate to liberalize trade in all goods and service sectors. A "cultural exception" could have led to a possible unraveling of a broad and unforeseen range of trade commitments and obligations in the WTO, undermining the stability of the organization;

2 Although few countries have made specific commitments for audiovisual services, general GATS rules, such as MFN and transparency apply to the trade in this sector (unless specific MFN exceptions are taken), helping both established and new motion-picture exporters;

3 The WTO dispute settlement mechanism remains applicable to audiovisual and culture-related activities, as it applies to all covered goods and services, for example, the Periodicals case (which prompted Canada to initiate the search for a new instrument to address "cultural" issues) and the current US–China market access case involving copyright-intensive industries, recently resolved in favor of the US.(Cf. Cody and Shin, 2009; Szalai and Frater, 2009);[18]

4 The US Objectives Paper of 2000 has helped to highlight the flexibility of WTO disciplines to accommodate the "special cultural qualities" of audiovisual services, and has suggested avenues to explore in future WTO negotiations, for example, negotiating a special subsidies code for audiovisual services, that could build a broader consensus to support liberalization of the sector;

5 Applying trade disciplines to audiovisual services helps to stimulate the development of related service sectors such as telecommunications, dependent on obtaining quality audiovisual product through trade in order to attract investment in advanced telecommunications infrastructures;

6 Including audiovisual services within trade disciplines offers countries with emerging motion-picture exporters or online content uploaders an opportunity to benefit from trade rules and the new technologies to which these trade rules apply. These are the countries most likely to benefit from application of WTO trade disciplines to the audiovisual sector, and the ones with the most to lose from the collapse of the Doha Round in July, 2008.[19]

Notes

Another version of this chapter appears in Toshiyuki Kono, Jan Wouters and Steven Van Uytsel (eds.) (2010). *The UNESCO Convention for the Promotion and Protection of Diversity of Cultural Expressions*. Antwerp: Intersentia.

1. The reports included the following service sectors: telecommunications, data processing and information services, motion pictures, engineering and construction, maritime, banking and related financial services, insurance, professional services, advertising, travel and tourism, franchising, lodging, and aviation.
2. Carol Balassa (1981) "Trade Issues in the Motion Picture Industry," Office of the United States Trade Representative. An edited version of this report, along with 11 others, was later included in the US Government Printing Office, 1984.
3. The cost was approximately $60 million in 2008.
4. The two basic principles of the TWF Directive were to ensure the free movement of EU television programs within the EU market and to require EU television channels to reserve, "wherever practicable," a majority of their transmission time for European works ("broadcasting quotas"). http://europa.eu/scadplus/leg/en/1vb/124.101/htm. Accessed October 25, 2008.
5. The blank tape levy issue remained an ongoing problem for the US motion-picture industry, cf. Press Release, Office of the United States Trade Representative, "USTR Announces Results of Special 301 Annual Review," May 1, 1998, p. 11.
6. USG, "Suggested Remarks on EC Directive, on Programming Quotas," n.d.
7. Each services sector had a Friends group comprised of like-minded countries interested in working together to advance liberalization of the sector.
8. Author interview with member of the US delegation to UNESCO, October 27, 2008.

9. UNESCO, Convention on the Protection and Promotion of the Diversity of Cultural Expressions, Article 6.
10. Coalition francaise pour la diversite culturelle, "The French Coalition Hail Successful Conclusion of UNESCO Negotiations for Treaty on Cultural Diversity in spite of the Hostility of the United States," French Coalition News Release, Paris, June 8, 2005, in *The Diversity of Cultural Expressions Newsletter* (Archives), vol. 5, no. 19, June 20, 2005, p. 10. Available at http://www.mcc.gouv.qc.ca/diversite-culturelle/eng/events/events05-06-20.html. Accessed January 24, 2008.
11. For a detailed discussion of these issues, see Balassa (2008, pp. 18–25).
12. To be noted, however, are federal and state-level tax incentives, including the tax benefits that a number of states offer to attract film production.
13. Unlike many European countries, for example, the US has no history of royal patronage of the arts.
14. A direct per capita comparison between the budgets of European cultural ministries and the $130 million of the NEA is unrealistic, points out former NEA Chair Bill Ivey, because European cultural ministries have responsibilities that far exceed those of the NEA, "often footing the bill for the operation of national and regional museums and performing arts centers while also financing the kind of trade and regulatory programs that lie totally outside the Endowment's portfolio." Nonetheless correcting for this disparity by adding into the NEA budget arts funding to other federal agencies and state and local arts commissions still leaves a major per capita disparity: in Europe, the per capita funding is between $60 to $80, while the adjusted NEA budget of $2.8 billion weighs in at just around $9 per American (Ivey, 2008, pp. 237–8).
15. Membership total of the WTO as of July 23, 2008.
16. See discussion on power politics in the accession process. Available at http://www. allacademia.com//meta/p_mla_2pa_research-citation/2/5/1/1/0/pages 251109. Accessed October 27, 2009.
17. Available at http://ec.europa.eu/avpolicy/ext/multilateral/gats/index_en.htm. Accessed October 27, 2008.
18. MPAA, "MPAA Applauds USTR WTO Action to Spur China IP Enforcement." Press Release, April 9, 2007.
19. *New York Times*, "After 7 Years, Talks on Trade Collapse," July 30, 2008. While WTO and member government officials have avoided officially announcing that the Doha Round has ended in failure, even its most optimistic supporters admit that it will take some time for the negotiations to resume.

9
Cultural Diplomacy: The Humanizing Factor

Cynthia P. Schneider

> *You cannot demonize people when you're sitting there listening to their music. You don't go to war with people unless you demonize them first.*

Former Defense Secretary William Perry's comments after attending the ground-breaking concert by the New York Philharmonic in Pyongyang (February 26, 2008) capture the essential power of cultural diplomacy. To paraphrase the Nigerian author Wole Soyinka (2000), "culture humanizes while politics demonizes." Through its capacity to move and persuade audiences, and to shape and reveal identities, creative expression has the potential to increase understanding and respect between disparate cultures and peoples. This is not a trivial concern; the reverse produces catastrophic results. Lack of respect and understanding lies at the core of the most threatening conflict today, that between the West and the Muslim world.[1]

President Obama indicated his understanding of the importance of respect in international relations generally, and the US–Muslim world relationship specifically, in his inaugural address, with one important line: "To the Muslim world, we seek a new way forward, based on mutual interest and mutual respect." While cultural diplomacy will not solve the political crises in the Middle East, it could help to reverse the decline in relations between the West and the East by increasing understanding and respect.

As the reputation of the US in the world, and particularly in the Muslim world, has declined over the past eight years, there have been repeated calls to remedy the situation through improved "public diplomacy." This overused, but little-understood term basically encompasses everything a country does to explain itself to the world (Cummings, 2003, p. 1).[2] Cultural diplomacy, or "the exchange of ideas, information, art and other aspects of culture among nations and their peoples to foster mutual understanding" provides much of the content of public diplomacy. Public diplomacy is more closely aligned with policy and can involve garnering support for and acceptance of policies. Cultural diplomacy is a prime example of "soft power," or the ability to persuade through culture, values, and ideas as opposed to "hard power" which conquers or coerces through military might (Nye, 2002, pp. 8–9; 2004). With creative expression, values or ideas tend to be communicated implicitly, rather than explicitly, and are communicated by touching the audience's emotions. This was true of rock music behind the Iron Curtain during the Cold War. As Andras Simonyi, former Ambassador of Hungary to the US, himself a rock musician, remembered, "Rock and roll was the internet of the '60s and early '70s. It was the carrier of the message of freedom ... Rock and roll, culturally speaking, was a decisive element in loosening up communist societies and bringing them closer to a world of freedom."[3]

Developing successful public and cultural diplomacy strategies first requires adopting a broader, and more realistic concept of the role the US plays in the world today. International relations between countries no longer reside exclusively, or even primarily in the political realm of treaties and international relations. Rather these relations involve a complex web of fields and actors, including media and culture, business, science and technology, and education, to name a few. More and more, experts are calling for the development of a more synthetic, complex, integrated approach to public and cultural diplomacy (Lord, 2008).

Even with a more comprehensive approach, however, public or cultural diplomacy will not be able to compensate for unpopular policies, or for policies which contradict the values or ideas espoused through cultural diplomacy. Fareed Zakaria's (*Newsweek*, October 2002) comments one year after 9/11 seem sadly prophetic: "America remains the universal nation, the country people across the world believe should speak for universal values ... The belief that America is different is its ultimate source of strength. If we mobilize all our awesome power and lose this one, we will have hegemony ... but will it be worth having?" The decline in America's image in the world directly impacts the ability to influence and persuade. But if cultural outreach is conceived as part of a long-term relationship, it can help to separate people from policies. This is the critical element of success in people-to-people programs, including the flagship Fulbright program, which funds exchanges of students and faculty. Even the founder of the program, Senator William Fulbright was surprised by its impact. "Since the program has gotten under way, the Russians have attacked it as being a clever propaganda scheme. I can agree that, as matters have developed, this program of exchange of persons is one of the most effective weapons we have to overcome the attack of the Communists ... So, while the program was not designed to meet specifically the attack of the Soviet Union, it is the most effective weapon we have in the propaganda war or the war of ideas" (Fulbright, 1951, p. 26).

The globalized, digital age holds the promise of dramatically expanding the reach of interpersonal contact that is at the core of all exchange programs.

Now people can be connected online, and can "speak" to counterparts in other regions through programs and initiatives such as *Soliya* which involves college students across cultures and continents in weekly conversations, or the webisodic series *Hometown Bagdad* which brought the human impact of the war onto the computer screens of millions.[4] Commercial culture ranks as one of the most significant exports of the US, and foreign sales outpace domestic ones for many cultural products (Arango, December 1, 2008).

All of these conditions appear ripe for effective cultural outreach, but instead, support for cultural diplomacy from both the public and private sectors has declined dramatically since the end of the Cold War. As America's reputation has plummeted, one might have expected arts, culture, and media to have been deployed to the front lines to strengthen ties to foreign publics and to increase understanding across cultures.[5] Yet, that has not happened. Instead, various commissions and groups of experts have churned out reports calling for reinvented and reinvigorated public diplomacy. In the years since the World Trade Center attacks, public and cultural diplomacy have been analyzed extensively, but executed minimally. Forty-odd reports on public diplomacy have produced the consensus that it is in crisis, but not much more.[6] With the exception of the commendable but largely ignored *Report of the Advisory Committee on Cultural Diplomacy*,[7] most of the reports focus on improving process and structure, but neglect the content of public diplomacy, which mainly consists of cultural diplomacy.

Culture and diplomacy have had a mercurial relationship in modern American history. Typically arts and culture have been used as a rapid response tactic; the renewed interest in public diplomacy following 9/11 follows this pattern. Experience has shown that this strategy tends to alienate foreign publics even further. For example, a Southeast Asian diplomat spoke of a US library that had opened six times during the 1960s, always in response to a crisis. Each time the crisis abated, the library was shut down.[8] Cultural diplomacy initiatives are not purely altruistic, but a cynical approach to cultural outreach inevitably backfires. In addition, the "put out the fire" approach to cultural diplomacy violates a basic principle of effective cultural outreach: it should form part of a long-term relationship that continues unabated through political ups and downs.

Whether arts and culture belongs inside or outside the Department of State has been debated over the last 50 years, and likely will be debated again in the future. From early cultural initiatives of the US government, such as the efforts to counter the Nazis' propaganda in Latin America during the 1930s, to the present, there has been a consensus about the importance of promoting understanding of the US among other countries, but not about how to accomplish that goal (Ninkovich, 1965; Tuch, 1994). Not long after cultural diplomacy was given its own agency, the United States Information Agency (USIA), founded in 1953, questions arose about the wisdom of separating cultural programs designed to promote understanding of the US and its policies from the State Department, where the policies were promulgated. Nonetheless during the peak of the Cold War, both government and private initiatives flourished under President Eisenhower, who was personally committed to cultural diplomacy (Cummings, 2003, pp. 8–9). Soon after his inauguration in 1961, President Kennedy chose to maintain the separation between State and USIA (Center for Strategic and International Studies, 1975, p. 77). USIA's brilliant director at the time Edward R. Murrow exerted more influence than anyone in his position before or since, but even he expressed frustration in his famous plea to be "present at the take off, as well as the crash landings" of foreign policy.

As part of the Foreign Affairs Reform and Restructuring Act of 1998, and in the name of increased integration and efficacy, USIA was merged into the State Department in 1999.[9] Although public diplomacy was described as a "national security imperative" by Secretary of State Madeleine Albright at the ceremony marking the consolidation, the precipitous decline in funding during the 1990s indicated that others in the government did not share her commitment.[10]

The reduction in budget, personnel and effectiveness of public and cultural diplomacy that resulted from USIA merging into the State Department reflected a profound misunderstanding of diplomacy in the post Cold War world, as well as over-confidence in the wake of the collapse of the Soviet Union. Warnings of the long-term dangers of diminishing cultural diplomacy by Walter Laqueur (1994, p. 20), the prolific political historian, went unheeded:

> Nor can it seriously be argued—as some have—that these tools of U.S. foreign policy are no longer needed now that the Cold War is over and America no longer faces major threats ... far from being on the verge of a new order, the world has entered a period of great disorder. In facing these new dangers, a re-examination of old priorities is needed. Cultural diplomacy, in the widest sense, has increased in importance, whereas traditional diplomacy and military power ... are of limited use in coping with most of these dangers.

A comparison between cultural diplomacy during its peak in the Cold War period helps to illuminate the potential of the arts in the service of diplomacy, and the special challenges of the current geopolitical climate. During the Cold War period, the US armed itself with jazz, abstract expressionism, and modern literature. In the late 1950s more than 100 acts were sent to 89 countries in four years. Musicians such as Louis Armstrong, Dizzy Gillespie, and Charlie Parker departed on tours of one to two months, playing in Iran, Iraq, Egypt, Nigeria, and many other Muslim countries, as well as in the Soviet Union and Eastern Europe. The legendary radio host Willis Connover captured the intangible qualities that made jazz such a meaningful symbol of freedom: "Jazz is a cross between total discipline and anarchy. The musicians agree on tempo, key, and chord structure but beyond this everyone is free to express himself. This is jazz. And this is America ... It's a musical reflection of the way things happen in America. We're not apt to recognize this over here, but people in other countries can feel this element of freedom" (cited in Wilson, September 13, 1959).

Cultural diplomacy succeeded during the Cold War in part because it allowed and even fostered dissent. Artists, actors, musicians, writers in any culture act as the national conscience, reflecting, often critically, on society. Jazz's power as a cultural ambassador stemmed from the inherent tension created by black musicians traveling the globe trumpeting American values during the era of segregation. The musicians themselves did not shy away from exposing this hypocrisy.[11] When summoned to the State Department for a pre-tour briefing, Dizzy Gillespie declined, noting that "I've got three hundred years of briefing. I know what they've done to us and I'm not going to make any excuses ... I liked the idea of representing America, but I wasn't going to apologize for the racist policies of America" (Von Eschen, 2000, p. 170). Musicians such as Louis Armstrong, Dizzy Gillespie, Charlie Parker brought abstract concepts of liberty to life by democratizing their concerts and insisting that ordinary people, not just elites, be allowed to listen. That the US permitted critical voices as part of government-sponsored performances and emissaries astonished audiences everywhere, particularly behind the Iron Curtain. During a visit to the Soviet Union, American author Norman Cousins was asked if US writers would not be punished for criticizing the government openly, he surprised his Soviet interlocutor by countering that any government official who complained about their criticism would be more likely to encounter difficulties (Schneider, 2007, p. 152).[12] Another American writer recalled the impact of the exchanges as follows:

> What I sensed they got out of visiting American writers was, to them, our spectacular freedom to speak our minds. I mean, there we were, official representatives of the U.S—sort of the equivalent of their Writers Union apparatchiks—who had no party line at all ... and who had the writers' tendency to speak out on controversial issues ... In other words, the exchanges enabled Soviet writers, intellectuals, student's et al. to see that that the "free world" wasn't just political cant.
> (Richmond, 2003, p. 154, quoting Ted Solotaroff.)

Until recently, voices of dissent have been notably absent from attempts to instill ideas of democracy, which for the last eight years have targeted the Arab and Muslim world. In the wake of 9/11, public diplomacy, and the cultural diplomacy programs within it, has been misconstrued as a form of public relations. When President Bush's first appointment to the top public diplomacy position, Undersecretary of Public Diplomacy, advertising executive Charlotte Beers applied her considerable knowledge and experience in public relations to "selling" the US, her efforts fell flat. Beers commissioned infomercials extolling life in America for Muslim Americans for distribution to television channels in the Middle East, but the videos received very little distribution. Her successors have continued to advance the model of "winning the war of ideas," which reveals a profound misunderstanding of the challenges facing the US in the twenty-first century, and of the capacities of public and cultural diplomacy to meet them. The most challenging conflict in the world today, the divide between the US and the Muslim world, is not a win–lose situation. Rather data from largest survey ever taken of Muslim populations worldwide points to lack of respect for and understanding of Muslims and Islam as the most significant driver of the intercultural divide (Esposito and Mogahed, 2008).

In the Gallup poll, whose results were published in *Who Speaks for Islam: What a Billion Muslims Really Think*, a majority of Muslims polled identified a sense of humiliation and a perceived lack of understanding from the West as key factors in shaping negative attitudes toward the US. At the same time, a majority of the Americans surveyed, when asked to identify what they admired about Muslims and Islam, responded with either "nothing" or "I don't know." The data reinforce the urgent need for more accurate information about Muslims and Islam in the US, and for more nuanced and accurate portrayals of America and Americans in the Muslim world, not to mention greater cross-cultural engagement. It also provided further proof that the often-troubled relations between the US and the global Muslim community reflect in part a cultural problem that could be responsive to cultural solutions.

At a time when greater understanding across cultures is needed more than ever, as the gap between the West and the global Muslim community widens, the arts have an increasingly important role to play as they offer windows onto different societies and belief systems. In a world made smaller by globalization, and one in which non-governmental actors and organizations (NGOs) exert increasingly greater influence, public opinion matters more, not less. The opportunity for building cultural connections, and the consequences for neglecting cultural diplomacy in this arena, are nowhere more evident than in the relationship between the US and the Muslim world.

A key strength of arts and culture within the context of diplomacy and international relations is their ability to tap into emotions, to communicate on more than a rational level, and to precipitate alternative ways of seeing the world. The emotional potency of creative expression, together with the critical role of arts and culture within Arab and Muslim societies, underlines their importance within the US–Muslim world relationship. Creative expression, in its various forms, can help to build bridges across cultures as well as to facilitate understanding of cultural differences. This often happens in unpredictable ways. For example, during a talk at the Georgetown University campus in Doha, Qatar, author Amy Tan was surprised to learn her novel *Joy Luck Club*, about ethnicity and identity in the Chinese-American community, had inspired Qatari and Palestinian girls as they struggled with their own personal issues of tradition and modernity, homeland and identity.

Since 2001 the State Department has steadily increased the budget for cultural programs, to $7.9 million in 2007, up from only $1.4 million in 2001. This sum is still a pittance in comparison to the per capita spending on cultural programs of the French, British, or even the Dutch, or in comparison to spending at the peak of cultural diplomacy during the Cold War, but it represents, nonetheless, a positive trend.

Along with the increased funding for cultural programs in the past few years has come greater openness to a diversity of opinion and artistry among the cultural envoys sent out by the State Department. The choices of artists and the locations of their tours reflect the State Department's current focus on reaching youth, who dominate the populations of most Muslim and Arab countries. Arguably, hip-hop is in today's world what jazz and rock n' roll have been in the past: the musical language of dissent. A genre conceived as outsiders' protest against the system, hip-hop resonates with those marginalized from the mainstream. From the suburbs of Paris to Kyrgyzstan in central Asia, hip-hop music reflects the struggle against authority (Brooks, 2005). When terrorism expert Jessica Stern asked Muslim youths in Amsterdam about Americans they admired, rapper Tupac Shakur was mentioned.[13] In the words of hip-hop artist Ali Shaheed Muhammad (of the legendary Tribe Called Quest), "People identify with the struggle. It doesn't really matter where you come from, we all have the same story. The music has an aggression to it, and it taps into the emotion or the spirit or the soul. Lots of times, people may not understand what you are saying, but they also feel the pain."[14]

In the summer of 2007 the State Department funded highly successful tours of the Latin fusion hip-hop group Ozomatli (to the Middle East and Asian subcontinent), another hip-hop group Opus Akoben (to China), and the HaviKoro hip-hop and break dance ensemble to Denmark (with focus on urban minority communities). The Ozomatli tour, in particular, signaled a change in approach for the State Department because the members of the band are outspoken opponents of the Iraq war, and have played at many anti-war rallies. Why, then, would they agree to tour for the State Department? "Our world standing has deteriorated," said Ozomatli saxophonist Ulises Bella in an interview in August. "I'm totally willing and wanting to give a different image of America than America has given over the last five years." One of the thousand-plus audience members of the Ozomatli concert at the Citadel in Cairo commented, "Music more than language is a cultural bridge." The young Cairene added that he still objected strongly to US policies. But that is no surprise. Nonetheless cultural diplomacy never pretended to compensate for policy, but by showcasing artists such as those in Ozomatli, the State Department began to give foreign audiences a sense of the diversity of cultures and of opinions in the US, of the respect within the US for Muslims and Muslim artists, and of what freedom of speech really means. In the words of the American Ambassador to Cairo, Francis Ricciardone, "These things cost a little bit of money, but compare it to the cost of not having the standing we had in the past, when people thought they knew us and what we stood for. People talk about it as soft power. But it's real power."

Artists in all fields act as the conscience of any society, reflecting on its good and bad points, and challenging the status quo. During the Cold War period, musicians and writers brought abstract concepts of liberty and freedom of speech to life by speaking openly, and sometimes critically, about aspects of American society, notably segregation, while traveling on US government sponsored tours. As was true of jazz during the Cold War, hip-hop can offer pleasure and enjoyment as a musical experience, as well as social commentary and criticism. As we struggle to find ways to connect with the predominantly youthful population in the Muslim world, hip-hop provides a ready opportunity: artists from the Muslim world admire American artists, especially politically engaged rappers such as the late Tupac Shakur, and many leading American hip-hop artists are Muslim, such as Nas or Talib Kweli.

Hip-hop also offers a possible medium for advancing ideas of social change. Hip-hop artists throughout the Muslim world, from Morocco to Malaysia, and especially in Palestine, have adapted the beats as well as the language of the disenfranchised. Groups such as Dam, featured in the recent documentary *Sling Shot Hip Hop*, express in their music their frustration with politics and society, but also their hope for the future. Although governments in the Middle East and Iran (where hip-hop is very popular) have recognized the power of music to effect political change, the US government, and to a lesser degree private funders, tend to view music, arts, and media separately from politics and social change, and therefore underestimate their potential impact.

Equally independent media and new technologies such as social networking have the potential to influence, or even bring about social change, but, with the exception of the NGO Search for Common Ground, they are not yet regularly integrated into political or developmental strategies. Foreign governments, however, recognize the power of social networking, particularly when connected to social action. The Egyptian government imprisoned a young woman who advertised a general strike on her Facebook page. New media and social networking have untapped potential to provide online "groups" that Muslim youth could join, as well as unrealized capacity to facilitate cross cultural dialogue and interactions. Extremist groups attract youths because they fill a vacuum; the positive potential of new technologies to engage youth in the Muslim world in alternative ways has not been explored, although the framework is already there, in the widespread Internet access in the Muslim world. What is missing is the creative collaboration between new media and technology experts and leaders in music, film, and other forms of creative content to set up social networking groups.

From soap operas whose narratives capture government corruption or envision improved rights for women, to local versions of *American Idol* such as *Afghan Star*, media has the capacity to influence social change because of its broad reach and powerful, emotional impact. The Bush administration approach of advocating "American" values of democracy and individual freedoms has had limited success. Indigenous media and entertainment communicate local values and ideas implicitly, and in the context of the region, and often those concepts will align with positive societal change. For example, *Afghan Star* introduced the radical notion of a merit-based competition, with the winner selected by popular vote, precluding any corrupt practices. The program succeeded in uniting the population where the US and Afghan governments have failed: 11 million viewers, or one-third of the population, watched last season's finals, which included two women among the ten finalists. In the first three seasons of *Afghan Star*, people have crossed ethnic lines to vote for the "best" singer—the winners have come from different ethnic backgrounds every time.[15] Mohammed Gohar has adapted the reality TV model to document everyday examples of corruption, inefficiency, and other problems in the streets of Cairo. In organizing the Middle East International Film Festival (MEIFF), Nashwa al Ruwaini has introduced special categories such as documentaries, films by women directors, or films on environmental issues that have increased the number of films in MEIFF that grapple with social issues.

Recognizing the power of arts and culture to shape opinions and identities, as well as the influence of leaders in arts and culture within their own regions and around the world, the Saban Center for Middle East Policy at the Brookings Institution has formed the Arts and Culture Dialogue Initiative to convene meetings (including a workshop at the annual US–Islamic World Forum), conduct research, and spin out projects (Schneider and Nelson, 2008). The first of these, MOST or *Muslims on Screen and Television (MOST): A Cross Cultural Resource Center* (www.mostresource org), reflects the innovative fusion of policy and the arts represented by the Brookings Initiative. MOST aims to impact perceptions of Muslims and Islam in America and abroad, by working with content creators, providing them information to flesh out more nuanced characters, beyond the stereotypical portrayal of the "bad guy du jour" in the post 9/11 era. MOST was formed to address the serious need in the media landscape for broader and more accurate portrayals of Muslims in all societies. The successful launch of MOST at a panel in the Middle East International Film Festival, Abu Dhabi in October 2008 indicated that the project struck a chord among Muslim publics, who were surprised and pleased to discover an American organization that was concerned with the negative stereotypes that dominate popular culture.[16]

The relative absence of arts and culture from any significant role in American foreign policy is all the more ironic, given that commercial culture—music, movies, television, web-distributed media—comprises one of the US's most significant exports. In a world where arts and culture are supported and controlled partly or totally by governments, the private-sector context of culture in the US is alien and poorly understood. Thus, audiences in nondemocratic countries view films and TV from the US with subliminal questions like "why the US government wants me to see this," when, in reality, those choices were not made by a government agency, but by a private distributor. Yet, despite the negative stereotypes about American popular culture, recent polls indicate generally favorable attitudes towards individual experiences of American films, music, and other art forms, but albeit a resistance to "Americanization."[17] A young Egyptian explained how she could like Americans but hate American policies, even though she knew no Americans personally, with one word, *"Friends"*, the television program, which made her feel that she knew and liked Americans on the basis of her knowledge of Rachel, Joey, and the other "Friends" on the program.

On the one hand arts and culture in the US comprise one of the country's most significant exports, enabling global domination in entertainment; on the other hand, cultural diplomacy is a poor stepchild in the State Department, lacking sufficient funds or personnel to realize the potential of the creative arts in the commercial and nonprofit sectors to positively impact diplomacy. Failing to provide robust support for cultural diplomacy, or to integrate it into policy, means losing precious opportunities to increase understanding across cultures and to lay the foundation for positive diplomatic relations, based on respect and trust.

Thomas Jefferson understood the value of cultural diplomacy, for both foreign and domestic publics. On September 20, 1785, he wrote to James Madison from Paris: "You see I am an enthusiast on the subject of the arts. But it is an enthusiasm of which I am not ashamed, as its object is to improve the taste of my countrymen, to increase their reputation, to reconcile to them the respect of the world and procure them its praise." Jefferson, the polymath statesman/scientist/architect, understood the potential of cultural expression to positively shape world opinion about the fledgling republic. The goals he presents as the "object" of the arts—"to increase the reputation" of his countrymen, "to reconcile to them the respect of the world and procure them its praise"—are still relevant over 200 years later in the post 9/11 era of opinion polls charting world opinion.

Notes

1. The "Muslim world" is an admittedly imperfect term that is used here to denote Muslim populations throughout the world. It is recognized that they are scattered throughout the globe, with majority populations in the Middle East, and parts of Africa and Asia. This label inevitably defines people by faith, which may or may not be appropriate for any given individual. It is used here for lack of a better term.
2. For a catalogue of definitions of public diplomacy, see http://uscpublicdiplomacy. com/index.php/about/what_is_pd (accessed December 15, 2008).
3. Bill Nichols, "How Rock n' Roll Freed the World," *USA Today*, November 6, 2003.
4. http://ww.soliya.net (accessed December 15, 2008); http://wwww.chattheplanet. com (accessed December 15, 2008).
5. On America's declining reputation, see Kohut and Stokes (2006). Also see http:// pewglobal.org/reports/display.php?ReportID=252e (accessed December 15, 2008) for the most recent polling report, released June 13, 2006. Earlier reports: Pew Research Center, "America's Image Further Erodes, Europeans Want Weaker Ties," March 18, 2003, pp.1–2. Available at http://people-press.org/reports/display. php3?ReportID=175 (accessed December 15, 2008). Pew Research Center, "Views of a Changing World 2003," June 3, 2003, pp.1–2. Available at http://people-press.org/reports/display.php3?ReportID=185 (accessed December 15, 2008). Meredith Buel, "New Poll of Islamic World Says Most Muslims Reject Terrorism," May 2, 2006. Available at http://www.voanews.com/english/archive/2006-05-02.voa82.cfm?CFID=7176751&CFTOKEN=55381572 (accessed June 14, 2006).
6. For a summary of the reports and their recommendations, see Lord (2008, pp. 51–4), and Epstein and Mages (2005). On cultural diplomacy, see the excellent, if unheeded, report, Advisory Committee on Cultural Diplomacy, "Cultural Diplomacy, Lynchpin of Public Diplomacy," US Department of State. Available at http://www.state.gov/documents/organization/54374.pdf (accessed July 15, 2006). On public diplomacy with the Arab and Muslim worlds, see the May 2006 GAO report. Available at http://www.gao.gov/new.items/do6707t.pdf (accessed December 15, 2008).
7. Advisory Committee on Cultural Diplomacy, "Cultural Diplomacy, Lynchpin of Public Diplomacy," US Department of State. Available at http://www.state.gov/ documents/organization/54374.pdf (accessed July 15, 2006).
8. http://www.publicdiplomacywatch.com/091505Cultural-Diplomacy-Report.pdf (accessed December 15, 2008).
9. "The Public Diplomacy and Public Affairs Missions." Available at www.fas.org/ irp/offdocs/pdd/pdd-68-docs.htm (accessed June 24, 2004); see also http://ieie. nsc.ru:8101/nisnews/let5/easa.htm (accessed June 29, 2004).
10. http://www.wtcsglobal.org/cie/fedspeech.htm (accessed December 15, 2008).
11. Armstrong and Brubeck's 1962 musical revue "The Real Ambassadors" satirized the contradiction. See Von Eschen (2000, p. 168).
12. See also Richmond (2003, p. 158). On Soviet reactions to encounters with American freedoms, see Barghoorn (1960).
13. Conversation with Jessica Stern, March 2005.
14. Press release for the 2006 US–Islamic World Arts and Cultural Leaders Seminar, US–Islamic World Forum, Doha, Qatar, February 20, 2006. Available at www.us-islamicworldforum.org (accessed December 15, 2008). A four-time Grammy winner, Ali Shaheed Muhammad is the founder of the group "A Tribe Called Quest". See also Brooks, "Gangsta."

15. On the positive impact of independent media in Afghanistan, see David Ignatius, "What Afghans Want", *Washington Post*, December 18, A25. Available at http://www.washingtonpost.com/wp-dyn/content/article/2008/12/17/AR2008121702924_pf.html (accessed December 15, 2008).

16. http://www.thenational.ae/article/20081016/ART/379304135; http:///www.meiff.com (accessed December 15, 2008).

17. Pew Research Center for People and the Press, "Global Unease with World Powers". Available at http://pewresearch.org/pubs/524/globsl-unease-with-major-world-powers-and-leaders, p. 6 (accessed November 12, 2007).

10
Power in European Union Cultural Policy

Patricia Dewey

The European Union and cultural policy

> ... *Political union, if it is to be true union, has to be a com-
> bination of economic interests and shared cultural values. ...
> [A European cultural policy] would serve three principal func-
> tions. It would be a factor of cohesion making the most of
> diversities as a richness shared, not as grounds for division. It
> would be a factor of identity in the world, an identity that is
> not self-centered and over-protected but open to world. And,
> it would be a factor empowering all European citizens to take
> democratic part in their common destiny. It would be a way, in
> short, to instill a "feeling of Union." (Ruffolo, 2001, p. 11)*

Many systems of regional integration exist in the world, but none is as broad
and deep in nature as that of the European Union (EU). In the 50 years since
the Treaty of Rome was signed, the EU has evolved to become the world's
newest superpower and largest trading power. The EU defines itself as "a
unique economic and political partnership between 27 democratic European
countries" that aims to achieve "peace, prosperity and freedom for its 495
million citizens—in a fairer, safer world" (http://europa.eu/abc/panorama/
index_en.htm). Indeed, the process of ever-closer integration among European
nation-states is one of the most distinctive features of contemporary Europe
and represents one of the most important political, economic, and social movements of our time. Participation in the EU has led to a new "European dimension" of politics and policies that infuses Europe's nations and societies.

As the need to promote "unity within diversity" or "a community of cultures" is increasingly emphasized in processes of European integration, the
cultural sphere is being called into action for purposes of fostering regional
identity, citizenship, intercultural understanding, and economic development (Dewey, 2007). In 1992, Article 128 of the Treaty of Maastricht (which
became Article 151 in the 1997 Treaty of Amsterdam and was subsequently

consolidated as Article 151 of the Treaty on European Union) became the first formal legal instrument supporting EU-level competency in culture. The inclusion of this culture article reflected a growing awareness that the EU needed to employ the power of culture in broadening and deepening a legitimate community of Europe's peoples. "Identity-formation and 'culture-building' have thus become explicit political objectives in the campaign to promote what EU officials and politicians call *l'idée européene* or 'European idea'" (Shore, 2000, p. 26). The cultural sphere has been politicized by European elites in an attempt to address the EU's chronic problem of legitimacy among European citizens. Arguing that that EU-level policies affecting the cultural sector are taking on ever-increasing importance, Sarikakis (2007) writes:

> The significance of cultural and media policy cannot be overestimated, as it transcends the fields of technology, politics, economics and social life in a number of ways. Not only have media and culture industries become increasingly central in the economies of European countries, they have also become the terrain of contestation and consensus regarding self-governance and cultural identity. The polity had to deal with these questions in its transformation from an economic coalition to a political and cultural entity. Media and cultural policies are themselves expressions of conflict of economic interests and political ideological positions. They have an impact upon rights, the legitimation of the polity, and the conditions for the materialization of citizenship. They occupy a peculiar position in the European Union agenda. Not only have they entered the arena of EU jurisdiction under complex and contradictory conditions, but they have also become the terrain where the essence and future of the polity is taking shape. Or at the very least, this is the domain where worldviews about the identity of the EU conflate and contest its present.
>
> (p. 14)

In addition to the perceived role of culture in Europe for purposes of enhancing a sense of transnational identity and citizenship, the EU considers the cultural and creative sector industries to be crucial to driving economic development in an increasingly global knowledge-based economy. The Commission of the European Union commissioned a study titled *The Economy of Culture in Europe* (2006), which profiles the impressive size and growth of Europe's creative sector. The study conceptualizes core arts fields (visual arts, performing arts, and heritage) as integrated into a much broader range of cultural sector industries: (1) the cultural industries (such as film, television, video games); (2) creative industries and activities (design, architecture, advertising); and (3) related industries (such as computers, software, and mobile phones). Many EU policies[1]—for example, the Lisbon Strategy, the Bologna Process, Media Policies, Cohesion Policy, Structural Funds— often drive cultural policy and provide significantly more funding to

Europe's arts and culture sector than policies specifically designed to do so. This chapter, however, is delimited to EU cultural policy that focuses on the core arts fields considered (at least theoretically) to be at the center of Europe's creative economy.

Power in EU cultural policy may be best conceptualized across two dimensions: the *content* of EU cultural policies, and the *process* of EU cultural policy making. This chapter is delimited to these two aspects of analysis, and presents a constructivist and neo-institutionalist lens in analyzing transnational cultural policy (Finnemore, 1996; March and Olsen, 1989; North, 1990; Peters, 2005; Powell and DiMaggio, 1991; Weaver and Rockman, 1993). Institutions are "persistent and connected sets of rules (formal or informal) that prescribe behavioral rules, constrain activity, and shape expectations" (Keohane, 1989, p. 163), and it is crucial to consider the role of international institutions in influencing societal norms, values, and preferences (Finnemore, 1996, pp. 3–6).

Policy networks, as well as procedures, practices, relationships, customs and norms matter enormously in understanding systemic policy-making processes and decisions about policy content. As Rifkin (2004) puts it, "the EU's very legitimacy lies ... in a code of conduct, conditioned by universal human rights and operationalized through statutes, regulations, and directives and, most important, by a continuous process of engagement, discourse, and negotiation with multiple players operating at the local, regional, national, transnational, and global levels" (p. 209). Policy making in the EU involves a procedural logic that has become an embedded EU policy style. The everyday actions of key stakeholders, policy actors, and institutions may be best understood as *low politics*, which is where institutional governance systems and incremental policy development continue to function in the EU, despite recent contextual changes (Richardson, 2006). Most often, cultural policy in the EU involves *soft law* instruments (such as non-enforceable recommendations and incentives) as well as *soft power* (the ability to shape the preferences of others (Nye, 2004)) in international relations.

As a policy area in the EU, culture is officially a competence shared with the member states, although EU-level competence in culture is negligible and restricted to certain actions. Member states hold authority for their own cultural policy development, and the EU may not exert direct, active cultural policy influence on member states or dictate harmonization of cultural policy at the nation-state level (see Chapter 11 by Johannison in this volume for Sweden's perspective). That said, as a transnational governance system, the EU provides an opportunity by which member states can learn about each others' national cultural policies. At the transnational level, the EU presents a forum where the *Europeanization* of cultural policy can occur. This chapter considers power in the content of EU-level cultural policy, in the process of EU-cultural policy making, and in the institutionalized European influence on nation-states' cultural policies.

European agenda for culture

The politics and legal bases associated with culture in the EU are complex, and many Europeans are adamant that no EU cultural policy exists. The EU does not officially have an explicit cultural policy, yet many transnational initiatives, actions, and programs that affect the cultural sector exist throughout Europe. As Mucica wrote in 2003, "The idea of a 'European cultural policy' has been advanced in recent years, especially in the context of the growing policy-making role of the European Union. But the concept of a common European cultural policy is a highly controversial one, and a number of critics disagree with the notion, considering that what is indeed needed is 'European cooperation', 'policies for culture in Europe', rather than a 'European cultural policy'" (as quoted in Obuljen, 2004, p. 30). At the heart of the controversy are conflicting views about the legal competence and power ascribed to EU-level cultural policy vis-à-vis that of European nation-states. And even more fundamentally, the term *cultural policy* is often very sensitive and politically loaded for Europeans.

Researchers and practitioners interested in comparing cultural policies in Europe and assessing EU-level cultural policies may find several approaches particularly informative. The Council of Europe (which, it should be noted, is an entity separate from the EU institutions) developed a comprehensive process to review and evaluate national cultural policies (D'Angelo and Vesperini, 1998; 1999; Schuster, 2002, pp. 213–34). The concept of cultural policy recognized by the leaders of this project included assessment of five criteria:

1   Explicit objectives of central government, in conjunction with regional and local government and the players in the cultural sphere;
2. Implicit objectives, which are reflected in various examples of action on the part of the state which, in retrospect, is organized and forms a coherent whole, since it is related to the real choices made by the players involved;
3   Action regarding the provision of culture—whether in terms of facilities, programming or artistic creation;
4   Resources allocated—not only financial but also administrative, structural human and creative;
5   Planning, that is preparing for government involvement in cultural activities, and planning the resources to be allocated.

(D'Angelo and Vesperini, 1998, p. 19)

Concepts of cultural policy articulated by both the Council of Europe and the United Nations Educational, Scientific, and Cultural Organization (UNESCO) are important considerations when analyzing EU-level policies. The current UNESCO (2005) concept of cultural policy from the *Convention on the Protection and Promotion of the Diversity of Cultural Expressions*, states:

> "Cultural policies and measures" refers to those policies and measures relating to culture, whether at the local, national, regional or international level that are either focused on culture as such or are designed to have a direct effect on cultural expressions of individuals, groups or societies, including on the creation, production, dissemination, distribution of and access to cultural activities, goods, and services.

(p. 5)

The Council of Europe and UNESCO concepts of cultural policy are very broad in nature, including both explicit and implicit measures. Potential policy actions include strategic development of both the supply side and the demand side of cultural production and expression. Further, these definitions emphasize multilevel governance systems involved in cultural policy formulation and implementation, as well as the potential for manifold points of investment and intervention in the cultural sector of societies.

In light of these two international organizations' expansive and inclusive orientations toward cultural policy, it is interesting that there is such reluctance in defining EU cultural policy as *policy*. As Alan Forrest (1994), then the Head of Division (Education, Culture, Youth) for the Council of the European Union, commented upon the passage of Article 128 in the Maastricht Treaty, "There is no Community cultural 'policy', but Community encouragement of action among Member States, supporting and supplementing their action 'if necessary'" (p. 18). Still, there is no question that a legal basis for EU involvement in culture is provided by Article 151 of the consolidated version of the Treaty on European Union (see Figure 10.1). Prior to culture officially coming within the EU's legal competence, various cultural programs such as the European Cultural Capitals program and the European Youth Orchestra had existed—despite significant concern expressed by many member states regarding EU involvement in culture. With the cultural sphere viewed by many to be solely under the purview of national policy, significant controversy ensued during negotiations that led to the highly restrictive version of the culture article that finally passed as Article 128 of the Treaty of Maastricht. It was only through an agreement on how the principle of *subsidiarity* (the principle in the EU that decisions must be taken as closely as possible to the citizen) and how a unanimous voting requirement would be included in the article that an acceptable compromise was reached (Gordon, 2007, p. 15). As Forrest (1994) explained, "Article 128 contains a balance struck between member States which wanted culture in the Treaty in order to allow wider Community action and those who wanted it mentioned in order to set limits beyond which it should not go" (p. 17).

The manner in which power can be exerted through both incentive measures and restrictive measures of formal cultural policy is exemplified

1. The Community shall contribute to the flowering of the cultures of the Member States, while respecting their national and regional diversity and at the same time bringing the common cultural heritage to the fore.

2. Action by the Community shall be aimed at encouraging cooperation between Member States and, if necessary, supporting and supplementing their action in the following areas:
   – improvement of the knowledge and dissemination of the culture and history of the European peoples;
   – conservation and safeguarding of cultural heritage of European significance;
   – non-commercial cultural exchanges;
   – artistic and literary creation, including in the audiovisual sector.

3. The Community and the Member States shall foster cooperation with third countries and the competent international organizations in the sphere of culture, in particular the Council of Europe.

4. The Community shall take cultural aspects into account in its action under other provisions of this Treaty, in particular in order to respect and to promote the diversity of its cultures.

5. In order to contribute to the achievement of the objectives referred to in this Article, the Council:
   – acting in accordance with the procedure referred to in Article 251 and after consulting the Committee of the Regions, shall adopt incentive measures, excluding any harmonization of the laws and regulations of the Member States. The Council shall act unanimously throughout the procedure referred to in Article 251;
   – acting unanimously on a proposal from the Commission, shall adopt recommendations.

Figure 10.1   Article 151 of the consolidated version of the Treaty on European Union (ex-Article 128 of the Treaty of Maastricht)

by Article 128/151. With reference to Figure 10.1, one can immediately see in the first clause of the article the inherent tension in the objective of EU cultural actions to both support the "flowering of the cultures" and the "common cultural heritage." The second clause provides more insight into the types of cultural activities that are to be encouraged through EU-level programs, complementing member states' cultural exchange, preservation and creation efforts. Importantly, this article restricts the EU to these specific areas of action. The third clause is significanct as the EU expands its focus on culture as an aspect of international relations and encourages increased cooperation with international organizations. For example, in 2005, the EU member states were represented *en bloc* in negotiating the UNESCO Convention on Cultural Diversity and remain key partners in implementing this Convention. Such international cooperation demonstrates—at least symbolically—Europeans' interest in cultivating international legal instruments to support and protect opportunities for cultural expression.

The fourth and fifth clauses in the culture article focus on process. The fourth clause—commonly referred to as the *transversality clause*—stipulates that other EU policy areas shall take cultural aspects into account in order to protect and promote cultural diversity. The article, however, does not provide clarification of the scope, extent, or processes required by this clause. The fifth clause very clearly outlines the cultural policymaking process that must be followed. In the cultural sphere, the EU may only implement soft law instruments such as incentive measures and recommendations, and is prohibited from attempting to harmonize the member states' cultural policies through adopting formal regulations and directives. Further, clause five specifies that the Committee of the Regions must be consulted, the formal co-decision procedure among the Council of Ministers and the European Parliament must be followed as outlined in Article 251, and the Council's final vote must be unanimous.[2] Culture is one of very few policy areas where a unanimous vote is still required. This clause means that any member state has the power to block cultural policy development at the transnational EU level.

Power in EU cultural policy content is symbolic and instrumental in nature. Despite the limited and restricted scope of engagement specified by Article 128/151, and the marginal position of culture in the EU treaties and institutions, the potential role of culture for the purpose of European integration is enormous. According to the European Commission's report, *A Community of Cultures: The European Union and the Arts* (2002), there are four major goals of European cultural policy: (1) to bring out the common aspects of Europe's heritage; (2) to enhance the feeling of belonging to one and the same community; (3) to widely recognize and respect cultural, national, and regional diversity; and (4) to help cultures develop and become more widely known (p. 2). As is evident in this report, the goals of instrumentalizing culture for purposes of identity-building, forging a sense of citizenship, and fostering intercultural dialogue are continually reinforced in the EU.

In recent years, the EU cultural policy agenda-setting process has concentrated on articulating and advocating for an EU "cultural agenda." A new soft-law instrument, titled the *Communication from the Commission on a European Agenda for Culture in a Globalizing World* (commonly referred to as the *Communication on Culture*) was endorsed by the Culture Council of the Council of Ministers in November 2007. In general, the council endorses three major objectives that aim to form a common cultural strategy for the European institutions, the member states, and the cultural and creative sector. These objectives are the promotion of cultural diversity and intercultural dialogue; the promotion of culture as a catalyst for creativity in the framework of the Lisbon Strategy for growth, employment, innovation, and competitiveness; and the promotion of culture as a vital element in the EU's international relations. These lofty and ambitious objectives are being addressed through diverse EU policy spheres, such as cultural policy, media policy, social policy, cohesion policy, competition policy, education policy, and foreign policy, although a very low level of human and financial resources is appropriated by the EU for the express purpose of implementing cultural policy.[3] As such, there appears to be a disconnect between the dimensions of power implicit in the content and formulation of EU cultural policy and in the implementation of the policy. The next section of this chapter analyzes institutional power involved in the process of EU cultural policy making.

Transnational cultural policy making in the EU[4]

The institutional structure of the EU influences the ways in which power can be exercised throughout the EU cultural policy-making process. As such, an analysis of the independent stages of the policy-making process reveals diverse actors, systems, and organizations in which power may be exerted. Richardson (2006) suggests that it is helpful to shift one's analytical focus according to the policy stage under investigation. For example, transnational epistemic communities may serve as the key players in influencing the policy agenda. In the policy-formulation stage, the roles of transnational advocacy coalitions, policy communities, and issue networks should be analyzed. An approach using institutional analysis and organizational behavior may be most appropriate in assessing policy decision and policy implementation stages of cultural policy.

The European institutions most directly involved in EU cultural policy-making are the Council of the European Union, the European Parliament, the Commission of the European Union and, to a far lesser degree, the Committee of the Regions.[5] In general, the commission proposes legislation, the Committee of the Regions advises, and the council and parliament together reach a decision on the policy following the formally required co-decision procedure. At the implementation stage, it is also important to understand the structure and operations of the Education, Audiovisual, and Culture Executive Agency (EACEA). Each of these EU institutions has key actors and units involved in cultural policy, as depicted in Figure 10.2. To provide a clear framework for understanding institutional structure and processes, the focus of this chapter is solely on a model of cultural policy making that has resulted in the Culture Programme, the EU program that is most directly linked to Article 151.

EU cultural policy agenda-setting involves numerous stakeholders in a transnational epistemic community. International organizations such as UNESCO and the Council of Europe play a key role in establishing major international goals for cultural policy (such as the promotion of cultural diversity and intercultural dialogue). Many research-based and information-exchange organizations exist in Europe's cultural sphere at the local, national, regional, and pan-European levels. Numerous conferences, symposia, and meetings also take place regularly among key cultural policy stakeholders in Europe, helping to articulate common themes and priorities

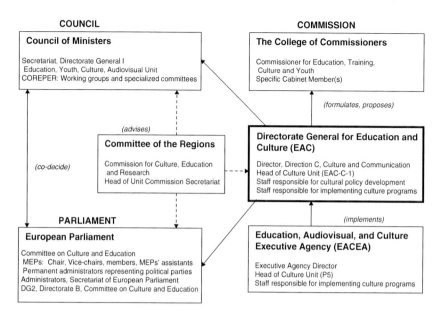

Figure 10.2   EU Institutions' roles in cultural policy decision-making

for the sector. Transnational cultural policy advocacy and lobbying efforts are nascent in Europe, represented most effectively by the recently renamed Culture Action Europe. Additional stakeholders in the agenda-setting stage of policy development include the interests of other EU policies, actions, and initiatives (such as the Lisbon Agenda), as well as European Commission personnel and soft law instruments (such as formal *communications*, and reports). Constant interaction among these stakeholders and the representation of their diverse interests informs ongoing development and agenda-setting for cultural policy (Dewey, 2008).

The Commission of the European Union (often referred to as the European Commission) proposes, executes, and manages policy. In its role as "Guardian of the Treaties" and with the objective to promote the common interest, the European Commission holds significant political and administrative power (Guéguen, 2006, pp. 24–5). The commission is the key EU institution involved in policy formulation and implementation. The Directorate General for Education and Culture (DG EAC) is the motor of cultural policy development; approximately five mid-level civil servants are involved in initiating and drafting cultural policy development on a daily basis. The commissioner responsible for culture (a political appointee) oversees the Directorate General. Policies the Directorate General drafts in cooperation with the field-specific commission are approved and formally proposed by the Commission of the European Union as a single entity. Cultural policy implementation involves personnel working in both the DG EAC and the EACEA. The executive agency, officially an independent institution reporting to the DG, is responsible for the day-to-day operations of various programs, such as the Culture Programme. Official communications state that the DG is responsible for cultural policy development and the executive agency is responsible solely for execution of programs, and there seems to be little recognition of the important policy-making power that can occur during implementation (see http://eacea.ec.europa.eu/ for an overview of agency structure and operations). Further, EU cultural programs of a "symbolic" nature, such as the European Capitals of Culture Programme or the 2008 European Year of Intercultural Dialogue, are administered by civil servants in the Directorate General, rather than in the executive agency. Power in EU cultural policy development, formulation and implementation is thus fluid as it shifts among the three divisions of the commission.

The Council of the European Union (most commonly referred to as the Council of Ministers) is the voice of the member states and holds the main policy decision-making authority in the EU. Civil servants from the member stages compose the committee of permanent representatives (COREPER), which is charged with preparing council decisions. The council is composed of nine technical councils, which are termed *configurations*; one of these is "Education, Youth and Culture." Personnel representing the cultural ministry of each EU member state participate in this council. COREPER working groups and specialized committees along with the council's secretariat work daily on preparing a basis for reaching intergovernmental compromises and preliminary agreements on policies under consideration. During each member state's rotating presidency of the EU, the member state and its COREPER operators thus have significant capacity to drive the agenda and timeline of meetings and negotiations.

The European Parliament is currently comprised of 785 Members (MEPs) representing seven Europe-wide political parties. Representing the people of Europe, the European Parliament is increasingly powerful in European policy-making processes. Where previously its power was limited to simple consultation, the parliament has evolved to now hold important authority as co-decider on many vital areas of EU policy. Each political party has numerous means of policy influence within the Parliament; each party has resources and specialized permanent administrators who prepare the agenda and drive the work of the committees and plenary sessions. A Committee on Culture and Education (CULT) is one of 20 parliamentary committees addressing specific policy areas. Despite being considered rather weak as a committee (that is, not attracting participation by powerful MEPs), the CULT committee nonetheless has a strong infrastructure with support of four permanent administrators, staff members of participating MEPs, and civil servants working in the parliament's secretariat.

Article 151 requires that the Committee of the Regions—a 344-member advisory body representing local and regional interests throughout Europe—be consulted on policy proposals submitted by the commission to the European Parliament and Council of Ministers. While the Committee of the Regions is identified as the guardian of the subsidiarity and proximity principles in EU decision-making processes, it remains an advisory body that is not particularly influential. However, its role may increase in importance as municipalities and regions engage more actively in EU policy making. As Europe's cities continue to focus on advancement of their creative industries as a significant factor of economic development, it is possible that local and regional perspectives will increasingly inform cultural policy development through this institutional channel.

An analysis of power in the institutions of EU cultural policy making reveals a constantly shifting institutional balance of power and some surprises in the locus of power within the institutions. As indicated above, the mid-level commission personnel hold tremendous power as the initiators and drafters of policy. Cultural policy involves low politics as policy decisions are negotiated between the Council of Ministers and the parliament. Here, the role of *comitology* (formal EU committee procedure) is very important as the legislation under review and consideration goes through proper policy decision-making channels in each EU institution. The ongoing meetings, discussions, strategic steps, and low-level negotiations that occur every day among civil servants in Brussels are crucial in ushering EU cultural policy from the initial proposal through revision to the final adoption of legislation. Also, the relative balance of decision-making authority is shifting as the parliament constantly gains more power and as Europe's cities and regions increasingly advocate for their interests at the EU level. Even more vital to consider, however, is the power of transnational influences on policy development exerted through institutionalized processes of Europeanization, discussed in the final section of this chapter.

Europeanization in cultural policy

Significant power lies in the EU's institutional structure and processes as well as in its legal basis for cultural policy. While cultural policy is considered to be mainly a policy area under the purview of national governance systems, institutional power at the transnational level must not be underestimated in its influential role in propelling policy learning and convergence. Institutionalized systems of *Europeanization* exist in the supranational and intergovernmental functions of the EU, and these systems may be highly influential in the cultural policy sphere across Europe.

In the EU, power flows throughout the EU's unique multilevel governance system and transnational policy networks. Europeanization may be best understood as an offshoot of multilevel governance, which conceives of the EU as a polity in which power and influence are exercised in networks that link public and private actors of regional, national, and European levels

(Heard-Lauréote, 2005; Nugent, 2006, pp. 555–7; Pollock, 2005, pp. 39–41). Rifkin (2004) observes that the EU "has become a discursive forum whose function is to referee relationships and help coordinate activity among a range of players, of which the nation-state is only one. ... It facilitates the coming together of networks of engagement that include nation-states but also extend outward to transnational organizations and inward to municipal and regional governments, as well as civil society organizations" (p. 215). As such, EU cultural policy research that uses policy network tools of analysis may provide deeper understanding of the dimensions of power exercised in this new model of governance. The analytical value of this approach lies in conceptualizing policy making as a process that involves diverse, mutually interdependent actors and institutions (Adam and Kriesi, 2007). "The value of transnational networks is their ability to make sense of dynamic policy-making processes in both the wider European and the local context as well as their contribution to political exchanges; policy-making and policy transfer below the EU level" (Heard-Lauréote, 2005, p. 37).

Europeanization is generally understood as a process "in which laws and policies in the member states have been brought into alignment with EU law and policy through a process of harmonization, or perhaps even of homogenization" (McCormick, 2008, p. 261). As such, Europeanization works as a powerful device, driven by the structural and administrative power of the EU and its civil servants (Shore, 2000). Lenschow (2006) explains that one key element of Europeanization is the fact that the extensive committee structure and consultative procedures of EU institutions routinely facilitate information sharing among national policy makers. This formal system of horizontal policy transfer is institutionalized through formal practices. "The Open Method of Coordination, for instance, is a device for the transfer of so-called 'best practice models' especially in areas where the EU lacks competency to exert top-down pressures" (pp. 58–9).

The Open Method of Coordination (OMC) is an institutional process established by the European Council in 2000, and is being increasingly used to address policy areas—such as education and training, culture, youth, and social policy—that have a limited and restrictive scope of EU competence. OMC is routinely utilized to foster agreement among governments to address a range of policy challenges where policy authority lies with national or subnational governments and where soft law instruments are appropriate. As a nonbinding and semi-voluntary form of policy coordination, OMC is based on collective establishment of policy goals that member states are pressured to meet by benchmarking, guidelines, indicators, timetables, periodic monitoring, and peer review (De Schoutheete, 2006, p. 51; Nugent, 2006, p. 584; Pollock, 2005, p. 44). "Instead of complying with rules, national actors are expected to widen their ideational horizon due to the exposure to European or neighbour country discourses and to reconsider previously held beliefs, expectations and preferences.

Europeanisation may take place because the EU had provided an arena for the exchange of ideas and shaped a discourse by identifying general goals or principles, disseminating information and pointing out examples of 'best practice'" (Lenschow, 2006, p. 66).

When the *Communication on Culture* (a soft law instrument setting an EU agenda for culture) was endorsed by the Council of Ministers in 2007, the Open Method of Coordination was formally introduced into Europe's cultural policy field. With this institutionalized process of policy transfer and coordination now a formal practice, transnational power exerted by the EU in cultural policy making enters a new stage. No longer are incentive measures and restrictions confined to EU-level policy content and policy-making processes. No research has yet been done on the impact of OMC in European cultural policy, and the potential long-term effects of implementing this institutionalized form of policy learning will require future study and evaluation. It may, however, be hypothesized that EU institutional structure and processes are reshaping cultural policy throughout Europe by profoundly influencing European policy makers' identities, preferences, and behavior.

In sum, as a nascent model of transnational multilevel governance, the EU provides fertile ground for ongoing exploration of supranational and intergovernmental power exercised in the content and policy-making processes of cultural policy.

Notes

1. Diverse EU policies are important considerations when analyzing EU cultural policy. The Lisbon Strategy pertains to a goal set in March 2000 for Europe, within a decade, to become "the most competitive and dynamic knowledge-based economy in the world, capable of sustainable growth with more and better jobs and greater social cohesion." Available at The Eurojargon glossary Web site, http://europa.eu/abc/eurojargon/index_en.htm [accessed April 25, 2007]). The Bologna Process has to do with harmonization of higher education in Europe. In general, Cohesion Policy and Structural Funds are designed to promote social cohesion and economic competitiveness by closing the gap between advanced and less developed regions in Europe.
2. At the time of writing this chapter, the Lisbon Treaty has been signed but not ratified. If the Lisbon Treaty is ratified, the unanimity voting requirement in the fifth clause of the culture article would be changed to a qualified majority voting requirement.
3. It is difficult to secure accurate data on EU financial resources allocated specifically to cultural actions. The EU program directly linked to Article 151 is the Culture Programme, which was allocated a budget of EURO 400 million for the current 7-year budget cycle (2007–13). A recent study on structural funds allocated to cultural initiatives can be found in German (Beckmann and Gedak, 2000) and a study on the use of structural funds in the domain of culture in the EU member states from 1994–9 is available on the European Commission's website. (see http://ec.europa.eu/culture/key-documents/doc1799_en.htm). A comprehensive analysis of EU resources invested in the cultural sector through diverse policy spheres is beyond the scope of this chapter.

4. This section of the chapter presents a summary of findings from field research conducted by the author in 2006. See Dewey (2008) for a more detailed discussion of research methods, data, and findings on transnational cultural policy making in the EU.

5. See Guéguen (2006); McCormick (2008); Moussis (2005); Nugent (2006); Peterson and Shackleton (2006); Richardson (2006); and Wallace, Wallace, and Pollack (2005) for comprehensive introductions to the institutions and policy making of the EU.

11
Making Geography Matter in Cultural Policy Research: The Case of Regional Cultural Policy in Sweden

Jenny Johannisson

Introduction

In Sweden, like in most late modern Western societies, contemporary cultural policy is considered to be permeated by and inseparable from globalization processes. Such processes are understood in this chapter as parallel processes of internationalization and decentralization, which contribute to shifting the allocation of power both within the political-administrative organization and between this organization and its surroundings (cf. Johansson 2000; Mitchell 2003). The local, regional and transnational levels of government are from this perspective given opportunities of becoming more self-sufficient agents, threatening and transforming—but certainly not eliminating—the hitherto dominant position of the nation-state (Smith 2001). Thereby, changes in the organization of political practices—here delimited mainly to policy making and policy implementation—can be identified. Rather than succumbing to formal rules applied in easily discernible sectors, policy making and policy implementation are increasingly portrayed as a muddy affair; a set of social practices enacted by a number of different agents, including not only politicians and civil servants from a number of different policy fields, but also professionals and business people (Beck 1994; Halonen 2005).

This chapter is based on research on local and regional settings; research which aims to explore the geographical and discursive shifts in cultural policy outlined above.[1] The objective of the chapter is threefold: first, to provide insight into contemporary Swedish cultural policy; secondly, to argue for a space/place-sensitive approach to cultural policy; and, thirdly, to indicate what I consider important points of analysis in space/place-sensitive research on Swedish regional cultural policy. The chapter is positioned in what is increasingly becoming an established research field, namely that of cultural policy studies. Internationally, two important forums and outlets for this research community are the biannual *International Conference on Cultural Policy Research (ICCPR)*, and *The International Journal of Cultural Policy* (Routledge). An underlying assumption in this chapter is that while existing cultural policy studies provide a growing body of critically informed research on national cultural policies and arts policies, there is a more urgent need for developing further critically informed research on regional and local cultural policies. In order to make such a critical understanding intelligible, however, I believe it is necessary to start with outlining the basic principles of contemporary Swedish cultural policy.

Swedish cultural policy in brief

Sweden is situated in Northern Europe and has nine million inhabitants. Since the twentieth century , Sweden has integrated cultural policy with what has internationally become known as a social democratic-oriented welfare model. Within the Swedish political-administrative organization, cultural policy is understood as "an ordered, structured means for expressing official endeavours in this area of public responsibility" (Swedish National Council for Cultural Affairs 1997, p. 8). In Sweden, cultural policy in this sense implies the fulfillment of the following criteria: "goals, methods, routines for evaluation, responsible political and administrative bodies, and financial resources" (ibid.).[2] This formation of cultural policy as a policy field in its own right is dated to 1974, when a united Swedish parliament supported the cultural policy bill produced by a Social Democratic government. In the same year, measures to fulfill this vision were also taken. Of central importance to the organization of cultural policy in Sweden is the division of political-administrative responsibility between three levels of government, each with its own decision-making agencies and power of taxation. At the national level you can thus identify the state, at the regional level the county councils/regions, and at the local level the municipalities. Taken together, these three levels of government subsidized cultural activities for Euro 1.9 billion in 2005 (Swedish Arts Council 2006).[3]

At the national government level, the Swedish Arts Council has the overall responsibility for implementing national cultural policy. Activities subsidized by the national government are limited to "theatre, dance, music, literature, arts periodicals and public libraries, and to the fine arts, museums and exhibitions" (Swedish Arts Council 2008). The activities are mainly produced, distributed and consumed in an institutional context, even though activities are also carried out in more independent settings. The national government includes a Ministry of Culture and Education, and the Parliament includes a Committee on Cultural Affairs. In addition to the Swedish Arts Council there are several national authorities specializing in different cultural policy subfields, such as heritage, archives, film and art subsidy. Regarding the media, the national government concentrates its support on public service activities. Popular education, which has a unique design and position in Sweden, as well as in the other Nordic countries, enjoys national government funding and coordination. Every activity supported by the national government should be in accordance with the seven objectives that the Swedish Parliament set for national cultural policy in 1996, objectives which include a very moderate revision of the 1974 objectives. These objectives concentrate on the freedom of expression, artistic quality and non-commercialization, pluralism and development, an increased participation in cultural activities, internationalization, education and the preservation and revitalization of cultural heritage (Swedish Arts Council 2008). The national government has the overall responsibility for objectives, funding, investigation and information within the cultural policy field. The Swedish Parliament is also responsible for legislation, which is limited to the areas of cultural heritage, the broadcasting media and the public library system. In 2005, the national government answered for 47 percent (or approximately Euro 0.9 billion) of total public expenses in the cultural field (Swedish Arts Council 2006). This figure includes contributions to cultural activities on the regional and local levels.

The regional level of government is organized in 18 county councils and two regions. Public healthcare constitutes the main bulk of their budgets (approximately 80 percent), even though they also play an increasingly important role in regional development. Mainly as a consequence of the national cultural policy decisions of 1974, the county councils have generated cultural policy strategies of their own. Regional government bodies also act as owners of regional cultural institutions, as well as funding bodies of regional and local cultural activities. In 2005, the county councils and regions answered for 10 percent (or approximately Euro 0.2 billion) of total public expenses in the cultural field (Swedish Arts Council 2006). Experiments with political-administrative regionalization, carried out in Sweden from 1997 onwards, have led to heated debate on regional cultural policies. These experiments are partly a result of Sweden entering the European Union in 1995. The experiments consist of the amalgamation of county councils into larger regions, which not only coordinate their own activities, but are also delegated responsibilities that previously belonged to the national government.

At the local level, Sweden is divided into 290 municipalities. Of great importance is the right to self-determination that has been granted to Swedish municipalities since 1862, where a distinction is made between duties that the municipalities are obliged, by law, to fulfil, and duties that are voluntary on their part. Cultural policy is part of the latter, apart from the public library system and parts of the cultural heritage field. The funding of public libraries is the key responsibility of the local level, supplemented with funding in the areas of popular education, music schools and cultural environment. On an average, cultural activities take 3 percent of the municipal budgets, while public education and social services are the dominant items of expenditure. In 2005, the municipalities answered for 43 percent (or approximately Euro 0.9 billion) of total public expenses in the cultural field (Swedish Arts Council 2006).

My ongoing research, financed by the Swedish Arts Council, consists of a comparative study of cultural policy in Region Västra Götaland and Region Skåne, two results of the experiments with regionalization that were mentioned above. Against the backdrop of globalization processes, the overall research question is directed at identifying alliances and conflicts between different levels of government in the cultural policy field, as well as between cultural policy and other policy fields. In the next section, I will turn to an analysis of what I consider to be the basic guiding principles—what will henceforth be referred to as discourses—of Swedish cultural policy. The analysis has two purposes: to provide a deeper understanding of Swedish cultural policy at all levels of government, and to illustrate what I consider to be a shift from the hitherto "placeless" character of both cultural policy and cultural policy studies to cultural policy where place makes a difference.

A Sense of place? Art, welfare and new alliances

My ongoing research on regional cultural policy in Sweden partly emanates from and builds on findings made in relation to the study presented in my doctoral thesis (Johannisson 2006). The latter explored the use of different cultural policy discourses in cultural policy (re)construction in the City of Göteborg, Sweden, during the 1990s. Theoretically, I thus strived to make a contribution to the growing body of cultural policy research informed—in very different ways—by discourse theory (cf. Bennett 1998; 2003; McGuigan 1996; 2004; Miller and Yúdice 2002; Volkerling 1996). Using a neo-pragmatist, discourse-oriented approach inspired mainly by the works of American philosopher Richard Rorty (1979; 2000), French philosopher Michel Foucault (1991; 1994) and American political scientist Frank Fischer (2003), I studied statements[4] put forward in documents and interviews in relation to the shaping of both new visions for, and a new organization of, the city's cultural policy. The statements were produced mainly by agents at the local level of government, but statements by agents on the national and international levels were also included.[5] The discourses used in this process of (re)construction were identified by relating the statements by cultural policy agents to statements put forward in research-based literature on cultural policy or closely related areas. Policy making was thus understood as defined by Fischer, namely as:

> a constant discursive struggle over the definitions of problems, the boundaries of categories used to describe them, the criteria for their classification and assessment, and the meanings of ideals that guide particular actions.
>
> (Fischer 2003, p. 60)

Table 11.1 Summary of the discourses used by institutional agents in the cultural policy (re)construction process in Göteborg 1991–8 (Johannisson 2006, p. 239)

	The quality discourse	The welfare discourse	The alliance discourse
Aim	Professional, artistic quality	Broaden participation in cultural activities and create a good living environment	Sustainable development (financially and living environment)
Concept of culture	Aesthetic	Anthropological (group-oriented) and aesthetic	Anthropological (individual-oriented) and aesthetic
Concept of place/space	Artistic, universal space	National space	Glocal places
Rationale	Humanistic	Sociological	Market-oriented
Model of governance	Profession-oriented patron model	Legal-bureaucratic architect model	Network-oriented architect- and patron model

The analysis resulted in the identification of three cultural policy discourses, summarized in Table 11.1.

While strongly emphasizing that discourses cannot be separated from the specific articulations—in this case statements in the cultural policy (re)construction process in Göteborg—which manifest the discourses, I regard them as useful tools of analysis in relation to regional cultural policy. The discourses should be considered a working tool, and its deployment could and should result in modifications of the discourses described above. Having said this, I still believe that they can be used in the study of cultural policy in other places and other processes than those of a specific Swedish municipality in the 1990s. In the following, I will therefore briefly introduce the three discourses, tuning in on their theoretical inspirations rather than their specific and empirical articulations in Göteborg.

The quality discourse

To identify a discourse is to identify a specific set of rules according to which specific categorizations—distinctions—are made (cf. Bartelsen 1993, p. 62). When categorizing the sets of rules at play in Swedish local cultural policy, I am greatly indebted to the Danish cultural policy researcher Dorte Skot-Hansen. In a seminal article (Skot-Hansen 1999), she describes three main rationales that have guided Nordic—and, to a certain extent, other West European—cultural policies since the 1930s. Skot-Hansen labels these the humanistic rationale, the sociological rationale and the instrumental rationale. The aim of cultural policy within the humanistic rationale is to further the citizens' progress towards "Bildung" by subsidizing professional artistic activities of high quality. The main instrument of cultural policy is to spread such artistic excellence to as many citizens as possible, that is, the role of the state is to "democratize Culture" (Skot-Hansen 1999). The humanistic rationale, employed by Swedish national government bodies especially in the formation of cultural policy between the 1930s and 1960s, is based on a sector-oriented and aesthetic concept of Culture; culture with a capital C (cf. Vestheim 2001). It provides the quality discourse with its central moments, a discourse which transcends the specific places where cultural policies are enacted in favor of the specific quality criteria set up in an artistic, universal space. When related to the organization of public cultural policy agents, the quality discourse includes what the Swedish political scientist Bo Rothstein (2001) labels a profession-oriented model. This is a model where the professional interests in a specific policy field are allowed a great deal of influence on what cultural policy should be and how it should be organized. In Sweden, and in the other Nordic countries, professional artists and art mediators have traditionally had this kind of influence; the level of corporatism in the cultural policy field could thus be considered quite high (Mangset et al. 2008). In the quality discourse, this profession-oriented model of governance is expressed in what Canadian cultural economists Harry Hillman Chartrand and Claire McCaughey (1989) have labeled a patron model. The patron model, often exemplified in British cultural policy, stipulates that there should be an "arm's length" between artistic activities and the state. I would therefore argue that the patron model is primarily an arts policy instrument, rather than a welfare policy instrument—the latter being the central moment of the welfare discourse to which I will now turn.

The welfare discourse

The welfare discourse includes the sociological rationale, which Skot-Hansen (1999) presents as an important addition to—but certainly not a replacement of—the humanistic rationale in Nordic cultural policies, on all levels of government, from the 1970s onwards. The aim of the sociological rationale when applied to cultural policy is to liberate the citizens, that is, to provide the citizens with possibilities to engage in cultural activities on their own terms, rather than being the passive recipients of professional artistic activities. The main policy instrument of the sociological rationale is, therefore, "cultural democracy," where democracy refers both to a broader, anthropological concept of culture, and to a potentially broader number of people allowed to engage in cultural and artistic activities. In the welfare discourse, the sociological rationale is applied in relation to groups rather than individuals—in Swedish cultural policy this is expressed in the priority given to what is considered marginalized groups, such as children, people with other ethnicities than the Swedish, and people with physical or mental impairments. Due to its universalistic welfare moment, the welfare discourse, like the quality discourse, tends to be rather placeless, relating instead to national space and national cultural policy, that is, where welfare policy is discursively positioned in Sweden.[6] The model of governance activated in the welfare discourse is what Rothstein (2001) labels a legal-bureaucratic one, that is, a model based on the traditional Weberian notion of a strict division between decision-making politicians and neutral, implementing civil servants. Cultural policy is in this model considered as a policy field among others, the utmost aim of which is to contribute to the overall welfare of the citizens. This model presupposes a strong state, which does not always keep an arm's length in its interventions in the cultural field, but rather plays the role of the architect as pointed out by Hillman Chartrand and McCaughey (1989). The Nordic countries are often given as examples of the architect model (cf. Vestheim 1995). They have also, by Nordic cultural policy researchers (Mangset et al. 2008, p. 2), been portrayed as a combination of "the French Ministry of Culture model and the British 'arm's length' model," which points to the parallel use made of the quality discourse and the welfare discourse in Nordic cultural policy.

The alliance discourse

In opposition to the rather placeless character of both the quality discourse and the welfare discourse, place is a central moment in the alliance discourse. In the alliance discourse, the inherent instrumentalism of all political practices—including cultural policy—becomes an overt tool in furthering the aim of sustainable development, both in a narrow economic sense and in a broader sense, alluding to the general living environment of the citizens. The alliance discourse doesn't hide the "double technique" that Swedish cultural policy has made use of since its formal establishment in the 1970s, that is, to simultaneously claim the autonomy of the arts in relation to the political-administrative organization and the positive role of culture in local, regional and national development. It is based on the rationale that Skot-Hansen (1999) labels instrumentalist, thereby illustrating the turn that Swedish and Nordic cultural policies took in the 1980s towards market-oriented arguments for public intervention in the cultural field. In order to illustrate the fact that all cultural policy is instrumental (cf. Vestheim 2008), in the sense that cultural policy is inherently about promoting culture in order to reach objectives beyond culture itself—whether the objective be that of facilitating the citizens' access to culture, promoting freedom of speech, or urban regeneration—I label the rationale at play in the alliance discourse "market-oriented" rather than merely instrumentalist.[7] It is this obvious (re)turn of cultural policy to the market's way of working that is specific for the use made of culture in the alliance discourse. Like the welfare discourse, the alliance discourse is tied up to an anthropological concept of culture, but in the alliance discourse this concept is directed at the individual rather than at groups. Cultural policy is about facilitating the fulfilment of individual preferences and lifestyles in a global setting where everything has become "culturalized" (Skot-Hansen 1999), not about helping marginalized groups to take part in a predetermined range of activities. And in order to further individual lifestyles, cultural policy has to start off from what makes a specific place unique regarding cultural resources.

As the label indicates, the alliance discourse is about creating and using the networks that policy making is in this discourse based on (cf. Rothstein 2001); networks that transcend both the political-administrative organization and professional bodies and extend to all agents involved in shaping a place. Traditional distinctions and borders—between public interests and market interests, between professional and non-professional activities and between high and low culture—are contested and give way to partly new power hierarchies. In my study of cultural policy (re)construction in Göteborg, the empirical political practices that the quality discourse is used to underpin is arts policy while cultural policy is mainly based in the welfare discourse. The alliance discourse is used in Göteborg when promoting new perspectives in cultural policy, for example, in the shape of what has come to be known as cultural planning (cf. Bianchini 1993). The alliance discourse thus puts place into cultural policy, both as a commodity to be sold on a global market, and as an aesthetic and cultural artefact to be shaped, reproduced and transformed by those who live there (cf. Stevenson 2004, p. 122). In my study of Göteborg, the place was a city; in my ongoing research, the place is the region. In both cases, a city or a region is not understood as something given or static, but something that is continuously shaped, reproduced and transformed in social interaction between a wide range of different agents. As British political scientist Louise Fawcett (2005, p. 24) puts it: "a simple territorial definition might not take us very far—we need to refine regions to incorporate commonality, interaction and the possibility of cooperation." I find her definition of region as "units or 'zones' based on groups, states or territories, whose members share some identifiable traits" (ibid., cf. also Massey 1994; 1999) a useful starting point for exploring regional cultural policy in Sweden. I am interested in exploring how regions are created as "zones" through statements given by cultural policy agents, that is, how cultural policy is used as a tool in regional identity construction.

New places, old stories? Filling the region with meaning

The regions chosen for my ongoing study—Region Västra Götaland and Region Skåne—are chosen not for representing how regional cultural policy in Sweden is organized, but for being examples of current experiments with how regional (cultural) policy could be designed in the future. Both regions are the result of a political process that was formally initiated with the appointment of a national parliamentary committee on regional affairs in 1992. In the instructions to the Committee (Kommittédirektiv 1992:86), given by a conservative government, it was argued that the existing division of responsibility between different levels of government in Sweden was not working efficiently, neither from a democratic nor from a financial viewpoint. From the national government perspective, the regional government level in Sweden, which was at the time divided into 24 geographically based administrative units—the county councils—was not considered to function properly. The increasing internationalization of the Swedish political-administrative organization was pinpointed as an important reason for a readjustment toward the formation of regions better suited to further the aim of "sustainable development." This aim is clearly formulated within the framework of New Public Management (NPM), where the border between public and private interests and organization is blurred and cost-efficiency is a dominant theme.

In the final report given by the National Committee on Regional Affairs in 1995, culture is not a dominant theme, although the role of culture in supporting sustainable development is highlighted: "a rich cultural life strongly endorses an improvement of the citizens' quality of life, furthers their creativity and thereby fills an important function in identity construction" (SOU 1995, pp. 27, 341, my translation). But, the Committee argues, this role can never replace the fact that "culture also has an independent value" (ibid., p. 342, my translation). The Committee hereby provides an evident example of "the double technique" introduced above, where all discourses— the quality discourse, the welfare discourse and the alliance discourse—are put to use. But it is also evident from the report that the Committee does not consider cultural policy a key instrument within a predominantly market-oriented welfare policy which primarily aims at creating financially sustainable regions.

The government bills, issued by a Social Democratic government as follow-ups to the committee report, led to decisions in the Swedish Parliament on the formation of four new regions on a trial basis. Region Skåne was formally established in 1997 and Region Västra Götaland in 1999. They are the only regional experiments still active. There are both important similarities and differences between the two regional experiments. The main responsibility of both regions is, as was the case with the former county councils, to coordinate public healthcare in the 33 municipalities (1.17 million inhabitants) of Region Skåne and the 49 municipalities (1.5 million inhabitants) of Region Västra Götaland. In 2008, the total budget of Region Skåne was Euro 2.9 billion, and the total budget of Region Västra Götaland was 3.9 billion Euro. The two regions share an organizational model, where the publically elected county councils conglomerated into a new publically elected regional parliament, which have been granted authority over certain regional development issues by the national government. In the cultural policy field, however, Region Skåne has also been granted authority to allot national government funds to regional cultural institutions

(SFS 1996, p. 1414, § 2), while Region Västra Götaland is working together with the Swedish Arts Council in allocating the corresponding funds to its regional institutions. In addition, Region Skåne has the strategic responsibility for cultural policy in the region, including the operative responsibility for the regional cultural institutions. Region Västra Götaland has instead chosen a model where the regional board of cultural affairs commissions cultural activities from the institutions at hand (Johansson 2004). The two regions thus constitute examples of what cultural policy researcher Nobuko Kawashima (1997) labels political decentralization, that is, the transfer of political decision-making from the national to the regional level.[8] Finally, while Region Skåne is a formal, administrative region based on a supposedly identifiable and homogeneous cultural region, Region Västra Götaland, while also being a formal region, is considered a more heterogeneous entity and the result of regionalization rather than regionalism (cf. Malmström 1998, p. 50ff.; Trépagny 2003, p. 68–9; Törnqvist 1998, p. 60). As a result of a decision in the Swedish Parliament, both regions will continue on a trial basis until 2010.

Even though they are formally conducting their activities on a trial basis, both regions should be considered as established agents in the Swedish political-administrative organization. This includes their strategies and measures in the cultural policy field. Both regions have regional parliamentary decisions on comprehensive cultural policy strategies. Region Skåne adopted their cultural policy strategy in 2003, when the majority in the regional council was held by the Social Democratic Party. Region Västra Götaland adopted their strategy in 2005, in a council run by a minority coalition between representatives of the Social Democratic Party, the Liberal Party and the Centre Party. A preliminary analysis of the documents shows, perhaps unsurprisingly, that in both regions, cultural policy is a matter of combining different discourses. While both documents argue that the arts and culture have value in themselves, they should also be used in furthering sustainable development in the regions, both financially and socially. That culture can and should be used in order to further regional development is even more evident in the strategies for regional development that constitute the primary objective of both regions (Region Skåne 2004; Region Västra Götaland 2005).

As experiments with the Swedish political-administrative organization, Region Skåne and Region Västra Götaland are interesting to study in themselves, as examples of new and alternative ways of working with cultural policy at the regional level—even though the new moments at present seem to concern the organization of cultural policy rather that its objectives. In the research project outlined here, the regions can thus be identified as a new addition to the agents that shape, reproduce and transform the distinctions and hierarchies that constitute cultural policy; that is, as an addition to the agents that Michael Volkerling (1996) has labelled the "difference-engines" of cultural policy. Thus, the regions are not only interesting to study as formal agents in the political-administrative organization, but also as tools in the governance of regional identity in a more discursive sense. Hitherto, I have focused on the relation between the regional and national levels of government. In the following, I will briefly introduce the relation between the regional and local levels, where one important research question concerns how the local level relates to what I consider a new form of regional governance.

Swedish political scientist Jörgen Johansson, who has done extensive research on the democratic implications of Region Skåne and Region Västra Götaland, argues that an evident discursive shift has occurred concerning the ways in which the two regions present themselves as political agents (Johansson 2004, p. 22). When the regions were established in the 1990s, the rationale applied when arguing for the necessity of a new regional organization was clearly related to the European Union and the notion of "A Europe of Regions." At the beginning of the twenty-first century, however, focus lies instead on the relation between the regions and the municipalities they encompass, and how the regions can best serve the interests of the local communities they are set to coordinate. Regardless of this discursive shift, it is of course interesting to note that the national level is in neither case mentioned, even thought the national level implicitly is an active agent, portrayed either as an obstacle or a vehicle in the furthering of regional and local interests. It is in order to illuminate these shifts in relations between government on local, regional, national and international levels that I have chosen two municipalities—one in Region Skåne and one in Region Västra Götaland—as additional case studies. Furthermore, these case studies focus on one cultural activity in each municipality, since I not only seek to create an understanding of cultural policy at the comprehensive, strategic level of the municipalities, but also to develop knowledge on the relation between strategies and measures in the cultural policy field. Since I believe that the relation between centre and periphery is a key dimension in regional iden-tity construction, I have chosen two small municipalities, which at least on the surface represent the periphery in relation to the region.

The two smaller municipalities chosen for the project is Vellinge in Region Skåne and Mellerud in Region Västra Götaland. The smaller munici-palities are not chosen for being similar to each other; on the contrary, the differences between the municipalities by far overshadow their likeness. The point of comparison between the two focus on the fact that they are small municipalities but have both succeeded in receiving funding from the European Union's regional programmes (Interreg IIIA). In addition to highlighting the relation between the regional and local levels of govern-ment, they are included to illuminate the relations between local cultural policy and international policy agents (cf. Mitchell 2003). Furthermore, the activities chosen are run on a project-basis and relate mainly to the alli-ance discourse, as opposed to the primarily institution-based and quality discourse-oriented activities of Region Skåne and Region Västra Götaland. Finally, my interviews with cultural policy agents show how both municipalities relate to informal, functional regions rather than the formal, administrative regions of Region Skåne and Region Västra Götaland.[9] With this observation, I move on to my concluding remarks.

Concluding remarks

In this chapter, I have tried to provide arguments in favor of a more place/ space-sensitive approach to cultural policy. On the one hand, my arguments concern the discursive shift in Swedish cultural policy, from a placeless focus on artistic and national spaces to an increased interest in how place matters. On the other hand, I have tried to show how this discursive shift is expressed in a very material sense in contemporary Swedish regional cultural policy. In my research, I highlight these shifts by exploring the relation between different levels of government, and how, as American urban theorist Michael Peter Smith (2001, p. 109) puts it, "jumping scales may be an economic, political or cultural strategy for transforming local or national power relations." I strongly believe that cultural policy studies that are to a greater extent infused by knowledge produced in the social sciences, such as political science and cultural geography, could contribute to a deeper and more nuanced understanding of such strategies.

Notes

1. This article draws on research that has been presented in Johannisson (2006; 2008).
2. This definition is well in accordance with the criteria given by the Council of Europe (1997, p. 33): "We define cultural policy as the overall framework of public measures in the cultural field. They may be taken by national governments and regional and local authorities, or their agencies. A policy requires explicitly defined goals. In order to realize these goals, there need to be mechanisms to enable planning, implementation and evaluation." This should not be considered a coincidence: Swedish national government bodies in the cultural policy field have been very active in discussions with international cultural policy agents such as the Council of Europe and UNESCO. For example, in 1998 the Swedish capital of Stockholm hosted a conference which produced an action plan on cultural politics for development (UNESCO 1998), a follow-up to the report of The World Commission on Culture and Development (UNESCO 1995).
3. As a point of comparison, private spending on the arts amounted to Euro 4.5 billion in 2005 (Swedish Arts Council 2006).
4. "Statement" is henceforth defined as a linguistic utterance that makes claim on having some authoritative force, in the Foucauldian sense of being classified as "in the true" (Mills 1997, p. 61).
5. As a whole, the empirical material consisted of cultural policy statements put forward by agents in the political-administrative organization in Göteborg and on other levels of government during the period 1991–8. The agents included were

primarily of the institutional kind and were mainly situated in Göteborg: the municipal council, the municipal executive board, the cultural affairs committee, the 21 city district committees, and adherent administrations. In addition, institutional agents on the national level were represented by the Swedish parliament, the Swedish government and the Swedish National Council for Cultural Affairs (now the Swedish Arts Council), but also by the committees responsible for Swedish Government Official Reports. Finally, institutional agents on the international level were included in the form of reports by UNESCO, the European Union and the Council of Europe. In total, 117 public documents were analyzed and six interviews with key cultural politicians and administrators in the City of Göteborg were conducted.

6. It is important to note that while welfare policy is discursively positioned at the national level of government, it is the regional—and, above all, the local—levels of government which have implemented the Swedish welfare model (cf. Bogason 1996). The expansion of the welfare state in Sweden was at its peak during the 1960s and 1970s, but has since then gone into a steady decline.

7. My understanding of cultural policy as inherently instrumentalist is derived from an understanding of politics developed in discourse-oriented political science, where it is understood as a set of social practices that primarily concern "disputes about the good life and the means of realizing it" (Fischer 2003, p. 26). This understanding is by no means uncontroversial in the cultural policy studies community, which is mainly populated by researchers coming from the humanities and thereby displaying a basic (and often well-founded) skepticism towards any arguments which consider the arts as a tool to reach other objectives. The interested reader is referred to Belfiore and Bennett (2008).

8. In the cases of Region Skåne and Region Västra Götaland, political decentralization also implies what Kawashima (1997) labels economic decentralization, since the regions are to some extent granted power over the allocation of national government funding. Currently there is a debate in Sweden on how far-reaching this decentralization really is, where Region Skåne and Region Västra Götaland argue for increased self-sufficiency in the allocation of national funds in their respective region. The debate is fuelled by the fact that a National Committee on Cultural Affairs is due to submit its report on national cultural policy submitted in February 2009.

9. In the case of Vellinge, the informal region is the Øresund Region, which comprises Zealand, Loland-Falster Møn and Bornholm in Denmark, and Skåne in Sweden (total population 3.6 million). The Øresund Region is actually a semi-formal organization representing municipalities and regions on the Swedish and Danish sides of the Øresund. The region has, of course, a long historical tradition, bearing on the fact that Skåne was Danish until 1658 (Øresund Region 2008). In the case of Mellerud, the informal region is equally transnational although it does not have any given name but comprises parts of municipalities in West Sweden and Eastern Norway.

12

The Importance of the Business Sector in Cultural Policy in Japan—A Model of Complementary Relationship with Government

Nobuko Kawashima

Introduction

Conventionally cultural policy refers to policy planned, financed and implemented by a government or its agency. While Dewey in this volume discusses the increasing importance of governance involving a range of players at different levels, most notably at supranational level of the European Union, this chapter argues that the business sector is an important player in the field of cultural policy in Japan. In order to avoid semantic contradiction and confusion, cultural policy in this chapter is defined to include decisions made and actions undertaken in relation to the provision of resource, regulation, and the organization of administration, by a variety of actors—government, its agencies, businesses, local communities and non-profit organizations—to influence and shape the cultural life of citizens. The term "governance" may often be used in recent literature to refer to such a definition, but the conventional term "cultural policy" can still work.

It must be noted, however, that the chapter is not going to present a critical view of business sponsorship of the arts as having a negative influence and imposing a perverse restriction of self-censorship for them. Neither is the chapter going to have a Marxist political economy critique and argue that global entertainment and content businesses manipulate and shape the culture to achieve their capitalistic goals (see, e.g. McChesney, 2002). Rather, it will present the view that in the case of Japan, although corporate support for the arts has been relatively minor in terms of the volume of financial and other kinds of resources provided, businesses have played a major role in advancing cultural policy in a way that reminds us of what ideal public policy-making should be like.

It is useful to refer, at this point, to the model of public policy-making as stylized by Hogwood and Gunn (1984). Put briefly, they assume policy to be a process of a number of stages, and explain the first stage as the identification of societal issues that policy needs to address and can help to solve.

140

Policy then moves on to identify policy options, chooses the most appropriate ones and secures necessary resources. A policy program is implemented, and the result is assessed in light of the goals and purposes and in relation to the resources deployed. Policy goes back to the initial stage to determine whether to be maintained, renewed, modified, or terminated, thus creating a "cycle."

The above process may look obvious, but in the government cultural policy of Japan, critics have argued, what has often happened in practice is that, to start with, government has a politically pre-determined project to implement. For example, when a municipality plans the establishment of an art museum, it is not necessarily because people in the community want one, or because there is a collection of art works donated to the municipality that needs to be housed in an appropriate space. It is rather because there is a space available for the municipality and some building must be erected there. Further, no marketing research as to the potential demand for the museum is undertaken, because the plan is already in place. When undertaken, research is for the purpose of justification. Thus, without a good reason for a particular policy program, it may well go ahead. After a few years, resources necessary to keep the program going may become tighter, with audiences decreasing, but assessment is made only in a formalistic way and does not really address the heart of the problem, which is that the policy should not have been adopted in the first place.

This chapter will demonstrate that the ideal policy cycle is more often found in corporate support for the arts in Japan, and make a sharp contrast to the governmental style of cultural policy much criticized for failing to achieve efficacy. In other words, more than half of the corporations that support the arts, about 500 blue-chip businesses in total, have mission statements and explicit policies of support (ACSA, 2008). The policies are not just general and idealistic like those of government but specific and tend to be realistic in relation to their available resources. Businesses also proactively identify problem areas to which their help can make a difference, try to be accountable for their projects and programs to a variety of stakeholders, and assess the impacts of their support. To make such an argument, this chapter starts by describing a brief history of corporate involvement with the arts, leading to the introduction and establishment of what is called *Mécénat* (a French word meaning support for the arts), or *méséna* (the domesticated version of the term in Japanese), as a new concept. It will then move to discuss the emergence of the influence and power of those companies providing *méséna* in Japanese cultural policy by illustration of some examples.

The background of *méséna* in Japan

The history of the relationship between businesses and the arts and culture goes back to the early twentieth century, when major business owners often had a personal interest and sophisticated taste in high culture. Many of them were art collectors or patrons of painters and musicians, and donated their personal collections to set up private museums and art galleries. At the corporate, rather than the personal, level, newspaper companies and department stores were notable examples of business involvement with the arts. In the period of the modernization project in Japan from the late nineteenth century to the early part of the twentieth century, while the state was busy in strengthening Japan's economic, technological and military powers to catch up with major imperial powers of the West, businesses in the above two categories saw themselves as having major responsibilities to introduce Western civilization and culture to the Japanese public. In the absence of highly developed national museums and venues for the performing arts, department stores often held art exhibitions and mini-concerts within their premises, attracting middle-class customers who aspired to the enlightening experience of Western culture. Quality newspapers, too, have been active in introducing Western art and culture by sponsoring exhibitions at museums and art galleries, developed later in an effort to enlarge the readership base of their daily publications, but also out of a sense of responsibility for educating the public in a developing state. Today still, though Japan is endowed with public and private museums and arts facilities all over the country, mass media companies (i.e., newspaper publishers and television networks) are often the planners of major art exhibitions and artistic performances, generally with loans from abroad. They also act as the wholesaler of the packaged arts programs to the presenting organizations and performance operators in Japan, which often are not capable of creative programming themselves (see Martorella, 1996, p. 208, for some examples of the department stores hosting art exhibitions).

After World War II, different kinds of businesses began involving themselves with the arts and culture, particularly during the 1970s and 1980s, the period of economic development with an annual growth rate of GNP at over 10 percent. The Saison Corporation, a conglomerate of retail business and property development, finance, and so on, epitomizes the innovativeness of *méséna* during this period. As a late-comer in the department store sector, it had to carve out a niche by presenting itself as a place where sophisticated lifestyles could be learned, experienced, and purchased by urban, young, and aspiring populations. For its image and brand building, the Corporation set up and ran a museum of modern and contemporary art next to its flagship department store in Ikebukuro, one of the major shopping areas in Tokyo, as well as a space for experimental theater; a bookshop specializing in art and design; and published specialist magazines focusing on avant-garde art.

In the following years of the late 1980s and early 1990s, Japan experienced a so-called bubble economy, when businesses got involved in sponsorship in the way that is conventional in the American and European contexts, namely, as a commercial transaction for the mutual interest of business and the arts. Used largely for marketing and promotion purposes of the company or its brand, sponsorship often provides the sponsor with good opportunities for corporate entertainment, links to opinion-makers and community leaders, assistance in enhancing supply-chains and staff relationships. All of these marketing and managerial motivations have been found in Japanese sponsorship, where sponsors were interested not only in sport events for mass appeal and extensive exposure, but also in artistic ones such as touring performances and exhibitions of prominent companies and museums abroad, including world-class opera companies and symphony orchestras in Europe and the US. Association with such prestigious arts gives the sponsor a respectable and prestigious image and can allow good access to specific segments of the population, the higher echelons of socio-economic classes more specifically. Thus, corporate involvement with the arts and culture up to this period was largely for marketing purposes and/or for the niche market appeal by importing and implanting flashy, established products of the arts from overseas.

The change in the economic climate and the introduction of *méséna*

From around 1990, however, such activities started to be seen critically, as they tended to rely on established names from abroad that required enormous investments, while it became apparent that the arts and artists of Japan received little support. Critics argued that in order for Japan to become more respected in the international community, namely, to have "soft power" (à la Joseph Nye, 2002; 2004) rather than being a faceless country of economic power, it was necessary for the state to develop cultural policies. Businesses, too, were criticized for being inattentive to societal concerns and issues. Such criticism arose in the emergence of the need for diversifying the governance base to tackle complex social problems, such as the ageing population, by examining not only the state but also the profit and nonprofit sectors. In the meantime, the mighty "iron triangle" between the bureaucracy, politicians and industry which had enabled rapid economic development since the twentieth century started to erode, with the economic shift toward service and high-technology industries which challenged the old coalition that was based on traditional manufacturing. The introduction of the concepts "corporate philanthropy" and "corporate citizenship" was a natural development under such circumstances.

Corporate citizenship activity with a focus on the artistic/cultural area in particular has been called *méséna*. It is interesting to note that the term *méséna* has a French origin, where the national government's, rather than corporate, support for the arts and culture is extensive and dominant. The term was consciously chosen to distinguish the new idea from traditional sponsorship explained earlier by the Japanese advocates of *méséna* who included industry tycoons such as the CEOs of Shiseido and Suntory (top cosmetics and beverage manufacturers, respectively, in Japan) when they gathered to discuss the possibility of setting up an organization to promote *méséna*. Equivalent to the Business Committee for the Arts, Inc. (US) and the then Association for Business Support of the Arts (ABSA, UK), the Association for Corporate Support of the Arts, Japan (ACSA), established in 1990, has been at the forefront of promoting the concept and encouraging businesses to provide support for the arts to fulfill corporate social responsibility without the expectation of tangible and immediate return (although expecting indirect and long-term return is accepted). ACSA is also engaged in research, advocacy, consultation, and matchmaking between business and arts organizations and artists. ACSA, thanks to support provided by its Board Members who were prominent industry figures, quickly came to be well-known in the same way as the concept itself, and attracted as many as 150 member companies in its first year, including those from the regions as well as from Tokyo.

It must be noted, however, that *méséna* in Japan is not quite the same as the corporate philanthropy widely seen in the US. Partly due to the heavily regulated tax-deductibility of charitable giving in Japan (whereas in the US traditionally charitable donations can be deducted from taxable incomes with relative ease (see Kawashima, 2001, pp. 9–10)), sources of money spent on *méséna* may well come from a company's advertising budgets. However, it is often used as a "cover" to increase the limited resources for *méséna*. Also to be noted as a distinguishing characteristic of corporate support for the arts in Japan is the direct operational activities in the arts and culture undertaken by the companies themselves rather than providing purely financial resources to third parties (i.e., artists and arts organizations independent of the companies). Artists and performers visiting Tokyo from abroad are often surprised to realize that the metropolis's first-class venues for the performing arts have been built and run by business corporations unrelated to entertainment and arts industries in any direct way. Indeed, the Tokyo equivalents to the Lincoln Center in New York City (run as a nonprofit organization heavily reliant on charitable contributions) or the South Bank Centre in London (built by government and relying on public subsidies) are run by business corporations outside the media and entertainment sector.

A good example is the Tokyu Bunka Mura art complex in Shibuya, a busy shopping area in Tokyo, built and run by the Tokyu Corporation (Tokyu being similar to Saison mentioned earlier as a conglomerate of public transport, property development, retail, hotels and resorts, and so on). This art complex houses a large concert hall with the seating capacity of over 2000, a medium-sized theater, two art house cinemas and two art exhibition spaces, as well as restaurants and shops, right next to Tokyu's flagship department store. Although the neighboring districts of Shibuya are one of the wealthiest areas in Japan, Shibuya had suffered from a lack of space for upper-middle-class Tokyo residents to come and experience highly sophisticated arts. Tokyu saw the opportunity to provide a magnet for people with a desire for refinement and with high purchasing power. In this way, thus, *méséna* may be for corporate citizenship, but also for corporate image-building and marketing promotion at the same time in a less direct way. Ideally, one would like to make a clear conceptual distinction between the areas of corporate philanthropy and corporate sponsorship and sort out statistical data accordingly (Schuster, 1997, pp. 153–4), but it is almost impossible to do so in the Japanese context of *méséna*.

Despite its quick entrance to public awareness, however, *méséna* subsequently suffered from the economic downturn starting in the early- to mid-1990s. The mass media loved the stories of company withdrawal from *méséna* activities, ascribing the shrinkage to a lack of philosophy in the companies and arguing *méséna* was only a fad to be abandoned in a time of economic difficulties. It is true that in the economic downturn lasting for ten years or so some of the companies did disappear from the *méséna* scene altogether, or cut down their budgets, and closed their arts facilities. The Saison Corporation, mentioned earlier, had to close completely its flagship art museum and performance space in Ikebukuro and theater in Ginza during the 1990s. The Casals Hall in Ochanomizu, created and supported by a major publisher in Tokyo and much respected for its excellent acoustics suitable for chamber music, changed its function from a presenting venue to a space for rent to avoid the programming costs and risks involved in selling the concerts.

While these examples are not few, however, statistically and seen as an aggregate, the continued presence of *méséna* can be confirmed. Figure 12.1

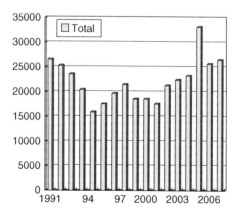

Figure 12.1 Total amount of spending for *méséna* by respondents 1991–2007 (million yen)
Note: The total number of the respondents was below 300 until 1999, but the survey was expanded to increase the number to about 400 in 2000.
Source: ACSA (2008: 3)

shows the total amount spent on *méséna* in 2007 by 404 companies, responding to the annual survey of the ACSA (and disclosing their spending), is not radically different from that of 1991. The average spending per company at first glance looks to have been halved from 14 million yen in 1991 to 6.6 million yen in 2007, but focused on those with *méséna* experience of more than nine consecutive years (75 companies in 2007), it has remained stable at around 14 million yen (ACSA, 2008, p. 3). It should be noted that the number of respondents has increased as ACSA membership has expanded, and the amount spent on *méséna* is very hard for most companies to specify because of the diversity in sources of support including support-in-kind and the existence of in-house operation of corporate arts facilities and programs. Such caveats set aside, however, it can safely be assumed that the level of spending by those companies remaining at the core of *méséna* has sustained. It should also be noted that there have been newcomers, alongside withdrawals, to launch new projects. On the whole, therefore, the concern that *méséna* closely follows the economic trend and inevitably fluctuates has been excessive.

Such sustenance has been made possible by the institutionalization of *méséna* within corporations. One feature of this is the establishment of a philosophy and mission covering the *méséna* activities, often in the framework of corporate social responsibility. According to the ACSA 2008 Survey, over 90 percent of the respondents place *méséna* as part of their corporate social responsibility programs (ACSA, 2008, p. 5). This is a quite significant development when one considers the confusion, puzzlement, and perplexity found in the early eras of *méséna* among corporate executives and their struggles to "theorize" corporate responsibility for the arts. The executives assigned to the responsibility for *méséna* often did not know how to explain what they were doing to internal and external stakeholders, not to mention what, in concrete terms, to do to become a good corporate citizen. Seminars, conferences, and study trips to the US and Europe to educate those executives were organized for *méséna* and broader corporate social responsibility projects. It seems now that the concepts are well-established and understood so that there is little need to explain what they are about. Each company has debated internally and developed its own language to justify its programs. Some have set up funding guidelines to streamline applications that come from all over the country and from various arts disciplines. The justified and authorized status of corporate social responsibility programs and projects is also mirrored in the prevalence of designated staff and budgets, without which *méséna* may well remain *ad hoc* and sporadic.

In contrast to the internally institutionalized status of *méséna*, many of the corporate supporters keep open-door policies; they welcome artists and producers to come and talk about their own project ideas all year round, rather than request they send in the completed application forms by certain due dates. In this way, corporations have nurtured good relationships and networks with key individuals in the cultural sector, having gained a good picture of the artistic world and an understanding of problems and issues confronted by artists and arts organizations.

To sum up the development discussed so far, what started as personal support by business owners who formed the élite class and had in-depth knowledge of and taste for high culture became toolkits for marketing and public relations with strong commercial orientations during the 1970s and 1980s. Since the early 1990s, however, businesses have learned the importance of corporate social responsibility as integral to the contemporary management of business corporations. *Méséna* is one of the areas for such activity and has become firmly rooted in many companies across the country. It must be recalled, however, that the total number of companies engaged in *méséna* is still small, 500 or less, representing a fraction of the whole corporate sector countrywide. The total spending for the arts and culture by businesses, as far as we know, is 26.5 billion yen in 2007, compared to 477.6 billion yen by national and local governments combined in 2006 (Yoshimoto, 2008, p. 82),[1] although the business sector fares well in terms of support for fine arts activities alone (thus excluding historical preservation and capital expenditures, see note 1 for explanation). To return to and further advance the argument that businesses are a major player in the field of cultural policy in Japan, it is necessary to discuss three features of *méséna* that will help to enhance this contention.

Méséna as a model of cultural policy

This chapter argues that *méséna* is far more interesting than government's cultural policy and presents features of an ideal model for cultural policy making. Firstly, the actual content and style of *méséna* activities has sometimes been innovative, subsequently adopted by government-run organizations. The aforementioned closing of the Saison Museum of Art, for example, may ostensibly be ascribed to the financial crisis experienced by the corporation, but also to the completion of its role in the introduction of modern and contemporary art to Japan when there was little interest in that field. The newly established, much larger, Tokyo Metropolitan Museum of Contemporary Art has in a sense taken over that responsibility, rendering the corporate museum no longer needed to fill a gap in the public appreciation of contemporary visual arts in Japan. The withdrawal of corporate involvement with the arts has often been ridiculed by the mass media, but in this case it can be argued that the ability of businesses to terminate or downscale *méséna* activities may well serve efficiency and the decision has been sensible. In other words, the flexibility and speed in responding to perceived needs is the very quality of businesses to be admired, not treated with contempt as if continuity of any operation represented the highest value in cultural policy implementation.

Another example of *méséna* followed by government cultural policy (or practice in this case) is the serving of wine and other alcoholic drinks in the foyer of the Suntory Hall before and during the intermissions of performances. The Suntory Hall is one of the most prestigious concert halls in Tokyo, built in 1986 in Akasaka by the beverage and food giant Suntory. Prior to that, the major venue for classical music concerts in Tokyo was the Ueno Bunka Kaikan, publicly funded and run, with a foyer serving no alcoholic drinks. Reference to wine is of little importance here, but the point is the ways in which high art is provided. The Ueno Bunka Kaikan was conceived as a shrine to classical music, the pinnacle of high culture from the West, delivered in a top-down, authoritative manner only to aficionados. The Suntory Hall, in contrast, because of its sponsor being a consumer goods producer, saw it important that the Hall serve audiences and meet their expectations and demands to be treated as guests. Music itself was thus seen as a vehicle to help audiences to enjoy an evening out and the Hall was to present lifestyles for Tokyo's mature adult population. It was a revolutionary idea for the Japanese in relation to the appreciation of classical music and also a new approach to arts marketing, and subsequently made even the Ueno Bunka Kaikan adopt a similar approach.

In a similar vein, it is interesting to note that through *méséna*, such penetration of business styles has affected independent arts organizations positively, where there is a surprising tendency to lack understanding about the importance of customer relationship management and marketing. The NEC Corporation, a global company in the IT/network solution business that has been giving financial support to orchestras and chamber music groups, has also transmitted basic and simple marketing disciplines to the groups. For example, when free tickets to NEC-sponsored concerts are distributed by lot to applicants, the company makes sure that it and the orchestra involved together will write letters of apology to those who unfortunately did not win tickets with a brief introduction to classical music and anecdotes related to particular composers. Such efforts are made to broaden the audience base, particularly considering the perceived profiles of those applying for the tickets to concerts that present introductory pieces from the popular repertoire of classical music. The NEC staff responsible for *méséna* would also go to chamber music concerts supported by the company and stand at the doors alongside staff from the music groups, giving out programs and saying a few welcoming words to the patrons. Thus they show customer support models to the music groups who tend to be more preoccupied with music itself than with customer relationships. On-site help also gives the NEC a clue to understanding the impact it makes on the arts scene, something governmental agencies would not bother with, delegating the task of examination to third parties.

The second feature of *méséna* that places the business sector in a higher esteem than government in cultural policy is related to the organization of *méséna* in individual corporations. Firstly, corporations engaged in *méséna* designated departments and budgets, and, secondly, developed the quality of officers specializing in this area. Around 1990 in Japan, the slowness of development in arts management at arts organizations, presenting venues, and, most notably, in public administration was often discussed as one of the major issues in developing cultural policy. In corporate *méséna* departments, too, at the beginning executives were assigned this new responsibility regardless of whether they had a basic understanding of arts management, not to mention training in the performing or visual arts. Nevertheless the executives were smart enough to realize that what they really needed was not so much detailed knowledge about the arts as a grasp of how the arts world functions and a good communication with arts people based on that understanding. On one hand, *méséna* managers have requested artists and arts organizations to be better prepared in presenting their project ideas and details in a language comprehensible to them and in discussing what support is needed in realistic and concrete terms. On the other hand, these executives have also taken time to attend meetings, seminars, conferences, and symposia where arts management and cultural policy issues are discussed.

They thus approached the arts by meeting a large number of people on various occasions, formally and informally, gradually identifying visionary figures in the artistic sector, and listening to the issues and problems they have. The business executives have also formed their own study groups across companies with the help of the ACSA to exchange information and ideas related to *méséna*, and discuss commonly experienced issues. By undertaking fieldwork to figure out the ways to make *méséna* most appropriate and effective, particularly by listening to what artists and producers have to say, *méséna* managers have become quasi arts managers. Obviously, there has been some turnover in staff in *méséna* departments, but implicit knowledge has been successfully accumulated to form a solid foundation for the sustainable development of *méséna* activities in individual companies. In government, both at national and local levels, however, such personally gleaned knowledge and expertise in managing the arts rarely exists. Not only is there frequent rotation of staff within government, it also does not equip its departments for arts and cultural policy with the professional competence needed for policy-making and service provision. Thus, there has exists an ill-developed relationship between government and the arts with reliable, visible personalities and continued mutual respect.

The third feature of *méséna* that makes a good policy-making model for the cultural sector is related to the importance of policy and project evaluation. This final stage of policy process also has started to attract attention in government, but the assessment undertaken is often a rather formalistic, quantitative evaluation done by collecting relevant figures such as audience numbers and the number of articles reporting the event in the mass media. What is far more important, however, is firstly qualitative aspects of the artistic events supported, which may well be difficult to assess but still merits attention in policy evaluation. Furthermore, if the aspects mentioned so far for evaluation are related to outputs, it is important to consider the outcome of the projects and compare what has been achieved and the long-term goals of the support. In other words, for the businesses concerned with short-term goals of *méséna*, then, if the events they support turn out to be of good artistic quality and please a large number of people, that should be fine. Many businesses, however, started to ask if their support could have any impact on society beyond the community of people relevant to the project. Particularly welcome in this context has been the idea of "audience development" that has been a vogue in the discourse of British cultural policy (see Kawashima, 2006a), or "outreach," a term long-established in the American arts management to refer to the importance of making the arts more widely available.

In Japan, arguably, the consumption of culture is not considered class-related; in fact the consciousness of class is much less conspicuous among the public in Japan than in the US and Europe. Nevertheless it does not mean that arts participation is equal among the entire population, and the management of the arts may partly be to blame. It can be argued that they tend to be inward-looking, not proactively seeking potential audiences by going outside their comfort zones and reaching out to those under-privileged in arts provision for physical, geographical, economic, or cultural reasons. Government may well have been concerned with geographical unevenness of arts provision, but seems to care less about other barriers to arts participation, assuming that the provision of excellent arts should automatically lead to wide dissemination.

Méséna managers in contrast are more ambitious about what they do, no longer complacent with the philanthropic character of their activities, and ask themselves and the artists involved whether they are making any difference to society at large. Nonprofit, service and intermediary organizations that specialize in arts education, artists in schools, audience development, and outreach activities in local communities have coincidentally started to crop up, and businesses have started to align with them (see Kawashima, 2003 for the business-nonprofit alliance in general). Nonprofits are newcomers to Japanese society in the first place, hence have rarely formed partnerships with government, except that nonprofits may be used for cost-saving in the provision of public services (see Kawashima, 2006b, pp. 81–7 for a general overview of laws regulating nonprofit activities in Japan). *Méséna* managers, in contrast, are encouraging the development of nonprofits, as they have realized the limitations of their support on their own in terms of volume and effectiveness. These managers by now have understood their *méséna* can gain more leverage in collaboration with nonprofits.

Conclusion

This chapter has traced the historical background of corporate support of the arts in Japan, or *méséna*, and argued that businesses are a major player in cultural policy in Japan. It has presented this view by pointing out three features of *méséna*: the early adoption of an innovative model in cultural policy by business to be followed by government, the development of in-house arts managers within the corporate social responsibility or *méséna* departments, and the recent interest among *méséna* providers in the implications and impact of their support on the wider communities in which artistic activities take place. The chapter has not argued that *méséna* has undermined government in any way, but has meant to suggest that *méséna* has greatly contributed to the development of cultural policy, as widely defined, in Japan. After all, government has more resources to deploy, at least financially, but a critical examination into the effectiveness of its spending will be promoted in light of the discussion laid out in this chapter. It is hoped that a role-division between businesses and government, with the advantages of the former being flexible, innovative and risk-taking while those of the latter being universal, large-scale and stable, and their complementary relationship will continue to shape a dynamic model of cultural policy in Japan.

Note

1. Such statistical data needs to be seen with care. A large portion of government spending for the cultural sector goes to the preservation of historical monuments, particularly at national level. Local authorities' spending for the cultural sector includes revenue grants to arts organizations as well as the capital costs of municipal cultural facilities. The above figures do not capture expenditure related to the cultural sector by other ministries and agencies such as the Ministry of Foreign Affairs, the Ministry of Internal Affairs and Communications, and the Ministry of Economy, Industry and Trade, among others.

Part III Cultural Voices: The Developing World

13
Coloniality, Identity and Cultural Policy

Kevin V. Mulcahy

> *Colonialism is not satisfied with snaring the people in its net or*
> *of draining the colonized brain of any form or substance. With*
> *a kind of perverted logic, it turns its attention to the past of the*
> *colonized people and distorts it, disfigures it, and destroys it.*
> —*Fanon, 1968/2004, p. 149*

Introduction: The consequences of coloniality

Any discussion of cultural policy must take into account the importance of public culture and tradition "in giving a sense of uniqueness and meaning to individual political cultures" (Pye and Verba, 1965, p. 19). Accordingly a comprehensive analysis of a nation's development involves not only its political institutions, but its cultural identity as well. "As with politics in general, cultural politics involves the expression of the collective values of a people, the feelings of people about their social and group identities, and above all else the tests of loyalty and commitment" (Pye and Verba, 1965, p. 19). The distinguishing characteristic of cultural policy in countries characterized by a legacy of coloniality is the importance of the issue of identity and the politics that are involved in formulating its definition.[1]

At root, coloniality is an experience involving dominating influence by a stronger power over a subject state. However, this is not just a matter of external governance or economic dependency, but of a cultural dominance that creates an asymmetrical relationship between the "center" and the "periphery," between the ruling "hegemon" and the marginalized "other." In these circumstances, what constitutes an "authentic" culture, and how this informs national identity, is a central political and social concern.

Moreover, the legacy of coloniality is often a deracination that renders a people deprived of an agreed-upon history. Coloniality is "one of the purest forms of cultural destruction" because "it insistently degrades the self-image of those who are colonized" (Hogan, 2000, p. 83). Consequently, a country's independence is akin to being born (Zolberg, 1993, p. 234); or, more exactly, to being reborn as a people emerge from cultural repression. Postcoloniality necessitates constructing both a unique public culture and a distinct political culture if full sovereignty is to be realized. The discourse on postcoloniality emphasizes the role of culture in the imposition of imperial rule and in liberation from this imperialism.

As Edward Said, the late Columbia University literary theorist (and a Palestinian Christian) observed, "The power to narrate, or to block other narratives from forming and emerging, is very important to culture and imperialism, and constitutes one of the major connections between them" (Said, 1979, p. xiii). While formulated by Western scholars, missionaries and administrators, the telling power of a construction such as "Orientalism" was that its "hegemonic power" was able to persuade the colonized that "the idea of European identity was a superior one in comparison with all the non-European peoples and cultures" (Said, 1979, p. 7).

Postcolonialism emerged when the colonized recognized and contested regulatory and hegemonic dominance (Ashcroft, 2001). In essence, culture and politics are inextricably intertwined as they are about the redefinition of national identity. This involves "legitimizing the nation to its own citizenry and (perhaps most important) to outsiders" (Zolberg, 1993, p. 235). The nation-building project for the newly independent is the creation of an authentic culture to replace that imposed by the colonial power. "At the level of cultural policy, this means a core of common cultural practices, beliefs, customs and such has to be allowed to become manifest" (Alexander, 1995, p. 216). "The search for authenticity, for a more congenial national origin than provided by colonial history or a new pantheon of heroes and (occasionally) heroines, myths and religions" (Said, 1994, p. 226) is an essential element in the creation of a postcolonial public culture. For the decolonized, a policy of cultural reclamation is a necessary commitment to political reconstruction. The past is reclaimed by a people as a necessary element of political sovereignty.

The consequences of coloniality are important in shaping such cultural policies if only because national identity typically cannot be assumed. These policies often involved the invocation of "imagined communities" (Anderson, 1983) that were constructed to define nations that were not states in the empires that ruled in Eastern and Central Europe from the mid-seventeenth century until the end of World War I. Educated elites formalized dialects into languages and folklore into national sagas while composing music and creating literature in the new national spirit. It also followed that political history was re-imagined to correspond with cultural identity. Similarly the consequences of coloniality have necessitated a re-imagined public culture to counter the suppression of their marginalized values.

Consequently postcolonization requires cultural policies that would assert influence over the discourse that defined national identity. In this way, such cultural policies have as a central goal the determination of whether the hegemon or the other controls the definition of identity. The classic question in politics asks: "who is ruled by whom?" In cultural politics, the "who/whom" question is the determination of "by whom are a people told who they are?" In essence, postcolonial societies seek to reclaim a voice in telling their stories; that is, in creating their own cultural distinctiveness rather than being defined as the "other" by another.

This chapter will review some major themes that have informed cultural policies where there is a legacy of coloniality. In particular, what will be discussed herein are the ideological arguments and developmental imperatives that couple cultural sovereignty with political sovereignty. Cultural policies are not simply about support for aesthetic expression, but also entail addressing major political concepts and redressing legacies of hegemonic dominance. There are a variety of conceptual case studies that could be considered: cultural reassertion (for example, Quebec); cultural reinvention (for example, post-apartheid South Africa); cultural redefinition (for example, post-1991 Ukraine). All of these exemplify efforts of nations (whether states or regions) to re-identify themselves as distinctive cultures.

The two conceptual examples considered herein concern the "cultural renaissance" sponsored by the Mexican government after the 1920 Revolution and the "cultural revivalism" found in the contemporary Islamic world. Although these examples are from different eras (early twentieth/early twenty-first century) and invoke different cultural values for reclamation (indigeneity/religious tradition), they share a common interest in valorizing identities that had been marginalized and distorted by hegemonic cultures. The concluding section will return to the broad theoretical theme of cultural identity. This discusses the generalized nature of efforts to reconstruct identity after the experience of coloniality and, in particular, the role that cultural policies play in realizing these goals.

Cultural renaissance: Mexico after the 1920 Revolution

The countries of Latin America became independent from Spain in the early part of the nineteenth century. However, many retained a dependency status: economically to the American "colossus to the North" and culturally to a Europeanized aesthetic and the values of a Hispanophile elite who subordinated their national identities to the perceived superiority of Spanish (and more generally European) cultural values. It is not surprising, then, that artists and intellectuals have been in the vanguard of Latin American political struggles of the twentieth century. Two of the distinguishing characteristics of modern Latin American culture are: "an intense interest both political and cultural in the past civilizations and present life of the original inhabitants, with an attempt to revive native forms (Indianism or *indigenismo*), and an intense role for the social role of the artist" (Gowing, 1995, p. 911).

Nowhere was this confluence of the political and cultural greater than in post-revolutionary Mexico during the 1920s. Strongly committed to cultural nationalism, the Secretary of State for Education, José Vasconcelos, believed that art should have a direct and didactic public role. To this end, he commissioned a number of monumental murals from young Mexican artists to decorate the walls of public buildings. The murals commissioned by Vasconcelos were part of a cultural policy designed to institute a state-sponsored program of promoting artistic creativity designed to realize a revolutionary nationalism that would bring about a cultural renaissance that celebrated Mexico's indigenous past and cast the "pre-Hispanic Indian as a symbol of the nation" (Rochfort, 1998, p. 17).

The names of the "Big Three" (*Los Tres Grandes*) are most familiar: Jose Clemente Orozco, David Alfaro Siqueiros and, especially, Diego Rivera. The complex phenomenon of Indian culture was not addressed solely in mural paintings. However, the murals were a staple of a revolutionary art whose goal was not simplistic political indoctrination, but to affect a change in "consciousness and sensibility" (Hennessy, 1971, p. 72). For Siqueiros, his experiences in one of the twentieth century's bloodiest civil wars gave him a heightened sensitivity to Mexico's popular traditions. "It led to a direct reflection of the immense cultural traditions of the country, particularly with regard to the extraordinary pre-Columbian civilizations" (Quoted in Rochfort, 1993, p. 28). This cultural policy, which valorized indigenous people and pre-Conquistador history, was at root a commitment to the realization of a social consciousness and a cultural renaissance.

In murals such as those of Rivera in the National Preparatory School, the National Palace in Mexico City, and the Palace of Cortes in Cuernavaca, the context of the iconography is "art in the service of politics." The themes represent a new comprehension of Mexico's identity as a nation, "replacing the previous colonialist ideology and subservience of its people" (Catlin, 1980, p. 198). The murals' images were meant to be pedagogical, "to convince their audience of certain virtues and to promote corresponding behavior" (Folgarait, 1998, p. 12). Rivera's murals "exude an air of revolutionary optimism and idealism, creating visual eulogies to the gains of the revolution with its new atmosphere of political liberation ... and seem to represent Rivera's attempts to give expression to what he saw as an authentic indigenous image" (Rochfort, 1993, p. 57).

As part of a broader, nationalist program of popular education, the murals addressed the theme "What is Mexico?" For Vasconcelos, this endeavor had spiritual overtures; his teachers were termed "Maestros Misioneros;" his motto was "to educate is to redeem" (Folgarait, 1998, p. 18). This approach gave precedence to Mexican national objectives and equated the importance of native cultural values with the generalized imperatives of the revolutionary process (Catlin, 1980). Vasconcelos's motives in forming a national culture through education echoed the sentiments of President

Alvaro Obregon. "The hope of every nation is the development of a morality among the people themselves. This is the great task of education and culture" (Quoted in Folgarait, 1998, p. 19).

The mural painting, with its popular accessibility and ideological iconography, was the revolutionary art without equal:

> Not only was it possible to convey to a wide audience a sense of con-tinuity with a largely forgotten past, and to give ordinary spectators a vicarious sense of participation in a great historical process, but also, being rooted in a popular tradition and employing popular themes, the art enabled painters to appeal over the heads of a philistine bourgeoisie, to break away from the exclusiveness of a narrow literary culture and to reach out to the wider illiterate society.
>
> (Hennessy, 1971, p. 73)

Moreover the murals were definitely intended to be important. "Even today they are spoken of in awe by Mexicans, and guided tours of Rivera's murals in the National Palace in Mexico City are conducted in almost ceremonial fashion" (Folgarait, 1998, p. 12). Rivera, and his fellow muralists, also repre-sented a cultural policy that succeeded in inculcating a "sense of nationality, with its own demos and ethos, for a major part of the Indian and Mestizo community in Latin America" (Catlin, 1980, p. 211).

The political agenda of the mural paintings was fourfold: first, creating a common national culture on a secular basis; second, formalizing an idealized version of the past; third, interpreting national history to give primacy to the contributions of the indigenous people; and fourth, representing a universe of commonly accepted national symbols and a pantheon of immediately recognizable national heroes (Hennessy, 1971). In this sense, the overall objective was less historical and more mythopoetic. Postcolonial nations must seek to create a history that will validate their new status and legitimize the new regime. Vasconcelos remarked about his history of Mexico: "I am not writing history; I am creating a myth" (Quoted in Hennessy, 1971, p. 76). Indeed, in 1925, after four years as Minister of Educaition, Vasconcelos argued in his book *The Cosmic Race* that the mestizo represented the essence of Mexican nationality. For Vasconcelos, "the mestizo was seen as embodying national consciousness" (Vasconcelos cited in Rochfort, 1998, p. 83).

The "invention of tradition" (Hobsbawm and Ranger, 1983) is not unique to developing nations, but it has a particular urgency when a new political culture is being created. In the case of the Mexican muralist movement, a public culture was mobilized to assist in the creation of a political culture. The murals spoke to a socialist-revolutionary ideal and to the integration of Indian and mestizo viewers into a working-class political and cultural ideology rooted in the Mexican experience.

Diego Rivera's distinctive aesthetic achievement was to have created a visual image of an indigenous culture that transcended the realm of memory. He carefully crafted a popular vocabulary of sociopolitical themes that were understandable to the general public. "Rivera managed to convey to this much wider audience the sense of community with a forgotten past and a feeling of participation in a historical process that had been largely ignore in the history of the country's colonial experience" (Rochfort, 1993, p. 87). "As such, Rivera's work stands as a kind of *Summa Theologica* of the modern Mexican revolution" (Catlin, 1980, p. 211).

Cultural revivalism: Islam and identity

The Ottoman Empire, "the sick man of Europe," was dismantled by the Sykes-Picot Agreement of 1916 that partitioned the Asian area of the Ottoman Empire (See Macmillan, 2003, pp. 382–8). The European conquests were granted independence by the end of the nineteenth century; Sykes-Picot established mandates under European control—Syria and Lebanon for the French, newly constructed Transjordan and Iraq for the British. The Balfour Declaration of 1917 had created a Jewish homeland in Palestine as a British protectorate. This dismemberment of the Ottoman Empire was codified in the Treaty of Sèvres as part of the post-World War I settlement.

In its 1300-year history, Islam had overwhelmed the Byzantine Empire, conquered Spain, the Balkans and twice reached the gates of Vienna. However, from the latter part of the nineteenth century until the mid-twentieth, the Islamic world became increasingly colonized by European powers. Algeria was annexed as part of metropolitan France in 1830 until independence in 1961 after a protracted civil war; Tunisia and Morocco became French protectorates in 1882 and 1912, respectively, with internal self-rule and strong francophone educational and cultural influences and French determination of military and diplomatic issues; Libya was a protectorate of Italy from 1911 to 1947; the British established protectorates in Egypt in 1882 and Sudan in 1889 (See Armstrong, 2002, pp. xxvii–xxx). It might be noted that none of these were very successful. King Abdullah, who was installed by the British in Jordan, was assassinated before the eyes of his youthful successor, King Hussein. The struggle for independence in Algeria was called a "savage war of peace." The British fought a ten-year war in Iraq before ceding rule to local elites. Lebanon has been in almost perpetual civil war among Maronites, Sunnis, Shias and Druzes.

A more general observation that can be offered is the artificial construction of these colonial entities. Lebanon, for example, has functioned through "consociational governance" in which key political positions are distributed on a confessional basis. Of course, this was always fragile and France traditionally supported the interests of the Maronite Catholics. Iraq may be the model of what not to do in creating a state, being an amalgamation of

Sunni (a minority, but predominant) in the central area; Shia (a majority, but oppressed) in the south, adjacent to Iran and the Kurds, non-Arabs with significant co-nationals in Turkey, Syria and Iran in the north. The only people that each group hates more than each other is an imperial outsider, as evidenced by a ten-year (1922–32) insurrection against the imposition of the British mandate (as well as against the current American intervention).

In essential ways, what has been called the "Middle East" has never been successfully reconstructed—politically or socially—since the fall of the Ottoman Empire. In the modern world, cultural constructions of Islam have taken place against the hegemonic influence of powerful colonial forces. Consequently modern Islamic identity cannot be fully appreciated apart from its struggle against coloniality and its association with a concept of modernity that is judged antithetical to Islamic values. Indeed, the relentless export of a unilateralized modernity has put the West (especially the US) on a collision course with the Islamic world. For a proud civilization, its eclipse by an aggressive Western culture understandably produces an identity crisis. It is within this context that new religious, political, and intellectual movements have sought to grapple with this crisis mentality.

Western hegemony has aggressively manifested its power culturally, as well as, politically (see Chapter 9 by Schneider for attempts to counteract these practices). In particular, the colonized area is marked by a stereotypical exoticism that sees them as the "Other." As such, the Other can never be fully assimilated into the hegemonic culture. These cultural attributes, which Edward Said termed, "Orientalism," became instruments of mental conquest (as well as cultural racism) (Said, 1979). Education was used to create an indigenous elite who were effectively co-opted by Western cultural values. This Westernized elite became disaffected from its traditional cultural norms and were rendered unable to appreciate the civilizational context in which they lived.

For Said, "Orientalism" signified a cultural discourse that stylized the population of the East as variously indolent, treacherous, passive, inscrutable, devious and inferior (Said, 1979, p. 12). This ideological construction was both persuasive and persistent in Western thought. The idea of the Other underpinned the asymmetrical relation between East and West in which cultural power augmented political power to constitute what Antonio Gramsci called "hegemony" (See Said, 1979, pp. 6–7). The essence of hegemony is its ability to destroy cultural diversity by subordinating it to a universal, homogenous culture. This is effectively the distinction between "colonialism" and "coloniality." The former is typically associated with direct rule by a foreign power while the latter denotes the internalization of a people of a belief in their cultural inferiority. With reference to the Islamic world, this involved devalorizing Koranic values and the assertion of Occidental cultural values as superior.

Arabic efforts at liberation from Orientalist constructions involved emphasizing the delegitimization of the coloniality principles as the first step in a postcolonial era. Much of the difficulty of Western nations in coming to terms with a resurgent Arabic cultural identity is associated with revising the status of Occidental culture as inherently superior. This is extremely difficult because the fundamental legitimization of hegemony over the "other" is "the conviction not just of technological superiority (military, economic, scientific), but of moral superiority" (Said, 1994, p. 17). The former can be said to be the empirical rationalization for *colonialism*, the latter is the normative justification for *coloniality*. It may be that the existence of the Middle East as a tinderbox is the result of Western resistance to granting cultural parity to a system of values different from its own. At the same time, the Islamic world needs to be vigilant in considering the proposition that modernization does not necessarily entail Occidentalization (or Americanization). There may indeed be means of realizing modernization that can be compatible with Islamic values. In sum, it is against the Western construction of the Islamic world as an inferior Other that the contemporary Islamic culture seeks to revalorize its identity, roots and future. That some of these efforts have been seen as "fundamentalism," which then becomes equated with "terrorism," necessarily hinders most opportunities for meaningful engagement. This is further exacerbated by positing these difficulties as a "clash of civilizations" (Huntington, 1998).

Globalization is largely dominated by American cultural values and is associated (whether correctly or not) with having deleterious effects on the social and ethical system of Islamic values. In the Islamic world, American culture is very often associated with corrosive individualism and rampant materialism. Moreover, as noted, the powerful economic and technological processes associated with globalization eclipsed traditional Islamic civilization and came to be seen as agents of alien domination. Again, as noted, it is not possible to understand the political, social and religious movements of the Arab world without understanding the context of the globalized world in which they emerged.

Western encroachment has given a centrality to politics in the Islamic quest for a renewed identity; the disruptions brought about by Western intrusions have been, for many Muslims, a sign that something had gone gravely amiss in Islamic history. In such situations, devout Muslims turned to religion to guide them in their new circumstances. To understand Islamic culture, it would be helpful to keep certain facts in mind:

- Far from monolithic, Islam is a highly variegated phenomenon.
- Modern Islam has been shaped by its experience with European colonization of the Arab world.
- Islam has always adapted to changing circumstances and uses a religious discourse to legitimize these changes.

- Islam has been in a state of crisis for several decades and a new guard of Islamic religious leaders has emerged.
- The most controversial, and most misunderstood, aspect of this postcolonial Islam has been the question of Islamic fundamentalism.

(Armstrong, 2002, p. 165)

Fundamentalist movements of all religious persuasions share certain characteristics. At root, they exhibit a deep disenchantment with modernity. Fundamentalists often look back to a "golden age" that existed before the corrupting influence of the modern experiment. All fundamentalist movements, regardless of their confessional nature, share a disenchantment with what are perceived as a pernicious state of affairs and/or a conviction that fundamental theological principles have not been compromised. Religious fundamentalism within Islam is essentially a revulsion against the secularist expulsion of the divine from public life paralleled by an often-desperate effort to reassert spiritual values as the proper basis for the Islamic community. "Indeed, the new emergence of fundamentalism has now problematized the relationship between nationalism and religious identity" (Barakat, 1993. p. 36).

It would certainly be a mistake to assume that the reaction of the Islamic world to modernity has only entailed fundamentalist dogma. Many Muslim intellectual, religious and political leaders have sought to achieve a rapprochement between the demands of modernity and religious belief. It is ever worse to equate fundamentalism with terrorism, rather than understanding terrorism as a reaction to deeply-felt grievances in the Islamic world. Osama Bin-Laden routinely refers to the "crusading hatred" of "global impiety" and to "its American secularization, which is the pagan idol of the age." Osama Bin-Laden's goal is to persuade Muslims that the world is divided into two irreconcilable worlds: Islamic and non-Islamic. A similar dichotomizing can be found in much of the Western literature equating "fundamentalism" with "terrorism" and mischaracterizing Islam as a belief system which demarcates the "Rest" from the "West." Yet, as has been manifested in discussions of the nature of cultural identity, herein, stereotypical thinking and confrontational assumptions can only hinder understanding and accommodation. Learning about Islamic culture, as with studying any worldview, requires a two-fold process by which "static and oversimplified views are replaced by a dynamic, analytical approach to a highly complex and contradictory reality" (Barakat, 1993, p. 181).

Coda: Culture and identity

This last section is not designed so much to offer definitive conclusions about cultural policy and colonized nations as to make a final statement about the relationship between culture and national identity. These represent the shared values and traditions, whether invented or inherited, that are the essential glue for sustaining a sense of collective cohesiveness. As discussed previously, nations that have been subject to coloniality are particularly sensitive to any legacy of coloniality whereby a hegemon seeks to aggressively impose cultural superiority. Particularly suspect are the requirements of modernization that, in fact, barely disguise the superiority attributed to Europeanized norms over indigenous values.

In the same vein, Ukrainians were historically stereotyped as "little Russians"—backward, cultureless peasants in need of advancement through Russification and absorption into the Russian state. The doctrines of "white man's burden" and "civilizing mission" rendered Africans essentially subhumans. Similarly the pure-blooded Spanish ruling class in Latin America asserted a racial, as well as cultural, suzerainty over the indigenous peoples and those of mixed blood. It has been noted that the destructive effects of colonialism are incalculable, and that these costs are largely associated with systematic cultural deracination. Since the cultural damage experienced by the former colony outlives the realization of political sovereignty, its cultural policy must attempt to define a sense of identity.

For example, with the local autonomy afforded by its commonwealth status within the US, the Puerto Rican government "made a concerted effort to define an official cultural policy and stipulate what could rightfully represent Puerto Rican culture" (Davila, 1997, p. 4). "The Institute of Puerto Rican Culture was founded at this time, with the official task of defining and disseminating the constituent elements of Puerto Rico's national identity" (Davila, 1997, p. 4). In sum, national identity became "institutionalized" through a cultural policy and a cultural agency. In all this, postcoloniality necessitates cultural policies that create official policies of cultural nationalism.

Puerto Rico is a synecdoche for cultural policy in many countries with conditions of "coloniality." As a commonwealth of the US, Puerto Rico is a culturally distinct, but politically subordinate, region that has adopted an official policy of cultural nationalism admitted by the Institute of Puerto Rican Culture. The difficulty is in formulating exactly what should be the nature of the national culture to be supported. Typically such a cultural policy takes on two forms. The first is to stand in opposition to the colonial power's hegemonic culture, particularly in opposing American commercial culture. The second is to invent a tradition that is typically an idealized nostalgia for a largely lost historical community. This might be a tenuous Gaelic revivalism (Hutchinson, 1987), the fabrication of clan-specific tartan regalia (Hobsbawm and Ranger, 1983, pp. 15–41), or a "Puerto Ricanness" involving agrarian folklore "and a romanticized and harmonious integration of the indigenous Taino, Spanish and African components of society, under the rubric of a Hispanic tradition" (Davila, 1997, p. 5). The construction of an idealized cultural identity can be judged a necessary response to the destructive effects of colonialism; on the other hand, the construction may oversimplify cultural complexities and marginalize inconvenient historical and societal realities.

What can also result from even the most benign cultural construction is a policy that consigns the formerly colonized country to a cultural cul-de-sac as a "traditional" society of only anthropological interest. This can render its cultural sector out of touch with contemporary developments and unable to mediate the impact of an increasingly globalized world. For example, the anthropological concept of culture was used to justify Greenland's political and cultural struggle for independence from Denmark that culminated in Home Rule in 1991. Greenland's cultural policy priorities for the first ten years of its autonomy were based on Eskimo cultural heritage. However, a younger generation of artists had little desire to see their artistic creativity and aesthetic idioms limited by ethnic, monocultural tradition, even as they had no wish to deny their origins. In 1991, the Greenland Parliament set up a national Cultural Council that drew up a comprehensive policy for funding "modern" arts activities while also promoting a revitalization of Greenland's Eskimo cultural heritage (Duelund, *Nordic Cultural Policy*, pp. 425–6).

In sum, the challenge that countries combating coloniality face in constructing a cultural policy is to value its redefined past while being receptive to aesthetic innovation and the possibilities of cultural syncretism. Obviously, this is not a challenge that can be easily addressed. The pervasiveness of cultural globalization, which, as noted, is in the minds of many synonymous with Americanized values, makes the retention of national cultural identity a difficult issue even for countries such as France and Canada, which were the principal sponsors of the UNESCO Declaration on the Protection of Cultural Heritage.

These difficulties are compounded for nations with histories of coloniality that are only recently defining distinct cultural identities after long periods of hegemonic subjugation. Moreover the hegemon faces comparable difficulties in formulating its own fully realized identity. As Edward Said noted, "[t]he thing to be noticed about this kind of contemporary discourse, which assumes the primacy and even the complete centrality of the West, is how totalizing is its form, how all-enveloping its attitudes and gestures, how much it shuts out as it includes, compresses and consolidates" (Said, 1994, p. 22). In this sense, identity and cultural policy are central means by which nations of the periphery maintain their eligibility to compete in a centralizing world order.

Note

1. See also Chapters 14 and 16 in this volume by Briano and Champenois in this context.

14
Valorization of World Cultural Heritage in Time of Globalization: Bridges Between Nations and Cultural Power

Isabelle Brianso

The 1972 UNESCO World Heritage Convention is the most recognized normative tool at the international level in terms of safeguarding and preservation of the cultural and natural heritage. In 2009, the World Heritage List[1] counted 890[2] cultural and natural goods with "outstanding universal value" distributed in 148 States Parties. This growing List in the course of decades marks a political awareness on behalf of States Parties manifesting a diplomatic will to make heritages of the earth a geopolitical stake in dialogue and in peace between cultures. In 1994, the Committee of the World Heritage launched its "global strategy for a balanced, representative and credible World Heritage List."[3] The fact that Europe and North America had the strongest concentration of registered sites, the representation of the cultural and natural diversity with "universal and exceptional value" was not exactly in compliance with the foundational text of 1972. The List has to be balanced and made consistent with cultural and natural plurality created by the human beings and nature on a world level. Since then, the new orientations and the initiatives coordinated by the World Heritage Center aim this way so that the least-represented categories[4] of heritages, as the natural landscapes, the forests, the deserts and the geologic sites, or certain geographical zones can be revalued. This slow progression toward heritage as a factor of development and socioeconomic resources was formed and structured in parallel with the great political changes and the new geopolitical orientations in Europe and in the world.

Creation of a political and administrative framework of management and an international competitive intelligence: The World Heritage Centre of UNESCO

Created in 1992, the World Heritage Centre has the principal mission to coordinate the whole of the activities concerning the World Heritage sites. This mission is quite broad for a structure that has inadequate human and financial resources due to the planetary task with which it must cope. Since its creation, the importance of the Centre's activities is derived partly from the notoriety of this arising partly from the increased number of[5] sites classified on its List and partly from the notoriety this List produces at the international level. Nevertheless the financial reality and the management of these cultural and natural goods under this institution do not fully guarantee the needs of the countries that have subjected these goods to inscription. The Centre has taken on a particular importance since the events of September 11, 2001 when States Parties played the card of the cultural and intercultural dialogue on the political and diplomatic scene. These goods became a stake in the dialogue in favor of the promotion of peace and tolerance throughout the world, without truly granting them material supports for their conservation and their safeguarding. They are exposed at the fore of the international scene with a plurality of recommendations, measures and educational and scientific activities for good management. However, the World Heritage Centre should see its activities reduced or stagnate in the coming years in order to allow for more action and power for the Culture Sector of UNESCO.

The States Parties, having signed the Convention of 1972, see this List as diplomatic, political and economic action responding to the positions or pressures of the most powerful countries with regard to sustainable development. They are committed to protecting their cultural and natural heritage for future generations and consequently are interested in the problems connected to the living conditions of local populations, to their education, in the problems bound to the exploitation of the natural resources, etc. Cultural heritage, regardless of its "world, national or regional" specificities, cannot be confined anymore to the "simple" protection of old or modern walls (industrial heritage), but need a coherent integration of the local population and its daily problems. Like the UNESCO field offices for culture, education, and sciences, the World Heritage Centre should be established abroad according to this same model so as to better answer the local, specific needs that require an integrated or transverse management of heritage. However, we can easily understand the difficulty of the implementation of such an operation.

The inscription process[6] of a site on the World Heritage List is long and relies on multiple-skills[7] to draw up a satisfactory and documented list of the sites appearing on the Tentative List[8] to constitute the file of the inscription proposal. Developed countries have central and regional services with varied competencies that profit from a lumping of technical aids (universities, specialized cabinets or offices, ministries, town halls, regions, etc.). The countries in either a developmental phase or post-war recovery situation often request help from the international cooperation[9] to constitute these files, and thus to fulfill the administrative requirements of the United Nations which is essentially Western in nature.

The archeological park of Angkor was classified on the World Heritage List in 1992 during the Sixteenth Session of the World Heritage Committee, which took place in Santa Fe (US). The designed site covers an area of approximately 400 km^2 on Siem Reap province including the forested area and villages. Since 2000, the site has seen constant growth in tourism, which generates undeniable socioeconomic resources in the small and expanding city of Siam Reap and its region. This political decision at the beginning of the 1990s concerning the safeguarding and the protection of Angkor temples, following upon the solemn call launched by His Majesty King Norodom Sihanouk to the international community, was marked by a geopolitical context of recovery after a long period of violent conflict. The day after the fall of Pol Pot regime (Angkar), Cambodia was a shadow of itself and the following years under Vietnamese occupation resulted in extending the political and human chaos caused by the "*Angkar*". The eradication of the Khmer elite plunged the country into an unparalleled, post-trauma situation with loss of know-how, identity and consciousness (see Chapter 13 by Mulcahy for effects of coloniality). The temples of Angkor did not undergo the same physical destruction, reserved then for cultural and artistic practices.It seems that the Khmer Rouge had abandoned the archeological site itself, but not the symbolic meaning that it conveyed. Angkor Wat, symbol of the Khmer national identity, is displayed today on the current national flag.

Twenty years of war had violent and direct impacts not only on humans, but also on cultural properties that were subject to plunder and other kinds of violence. Although Cambodia ratified two main UNESCO Conventions (1954 and 1970), the country was overcome by the extent of illicit traffic on its territory. The legal and political gap until 1990 concerning the protection of cultural property encouraged cultural despoliation for the whole Khmer population.The great UNESCO project of safeguarding Angkor temples marks the end of the lapse of memory. The rebuilding is moving, but it is a slow and deep process requiring people to reconcile in order to heal the wounds of the past. The special court for Cambodia has already started the long walk toward this individual and collective work. To solve the legal gap regarding the proper management of cultural properties in Cambodia, the APSARA National Authority (ANA) was created in 1995 by royal decree. Its principal mission was to ensure protection, conservation and development of the Angkor temples[10] as well as the region of Siam Reap/Angkor. In Tokyo in 1993, the first Intergovernmental Conference discussed the "Safeguarding and the Development of the Historic Site of Angkor," and a Coordinating Committee for the Safeguarding and the Development of the Historic Site of Angkor (ICC) was created. This institutional body, whose Secretariat is ensured by UNESCO, is co-chaired by France and Japan through their respective embassies. Although this first conference was fundamental for the protection and the safeguarding of the temples of Angkor, it also underlined the beginning of a Western management for the archeological park of Angkor, supported by a multitude of international and academic structures financing whole or part of certain fieldworks or field operations in connection with the local cultural heritage (tangible and intangible) in a framework of sustainable development.

The tourism sector plays an important role in the strategy of a sustainable development for the country. "The city of Siem Reap has clearly benefitted economically from tourism during the last decade. The World Travel and Tourism Council estimates that in Cambodia, the tourism industry generated about 1,108,000 direct and indirect jobs in 2007,[11] making tourism-related employment reach 15.8 percent of total employment" (Laurence Nhan, 2008). However, the supply side of tourism is still centralised in the Angkor region, forsaking other interesting areas such as Sihanoukville or Phnom Penh (the capital). The supply diversification could disperse tourists better, and could unblock Angkor temples and the small town of Siem Reap, which is suffocating. Siem Reap is experiencing urban development without a real urban plan. Therefore hotels, restaurants and guesthouses open everyday; in eight years the number of guesthouses had a growth rate of 504 percent (147 guesthouses in 1998 and 742 guesthouses in 2006). The political, economic and diplomatic stakes in Angkor and its region request an adapted policy of tourism development which is in the process of coming under the control of the International Coordination Committee for the Safeguarding and Development of Angkor (ICC).

The UNESCO World Heritage Convention of 1972

The drafting of the World Heritage Convention of 1972 falls within a political and international context of protection regarding cultural and natural heritage, ideas that can be sourced to the beginning of the twentieth century. The two World Wars of the last century marked a collective awakening concerning the protection of heritage at the international level as a powerful factor favorable to the peace between the people and intercultural societies. The 1920s saw the emergence of the League of Nations (1919), the Council of the League of Nations (1922), which created in its turn Intellectual Cooperation Committee (ICI) "whose purpose was to improve the working conditions of the educated workforce and to build up international relations between teachers, artists, scientists and members of other professions,"[12] before being transformed from 1926 into the International Institute of Intellectual Cooperation (IIIC). The 1930s launched and concretized the first actions in protection and conservation of the monuments with the introduction of the Charter of Athens of 1931 and that of the 1933 then, 30 years later (on 1964) by the adoption of the Charter of Venice[13] as "a document on the fundamental principles of conservation and restoration of the architectural heritage, the International Charter for the Conservation and Restoration of Monuments and Sites."[14] It is indeed in this international context of the first half of the twentieth century stemming from a collective reflection on the main stakes in the conservation and the restoration of built heritage and its natural environment that the intellectual and political framework of the World Heritage Convention of 1972 was designed. The rescue campaign of the temples of Nubia (1960–80) strongly influenced public opinion on the cultural and scientific importance of protecting and preserving this heritage of "outstanding universal value"[15] for future generations, which will be the first foundation of the Convention of 1972 defined in paragraph 49 of *Operational Guidelines for the Implementation of the World Heritage Convention.*[16] Although this concept is developed within the framework of the Convention of the World Heritage, it had already been noted of the greatest pioneers of French archeology in the first half of the twentieth century. Thus, Mr. Maurice Glaize[17] will write in his book *Les monuments du groupe d'Angkor* published in 1944, at Saigon (Vietnam), that "Angkor Wat is from all the buildings, the vastest and the best preserved, it is also the most impressive and the one which, of many, takes it by the character of big architectural composition, comparable to the most beautiful human creations of the whole world."[18]

The valorization of cultural heritage: A Western vision toward developing countries

The concept of "valorization of the cultural heritage" is an abstract French terminology that lacks precise elements of definition because it refers similarly to the preservation and restoration of the heritage as it does to cultural tourism—or even to the cultural policies of arrangement and development. It exists in France as several regional agencies dealing with heritage issues. That of the *Provence-Alpes-Côtes d'Azur* region, also called "PACA Region," was created in 2001, at the initiative of the regional institution PACA and the Ministry of Culture and Communication, to meet the new local demands for decentralization via the cultural promotion of the territories. This Agency "is located from this prospect of crossings and diversifications of the ways of knowledge and valorization of the monuments and the initiatives: publications, coordinations of studies related to the heritage, implementation of an observatory of the economic and social repercussions, documentation data bases, expertise surveys and supports with the local initiatives, diffusion of the good practices, the networking and the professionalization of the actors, fights against exclusion, teaching and mediation actions, participation in European programmes and international exchanges."[19]

Moreover, this concept is often used in a restrictive way, depending on the initial profession of the interlocutor (architect, curators, politician, administrative, etc.). It is nevertheless the global, not partial, development of the site of which we speak which requires a multidisciplinary approach to the issue. It is relevant to wonder about the final objective concerning "valorization" issues because, indeed, on that depend the expected results. A historic site classified on the World Heritage List has to join a process of sustainable development-generating productivity gains thanks to its socioeconomic dynamics, which will allow it, maybe, a partial and institutional financial autonomy with the help of the international cooperation. We are thus faced with a reality more complex and wider than the simple question of "valorization," which is too often discussed and written about in specific French literature.

Recently, groups of researchers[20] in France and Europe started working on the set of themes of "cultural mediation" applied to historic sites. This new field of research, developed at the beginning of the 1990s in Europe, finds its originality in the transversal strategy of its competences and its components while trying to answer the new cultural heritage stakes (audience, development, education linked to heritage, etc.) in a globalized world. Characterized by the interdisciplinary research fields, cultural mediation was considered, for a long time, by the greatest French cultural institutions' elite a new "smart" name. Today more and more French museums set up departments or services of "cultural mediation" within their establishments whose principal mission is to study the audience moving in a defined cultural environment.

Like this field of research, the valorization of the cultural and natural goods needs multi-competences requiring an integrated management in order to transmit to future generations a cultural message based on quality. UNESCO, which encourages the least developed countries to preserve their heritage in a sustainable way, orientates, directly and indirectly, these countries toward safeguarding measures inspired by the successes of the Western countries, although efforts are made and supported by local initiatives. The concept of the museum as a "non-profit making, permanent institution in the service of society and of its development, and open to the public, which acquires, conserves, researches, communicates and exhibits, for purposes of study, education and enjoyment, material evidence of people and their environment"[21] "is exported" throughout the world like an institutional guarantor of good management concerning national cultural goods. Thus, developing countries which preserve their heritage according to international recommendations try almost always to equip themselves with at least one national museum. The recent national museum of Siam Reap (Cambodia), near to the Angkor temples, opened its doors in November 2007. This so-called national museum has received Khmer masterpieces and manages artistic collections, but the administrative structure is supervised and controlled by its neighbor Thailand.

In Cambodia, the Department of Tourism Development of Angkor (DDTA) carried out field operations in connection with the concept of "valorization of the cultural heritage" in the temples of Angkor. APSARA National Authority launched in January 2007 a project of structuring the approach area (*parvis*) of the small pink sandstone temple of Banteay Srei, also called

"Project of Parvis." A general report of parvis' work was presented during the Sixteenth Technical Committee of the ICC, a meeting organized once a year by the APSARA National Authority. This project is presented as a pilot project that should be used as a model for the implementation of other approach areas applied to other monuments. The small temple of Banteay Srei, located in the northeast, 30 km from the town of Siam Reap, knows a regular growth[22] of tourist frequentation placing it in the third row of the most visited temples of the park after Angkor Wat and Ta Prohm. The heavy traffic of tourists entailed emergency measures,[23] including controlled access (audience is not allowed anymore) inside the central shrine, which is the most fragile enclosure of the temple called the first enclosure. Despite this decision-making, the problem of over-frequentation was not regulated. Thus, in January 2007 an interdepartmental working group called *Cell of Project* was set up. It was made up of a Technical Committee and a Piloting Committee where department directors and the general director of the organization worked for the orientation and the validation of the decisions. This cell was coordinated by a French architect until November 2007; since then, it has been coordinated by a Franco–Khmer tandem team. It is directly attached to the general direction of APSARA Authority National in order to give it the greatest margin of action in a country where corruption and political pressures are part of daily life. The Franco–Khmer team deals with multi-abilities techniques and includes in this working group a Swiss team which lies within the scope of international cooperation agreements. This project of the *parvis* has been developed to answer the increasingly large request of foreign tourists to visit this small Khmer monument. The temple is on an East-West historical axis like the majority of the Angkor temples, which are also integrated with Phnom Dei mountain located in the vicinity. The zoning plan is organized according to two differentiated zones: the zone of the actual approach area and the temple zone itself: "The temple involves the temple structure and its immediate surroundings, part of which has an existing landscape to be preserved and an area, amenities zone, landscaped commercial zone and archeological zone-the mound and two '*trapeangs*' (lake), along with the visitor and control center. This will be rounded out by the interpretation center."[24]

To make the *parvis*' project successful, the DDTA agreed with its Swiss partner to conduct a poll questionnaire[25] to survey tourists' opinion of and satisfaction with existing and potential facilities in the approach area work. This field research collected more than 1000 responses from visitors, mostly from Western countries. A section of this inquiry was dedicated to new valorization tools that would be designed and implemented in the future parvis' area. According to the replies received, visitors' satisfaction levels would improve significantly if APSARA National Authority could develop sign information panels and create a center of interpretation (second row of request with more than 30 percent).

The concept of the *parvis* harkens back to a structured and organized valorization process largely developed in the Western countries and in particular in the Anglo-Saxon nations. The valorization techniques used in cultural and natural sites are based on elaborate strategies involving the production of these cultural goods in order to "allow visitors to benefit as much as possible from the offer proposed."[26] The center of interpretation is one of these techniques that must allow the audience to be easily directed and to acquire quality cultural content through various supports of mediation, such as: numeric, interactive terminals, paper documents, pedagogical films, etc. Thus, this tool must "present in a living and a comprehensive way a site, a monument, a landscape, a museum collection design by taking account at the same time of its particular characteristics and the centers of interest and levels of understanding depending on the large categories of visitors."[27] It can also be seen as a small "site museum" able, through mediation techniques, to simply explain complex data linked to history, archeology and chronology.

Beyond the huge financial expense of the design and the realization of this specific type of mediation tools, in order to transmit a studied and structured cultural message according to identified visitors, it is important to consider the validity of this model of educational tool for developing countries as a majority of their cultural heritage might traditionally have relied on oral transmission.

The research group called MECSCIA[28] belonging to the French research laboratory *Centre d'Histoire Culturelle des Sociétés Contemporaines* (CHCSC)[29] of the University of Versailles Saint-Quentin in Yvelines carries out research studies on world heritage sites in connection with the concept of "valorization of the cultural heritage." The Marrakech Medina (Morocco), classified on the World Heritage List of Humanity in 1985, relies on mass tourism seeking foreign orientations, sun, and rest. Within a few meters of the Medina, there is the Jemaâ el Fna Square,[30] which was added to the World Heritage List in 2001 by the Moroccan association[31] called *Safeguarding of the Jemâa el-Fna Square*. The general secretary of this structure, Mrs. Ouidad Tebba,[32] did not herself apply any pressures on UNESCO for the inscription of this square as a Masterpiece of the Oral and Intangible Heritage of Humanity.[33] In 1997, an important meeting of international experts was organized in Marrakech in close cooperation with the association; "it made it possible to pose the bases of a consideration which later allowed starting the preparation process for the nomination files for the first proclamations, which took place in 2001. As a local citizen association, a nomination file was established in collaboration with the Moroccan Ministry of culture, which made it possible for the Jemaâ el-Fna Square to belong to the first Masterpieces proclaimed by UNESCO." Following this nomination, the idea to set up a center of interpretation was posed in order to explain to the tourists visiting the area the meaning of such international recognition. Mrs. Tebba explains that this mediation tool "allows to dig and to make visible this invisible [existing] of the Square. At the same time, what a center of interpretation is? And, how it will dialogue, if we install it on the Square, [...] with the Square itself? [...] How to make sure that it will be not a kind of outgrowth or transplant which does not take."[34] Then, how to explain to the foreign audience this oral cultural heritage resulting from the cultural and social bond (*Houma*)[35] transmitted during centuries by Moroccan families into Arab or Berber language? Mrs. Tebba explains that "the tourist can neither apprehend nor to understand part of this heritage and it is a tragedy. It is a real tragedy because the tales are told in Arabic and Berber language; Thus in a certain way it questions the appropriation of this heritage by the tourists."[36] How to explain specificities of the intangible heritage or the "invisible elements" living and developing in the Kasbah of Marrakech to people who come mainly to Morocco to get some sun?

The Jemaâ el-Fna Square is certainly a masterpiece of the oral and intangible heritage but it is increasingly divorced from its first vocation of producing conviviality and social bonding, from being a living theater of cultural and artistic practices drawn with deepest of human creation where storytellers, animal trainers, and travelling acrobats keep close to each other. Mrs. Tebba stresses that "the current development of tourism: caricature, schematizes, simplifies and makes folklore [...] the transmission is not carried out any more."[37] The water carriers of the Square do not have anything traditional or authentic any more, except in front of the camera of a tourist where the image copyrights are skillfully negotiated before one photograph is taken. We pass sometimes from a "museum status" regarding the Medina walls of Marrakech as a static cultural heritage by forgetting the social bonds that bring to life this heritage into a commercial and touristic folklore process that animates the historical center town before the entry of the souks. According to Mrs. Tebba "the Medina is losing all that makes its essence and its spirit, i.e. all its immaterial essence. How can we design a whole district, a 'Houma', where half of the dwellings are second homes?"[38] These social changes and the migration of the Moroccan local inhabitants such as the craftsmen towards the periphery of the town of Marrakech are explained in great part because of the real property speculation. At this time of culture generating remarkable economic gains as testimony of a certain power at world level, it is fundamental to think about a better redistribution of this wealth in favor of the local actors as the creators and the artistic producers of the Jemaâ el-Fna Square. This new orientation understands the definition of a status of the artist as a key actor between the Jemaâ el-Fna Square and the visitors, but also to establish footbridges between the various UNESCO Conventions since 1972 to give back to the cultural community the intercultural and cultural tangles from which the culture arose.

This cultural "superpower" as a phenomenon of attraction and tourist marketing has to allow the integration of local actors, the intensification of social linkages, and not the exclusion or marginalization of these last ones. They do not have to be transformed into passive spectators of their cultural heritage, but be cultural ferrymen linking Moroccan people, foreign visitors and future generations. This complex and difficult balance has to rest on a flexible legal frame to integrate the large plurality of the situations regarding entertainment sector and particular cases without destabilizing the roots of this artistic and traditional production based on oral transmission. How can economics, politics and culture come together and produce a dynamic process in this complexity? The intercultural history of the societies[39] brings forth elements of an answer by decomposing the historic breaks in human history. The intercultural dialogue has arisen from the genesis of cultures which built themselves upon religious, political, economical and technical interactions throughout history and through great societal moments defined by Mr. Jacques Demorgon.

Conclusion

The perception of cultural heritage has greatly evolved in industrialized countries, leaving to the institutional elites the responsibility for the study, the transmission, and the diffusion of cultural contents. The standardization of cultural practices regarding living arts in particular is diffused widely each day through the media. This very partial vision of heritage is reflected in a direct or indirect process in the least developed countries, where traditional practices are partly scorned by the consumer society. We destroy the ancient to make it new "beautiful and strong" following Western trends in the name of mainly economic development. This development is caricatured in Cambodia by the ownership of a motorbike, a television and a mobile telephone, coming mainly from the telecommunications sector, which is the *eldorado* of the multinational companies in a globalized economic system.

The drafts of the different Conventions of UNESCO since 1972 show that the concept of "heritage" is complex and diverse like human thought throughout its millennium of history. The criteria of the scope of cultural heritage have been reduced since the the late 1970s, especially the social and anthropological aspects that form an integral part of cultural heritage in its global representation. Thus, "in 1980 the six cultural heritage criteria were revised and their scope reduced. This 1980 version of the cultural heritage criteria, which remained almost unchanged until 1992, led to a number of problems. It seemed to privilege sites of architectural and artistic value over those whose significance lay in other, less tangible, heritage values. This in turn meant that the World Heritage system was seen as favouring nominations from Europe at the expense of other parts of the world, such as Africa or Asia and the Pacific, where the significance of places often lay not in monumental structures or artistic arrangements of buildings, parks and gardens, but in the way that their natural features were charged with religious or symbolic meanings and associations."[40]

This reduction has compartmentalized the heritages of the Earth and of human creation into clear and well-identified categories of heritage, such as: intangible, cultural diversity, tangible, natural, etc., and presented as independent of each other. The Jemaâ el-Fna Square is located within the Medina of Marrakech, both classified on the World Heritage List of Humanity. In the Medina, only its material walls are registered, which leaves doubt about the existing intangible heritage inside the districts of the historical center of Marrakech: local folklore without major anthropological value or social bonds woven into the deepest Moroccan practices and cultural roots? In Cambodia, Angkor Wat is the emblematic temple of the park of Angkor and symbolizes the national and cultural Khmer identity. It is 'protected' by one important *neak ta* (genius): local communities see the monumental statue of Ta Reak as a religious Khmer masterpiece in a living and natural heritage place. The question becomes how does one preserve and interpret such a complex cultural heritage permanently connected with several cultural times (sacred, profane, etc.) in time of globalisation? A cross-cultural approach of local cultural complexity could be part of the interpretation for tourists visiting Angkor temples.

Notes

1. As of April 2009, 186 States Parties have ratified the World Heritage Convention. The World Heritage List includes 890 properties forming part of the cultural and natural heritage, which the *World Heritage Committee* considers as having outstanding universal value. These include 689 cultural, 176 natural and 25 mixed sites properties in 148 States Parties. Internet Source: http://whc.unesco.org/fr/list (accessed August 1, 2008).
2. In 2009: 31 properties are included in the List of World Heritage in Danger. Internet Source: http://whc.unesco.org/fr/list (accessed August 1, 2008).
3. UNESCO website: http://whc.unesco.org/en/globalstrategy (accessed August 1, 2008).
4. UNESCO, 2007. *World Heritage: Challenges for the Millennium*. Paris, France.
   Classification scheme is non exhaustive but includes regional, chronological, and geographical set of themes.

   1   Classification by themes: archeological sites; world heritage cities; Monuments and groups of buildings; modern heritage; cultural landscapes; forests; marine sites; geological and geomorphological sites; mountain sites.
   2   Regional and geographical classification: Africa; Arab States; area Asia and the Pacific; Latin America and the Caribbean; Europe and North America.

5. In 2007, 22 cultural sites as well as the extension of 13 cultural sites and 2 natural sites were registered on the World Heritage List.
6. Five phases: 1. Tentative List; 2. The nomination File; 3. The Advisory Bodies; 4. The World Heritage Committee; 5. The Criteria of Selection. UNESCO website: http://whc.unesco.org/fr/nominationprocessus/ (accessed August 1, 2008).
7. We understand by "multi-abilities" or "multi-competences": the accumulation of various specialties in various cultural fields: management, administration, landscape architecture, archeology, sociology, tourism, cultural policy, etc.

8. A Tentative List is an inventory of those properties which each State Party intends to consider for nomination during the following years. States Parties are encouraged to submit in their Tentative Lists, properties which they consider to be cultural and/or natural heritage of outstanding universal value and therefore suitable for inscription on the World Heritage List. States Parties are encouraged to prepare their Tentative Lists with the participation of a wide variety of stakeholders, including site managers, local and regional governments, local communities, NGOs and other interested parties and partners. States Parties should submit Tentative Lists, which should not be considered exhaustive, to the World Heritage Centre, preferably at least one year prior to the submission of any nomination. States Parties are encouraged to re-examine and re-submit their Tentative List at least every ten years. Available at: http://whc.unesco.org/fr/listeindicative (accessed August 1, 2008) .

9. The international cooperation can take several forms: support from embassies and foreign universities, archeological missions, foreign museums, associations, etc.

10. The temples of Angkor were classified simultaneously on the World Heritage List and the List of Cultural Heritage in Danger by decision of the Sixteenth Session of the World Heritage Committee on December 14, 1992, (Santa Fe city, the US). Cambodia is a State Party which has subjected the proposal inscription of this cultural good in accordance with the Unesco Convention of 1972.
    Files of UNESCO available at: http://whc.unesco.org/archive/out/peril94.htm (accessed August 1, 2008).

11. Ballard, Brett M. As stated in *Pro-Poor Tourism in the Greater Mekong Subregion*, CDRI, 2007 (accessed August 1, 2008).

12. Extract text of p. 26 of the book *World Heritage: Challenges for the Millennium*. UNESCO, France, 2007 (accessed August 1, 2008).

13. Complete text of the Venice Charter. Available at: http://www.icomos.org/docs/venise.html (accessed August 1, 2008).

14. Extract text of p. 28 of the book *World Heritage: Challenges for the Millennium*. UNESCO, France, 2007.

15. Definition of the "Outstanding universal value" according to paragraph 49 of the official Unesco document titled *The Operational Guidelines for the Implementation of the World Heritage Convention* (February, 2005). The "Outstanding universal value" means cultural and/or natural significance which is so exceptional as to transcend national boundaries and to be of common importance for present and future generations of all humanity. As such, the permanent protection of this heritage is of the highest importance to the international community as a whole. The Committee defines the criteria for the inscription of properties on the World Heritage List.
    Available at: http://unesdoc.unesco.org/images/0013/001386/138676f.pdf (accessed August 1, 2008).

16. Original text available at: http://unesdoc.unesco.org/images/0013/001386/138676f.pdf.

17. Mr. Maurice Glaize (1886–1964) was an architect then the general curator of Angkor from 1936 to 1947.

18. Extract text p. 76 of the French book *Monuments du groupe d'Angkor*, Sixth edition, France, 2003 (accessed August 1, 2008).
    Original text in French: "Angkor Vat est de tous les édifices, le plus vaste et le mieux conservé, c'est également le plus imposant et celui qui, de beaucoup,

l'emporte par son caractère de grande composition architecturale, comparable aux plus belles créations humaines du monde entier."

19. Available at: http://www.patrimoine-paca.com/sommaire.php (accessed August 1, 2008).

20. French group of researchers called MECSCIA (CHCSC) belonging to the University of Versailles Saint-Quentin in Yvelines (UVSQ).
    Available at: http://www.chcsc.uvsq.fr/gptravail/MESCI.html (accessed August 1, 2008).

21. ICOM (International Council of Museums) Statues, art.2, para.1
    Available at: http://icom.museum/definition.html (accessed August 1, 2008).

22. APSARA National Authority, DDTA. *Annual Results: Tourist Frequentations, Year 2007*. ODP, 2008.
    Evolution of the tourist frequentation over the last 3 years:
    2004–5: +25%; 2005–6: +18%; 2006–7: +25%.

23. Measures taken following the sanitary state inspection of the temple carried out in 2001. Extract text of the p. 76 concerning the Sixteenth Technical Session, July, 2007, Siam Reap, Cambodia. "Risks on the monument have been analyzed. In 2001, the monument's condition was diagnosed and area with significant damage was located. Because of its size and the great finesse of its components, Banteay Srei is an extremely fragile temple. Risks were identified, including the growth of microbiology, a worn-down central causeway and looting. Emergency measures were taken in order to deal with these risks: 1. Barriers were put up to cordon areas off, controlling access and keeping people from going inside the central shrine where structures are particularly fragile. 2. Protective flooring was put up over sculptured thresholds. 3. Directional signing was put up."

24. Extract text of pages: 76 and 77 of the Sixteenth Report of the Technical Session, July, 2007, Siam Reap, Cambodia.

25. Poll questionnaire title "Understanding of Banteay Srei Temple's Visitor," August 2007, APSARA, DDTA.

26. Extract text p. 98 of the book *Tourisme et patrimoine*, Valéry Patin, La Documentation Française, 2005.

27. Extract text p. 101 of the book *Tourisme et patrimoine*, Valéry Patin, La Documentation Française, 2005.

28. French group of researchers called MECSCIA (CHCSC) belonging to the University of Versailles Saint-Quentin in Yvelines (UVSQ).

29. French group of researchers called MECSCIA (CHCSC) belonging to the University of Versailles Saint-Quentin in Yvelines (UVSQ).

30. Extract text p. 69 of the *Masterpieces of the Oral and Intangible Heritage of Humanity-Proclamations 2001, 2003 and 2005*: "The Jemaa el-Fna Square is one of the main cultural spaces in Marrakesh and has become one of the symbols of the city since its foundation in the eleventh century. It represents a unique concentration of popular Moroccan cultural traditions performed through musical, religious and artistic expressions. Located at the entrance of the Medina, this triangular square, which is surrounded by restaurants, stands and public buildings, provides everyday commercial activities and various forms of entertainment. It is a meeting point for both the local population and people from elsewhere. All through the day, and well into the night, a variety of services are offered, such as dental care, traditional medicine, fortune-telling, preaching, and henna tattooing; water-carrying, fruit and traditional food may be bought. In addition, one can enjoy many performances by storytellers, poets, snake-charmers, Berber musicians

(mazighen), Gnaoua dancers and senthir (hajouj) players. The oral expressions would be continually renewed by bards (imayazen), who used to travel through Berber territories. They continue to combine speech and gesture to teach, entertain and charm the audience. Adapting their art to contemporary contexts, they now improvise on an outline of an ancient text, making their recital accessible to a wider audience. The Jemaa el-Fna Square is a major place of cultural exchange and has enjoyed protection as part of Morocco's artistic heritage since 1922. However, urbanization, in particular real estate speculation and the development of the road infrastructure are seen as serious threats to the cultural space itself. While Jemaa el-Fna Square enjoys great popularity, the cultural practices may suffer acculturation, also caused by widespread tourism."

    Available at: http://unesdoc.unesco.org/images/0014/001473/147344e.pdf (accessed August 1, 2008).
31. Moroccan association for the safeguarding and the preservation of Jemaâ el-Fna Square carried the registration file as a masterpiece of the oral and immaterial heritage of humanity.
32. Mrs. Ouidad Tebba, Professor at the University of Cadi Ayyad (Marrakech, Morocco), is the person in charge for the diploma section "Tourism and Heritage." Co-drafting of the book *Jemaâ el Fna-Marrakech* with Mr. Mohammed Faïz, Edition *La croisée des chemins* (2004).

    Interview of the Morocco Hebdo International n. 471, talk collected in French by Mrs. Naïma Bouâchrine, June 29, 2001: "I am a girl of the Medina of Marrakech and in addition, I come from a traditional family in whom the oral culture, in all its forms, was omnipresent. Old aunts, nannies, grandmothers, deluded me with their tales and legends ... And each time one of the invaluable agents of this tradition disappeared, a side of this heritage died with him, forever. The Jemaa el-Fna Square is, of this point of sight, an emblem. Do the components of this square form a universe variegated, strange, imperceptible, where imagination and the dream are still possible, but for how long? Taken out of clipper by the motor vehicle traffic and the various forms of 'pollution', the square, in spite of its apparent vitality, was asphyxiated with the wire of time and an imperative action also was essential to give again its letters of nobility to an oral heritage fallen in disuse with the eyes of many Moroccans."
33. According to the 2003 Convention for the Safeguarding of the Intangible Cultural Heritage, the intangible cultural heritage (ICH)—or living heritage—is the mainspring of our cultural diversity and its maintenance a guarantee for continuing creativity.

    The Convention states that the ICH is manifested, among others, in the following domains:

- Oral traditions and expressions including language as a vehicle of the intangible cultural heritage;
- Performing arts (such as traditional music, dance and theater);
- Social practices, rituals and festive events;
- Knowledge and practices concerning nature and the universe;
- Traditional craftsmanship.

The 2003 Convention defines ICH as the practices, representations, expressions, as well as the knowledge and skills, that, communities, groups and, in some cases, individuals recognize as part of their cultural heritage.

The definition also indicates that the ICH to be safeguarded by this Convention:

- is transmitted from generation to generation;
- is constantly recreated by communities and groups, in response to their environment, their interaction with nature, and their history;
- provides communities and groups with a sense of identity and continuity;
- promotes respect for cultural diversity and human creativity;
- is compatible with international human rights instruments;
- complies with the requirements of mutual respect among communities, and of sustainable development.

Available at: http://www.unesco.org/culture/en/masterpieces (accessed August 1, 2008).
34. Remarks collected in French, April 2008, Marrakech, Morocco. Interviewed by Isabelle Brianso.
35. "Houma": Arabic word which means "community" or "district."
36. Remarks collected in French, April 2008, Marrakech, Morocco. Interviewed by Isabelle Brianso.
37. Remarks collected in French, April 2008, Marrakech, Morocco. Interviewed by Isabelle Brianso.
38. Remarks collected in French, April 2008, Marrakech, Morocco. Interviewed by Isabelle Brianso.
39. Jacques Demorgon. *L'histoire interculturelle des sociétés*. Anthropos, 1998.
40. Extract text of p. 39 of the book *World Heritage: Challenges for the Millenium*. UNESCO, France, 2007.

15
Reality TV Shows, Private Television Networks and Social Change in India

Lauhona Ganguly

This chapter explores the emerging significance of private television networks, in India, as a social force and its impact on social change. In particular the entertainment genre of "reality shows" is examined to understand the narratives of reality, representation and change that are offered night after night on prime time television. Reality shows have been very popular with audiences, appear on the schedules of almost all television networks and have been at the center of a booming private television industry in India. The central appeal of reality shows rests on the dramatic potential of "ordinary" individuals who assert entrepreneurial zeal, exhibit ambition, seize opportunities and compete to win (or lose) "extraordinary" prize monies. Such a narrative resonates with the socioeconomic reimagining of a market-oriented India. Since the 1990s India has shifted towards privatization, liberalization and deregulation as the necessary logic for operating in a global economy. Private enterprise and (global) competitive market relations have replaced state-controlled developmental models of economy.

The television experience is situated within the socioeconomic context, in this chapter, to argue that reality shows (and private television networks in general) provide a new market-driven social milieu, and enable new ways of living and making sense of the social shifts in India. The transformative world of reality shows, where ordinary people win extraordinary rewards, rearticulates the imperatives of market competition and profit motive within a new ideational framework of change and progress. The values, strategies and logic of a liberal-market driven economy becomes familiar and meaningful at the level of everyday cultural practices. The structural adjustments from the state to the market, from ideals of collective good to private consumption are mediated on prime time entertainment television. As such it is argued that social power intersects through the political, economic and cultural realms, and the battle to shape social change is, and will, increasingly take place on the cultural domain.

The analytical framework used in this chapter draws correspondences between the structural adjustments at the socioeconomic realm and the narratives of change offered on reality game shows. Discursive analysis focuses on the specific frameworks of meanings and ideas embedded into the show as selective organization of cultural material. The "text" is linked with the "con-text" to understand what are the limits and scope of possibilities that identify reality and social change. Two reality shows are considered for analysis: one, *Kaun Banega Crorepati*, *(KBC)* the Hindi adaptation of *Who Wants to be a Millionaire* and two, *Indian Idol*, the Indian version of the series *Pop Idol*.

KBC's "reach" among the Hindi-speaking general entertainment population has been the highest of any program in its day part, registering a high 15 percent in 2000 for *KBC* I followed by a higher 24 percent for *KBC* II in 2005 (*Hindu Business Line*, 2005). The third season in 2007 continued the trend, and competing networks have included reality shows on their schedules as well. But the popularity of reality shows is not limited to high viewer ratings. The number of participants who regularly turn up for the auditions from different corners of India forced the producers of *Indian Idol* to lower the age limit to 16 years in 2007 (Chakrabarti, 2007). In the third season of *Indian Idol* 70 million votes were cast to elect the winner (Bamzai, 2007). Reality shows have changed the nature of viewing television by spilling out of television screens into discussions in living rooms and offices; on communities rallying behind their favorite candidates on streets; on media editorials and debates on news shows. Television as a domestic technology opens up "techno-social spaces" (Rajagopal, 2001) where viewers negotiate social transformation. Today, India's 71 million cable and satellite homes (with private television networks) is the third-largest television market in the world, next to the US and China (*Hindustan Times*, 2007). This growing universe of people makes it important to examine the frameworks for social imaginaries provided on the reality shows in the context of ongoing social change.

Television in India: Public good to private consumption

Television began in India in September 1959 with an explicit social mandate: to forge national unity and promote social development. Technology was to provide greater access to the masses and facilitate state-administered programs of national development and socio-cultural integration. As a result the government-run broadcaster Doordarshan (DD) operated under the Ministry of Information and Broadcasting and enjoyed unchallenged access to television viewers across India. Initial broadcasts from the Delhi station featured only couple of hours of program on one channel for schools and rural areas. Gradually new *Kendras* (stations) followed (Bombay, 1972; Srinagar, 1973; Amritsar, 1973; Kolkata, 1975; Madras, 1975; and Lucknow, 1975); hours of programming increased and entertainment programs were included (Mankekar, 1993). DD however continued to function within a state-centric framework for planned economic growth and social-national integration.

The crucial transitions in the television experience can be identified in two distinct but related moments: one, the shift to commercially sponsored programming; and two, the launch of private cable and satellite television networks. Both these moments of transformation contributed to a shift in the operating logic of the television experience in India—from a social agenda to that of the market's profit motive.

By late 1980s the idea of market-driven economic growth redefined the vision for national development. State control was rejected in favor of market liberalization. In independent India, developmentalist policies of the state had allowed a nationalized public sector to support the domestic private sector which was weakened under colonial rule. The interest of the domestic elite had thus been secured without contradicting the rhetoric of social equity and "national" development. With time, new economic interests from within the private sector began asserting their demands for greater economic liberalization (Rajagopal, 2001). State-owned public sector units were marked to be disinvested by the state or required to find market-oriented revenue models. The focus shifted from capital-goods-based economy and macro-infrastructural development programs to a consumer economy. Relaxed import regulations allowed multinational corporations into the country and opened a dizzying world of commodity choices to middle-class Indian consumers. This created an incentive to advertise, and turned the market's attention to broadcast media.

Commercial sponsorship of television programming appeared on DD (while still under state control) in 1984 with the serial show *Hum Log* (*We People*) (Singhal and Rogers, 2001). Though advertising first began in 1976, less than 1 percent of DD's budget came from advertising in 1976–7 (Sinha, 2007). But the interest of new market forces and corporate clients, in the 1980s, to use DD's national reach to advertise their products and services marked a turning point. DD was under increasing pressure to generate revenue through advertising, instead of relying on government funding. Simultaneously, DD began to tilt the balance of its programming schedule from pro-social themes to entertainment genres in order to attract more audiences and cater to its corporate clients.

The entry of cable and satellite (C&S) television marked the second significant transition for the television experience in India. The 1991 Gulf War touched the lives of many expatriate Indians in the Gulf; their families in India rushed to buy dish antennas for their homes. Others turned entrepreneurs and flung cable over treetops to offer the signal to their neighbors for a fee. In the land of the elaborate licensing regulations instituted by the state (and historically referred to as "license raj") times had changed: the unregulated cable connections were allowed to flourish with remarkably little interference. The new mantra for national development favored private enterprise, minimizing state regulations and providing multiple choices for consuming publics. Though there were random debates on cultural invasion by the western C&S networks (Pathania, 1998), unlike many other countries including China, there were no attempts to ban the sprouting cable connections and roof-top satellites. McDowell attributes the government's ambiguous attitude and official tolerance to its prior commitment to economic liberalization (McDowell, 1997). The popularity of C&S networks made it clear to different political interests that "Indians turn to television for entertainment and not for lessons on national integration" (Melkote, Sanjay, and Ahmed, 1998, p. 176); while a landmark judgment of the Supreme Court in 1995 allowed private players by declaring that government monopoly of airwaves and broadcasting was unconstitutional. What emerged was a "new historical conjuncture" (Rajagopal, 2001) where rejection of state-centric development programs and (global) movements towards liberal market reforms intersected with a new legitimacy for private consumption and profit motive.

The result was a boom in the television industry. From two channels prior to 1991, Indian viewers were exposed to more than 50 channels by 1996 (Derne, 2005). In a deregulated and liberalized Indian economy, both transnational media entities and domestic media enterprises entered the growing television industry. A Federation of Indian Chambers of Commerce and Industry (FICCI)–Pricewaterhouse Coopers 2007 report indicates continued growth: television industry revenue is predicted to reach Rs. 519 billion by 2011 (Figure 15.1).

The growth potential for the television industry in the next five years is projected to come from new subscriptions – both from the increasing number of "pay TV" homes and increased subscription rates (Pricewaterhouse Coopers report, 2006). The advertising spends as a portion of the GDP is relatively very low in India compared to other developed or developing countries: 0.34 percent in India compared to an average of 0.98 percent elsewhere (Pricewaterhouse Coopers press release, 2006). But 30 to 40 million people

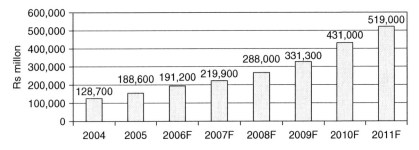

Figure 15.1   Projected growth of Indian television industry
Source: Industry estimates and PwC Analysis
(cited in FICCI–Pricewaterhouse Coopers 2007 report, p. 23).

join the "middle class" every year and illustrate "consumption patterns associated with rising income" (Pricewaterhouse Coopers report, 2006, p. 3). Consumption and leisure spending in terms of demand for commodities such as mobile phones, cars, credit goods, televisions, music systems and other goods are expected to increase. Private televisions therefore focus on new subscribers from urban and semi-urban areas—initiating them into the new world of consumption and choice navigation that reflects upward social mobility. The market makes it necessary to invoke the "ordinary individual" (rather than the affluent elite) as a legitimate actor in an emerging India—buzzing with entrepreneurial energy and profit-driven ambitions that fuel new consumptions and signify social mobility.

The world of private television, with its premium entertainment menu, global program formats and multiple viewing choices, offers more than a break from DD's lackluster programming and national-developmental agenda. It connects the "ordinary" Indian to a new way of life in a new, market-driven India. It is therefore important to ask what narratives of change are being offered to viewers in a fast-changing India and how the discursive claims define its progressive potential.

"Reality shows" on Indian television

The rapid growth of private satellite television industry in India was marked by the unprecedented popularity of a single program: *Kaun Banega Crorepati* (*KBC*)—the Hindi reproduction of the globally franchised format for *Who Wants to be a Millionaire*. The successful run of the program yanked its private network—Star TV—to the number one position in the television industry. According to a TAM study in 2000, Star TV's channel share went up from 2 percent to 25 percent for the 9 to 10 PM day part when *KBC* was broadcast. In the second season (2005), the channel share was 10 percent four weeks prior to telecast and increased to 38 percent with *KBC*'s telecast (*Business Today*, 2006). When *KBC* III was launched in 2007 it took the channel's share from 12.4 percent to 24.36 percent (Krishna, 2007). Other entertainment networks followed a similar strategy of reproducing success-ful global formats or introducing original formats – making reality shows a mainstay on Indian television.

Reality shows do not automatically guarantee success. But a reality format generates viewer interactivity and a unique opportunity for the network to establish its brand (that is not as accessible in linear program formats like soap operas, dramatic serials etc). In 2004, for instance, when the network Sony TV launched *Indian Idol* the senior vice president for marketing announced to the press that "The two critical words for *Indian Idol* are – involvement and entertainment" (Adesara, 2004). Sony's executive vice president for programming argued eloquently: "This is not just about who sings best. It is about who makes the nation sing" (Indiantelevision.com, 2004). However, the vast majority in the "nation" still cannot afford the average monthly subscription fee of Rs. 100 to Rs. 150 for Sony TV and other C&S networks. Poverty, malnutrition, and infant-mortality levels have been increasing at alarming rates in India (Global Hunger Index, 2006). But the Indian middle class itself constitutes a significantly large market for advertisers and corporate clients of private television networks. By invoking a "nation," of paying consumers from the middle classes, Sony TV creates a new world of aspirations and competencies for India at large. The realm of possibilities in this "nation" constructed on and through Sony TV allows ordinary individuals to seek unprecedented fame and multi million rupees of prize monies or simply consumption patterns that suggest participation in such an exciting new world. The first season of *India Idol* drew over 55 million votes (Miditech press release, 2007) and secured Sony TV as a serious contender in the industry—majority of votes came from small towns and areas outside the metropolitan cities.

It is significant to note that unlike Europe and the US, reality shows did not enter India in the context of cost cutting and creative labor strikes. Investments associated with the high scale of production, licensing fee and telephony infrastructure needed to host viewer participation in *KBC*, the first reality show on Indian television, was relatively higher. But the high "price point" was meant to signify a premium media product, and perhaps more significantly, a commitment to the Indian market made in the name of a national narrative of change. As a network executive with Star TV (part of Rupert Murdoch's News Corporation) declared to the press: "To me this is not about money. Ratings and revenue are a by product … Indian TV has to rise out of the Rs. 7–8 *lakh* (Hindi term for 100,000) bracket … look at the licensing and merchandising that accompanies *Baywatch* or *Ally McBeal*. This can happen here also. I passionately believe Indians are a global community. We have to adopt a global approach" (Aiyar and Chopra, 2000). Implicit is the idea that it is not only necessary to learn and adopt the sophisticated norms of the market (high-scale budgets, elaborate licensing and merchandising deals) if India is to fulfill its leadership potential, but it is in effect a legitimate goal to be a part of the global market-driven economy. Any discussion for alternative strategies of global community building, social interaction or reorganization of social relations becomes outside the scope of viable, reasonable possibilities.

Correspondences between the political-economic settings and the market-driven social milieu on reality shows do not suggest a causal mechanism between what transpires on television screens and its social impact. Social transformation is impacted by more than the television experience. Similarly, the popularity of reality-game shows may be influenced by a variety of reasons, including its new-ness, relation with film industry, celebrity appeal etc. But a media-centric analysis offers a unique everyday context to understand how cultural forms intersect with social contexts to render new realities. To that end, this chapter distinguishes the relationship between cultural products, such as reality-game shows, and the political-economic transformations in India. In exploring the social situated-ness of the television experience, the attempt is to understand how cultural processes may mediate and reshape social change. Consider the following sections.

The individual over the collective

The game structure of reality shows prioritizes the individual as the only legitimate actor. The quest for the final reward is almost always an individual journey—the test of an individual's dream, will power, hard work, talent and endurance. In *KBC*, ten participants compete for the "Fastest Finger First" round, in each episode. The winner is invited to walk across to the main stage to be on the "Hotseat"—away from other contestants and at the center of attention. She must then answer a series of 15 increasingly difficult questions leading to the prize money. The questions are accompanied by four possible answers and the contestant must choose one correct answer. If unsure, she may access four "Lifeline" options called "Audience Poll" (that is take the studio audience's opinion), "Phone a friend" (who may provide the correct answer), "50-50" (that is, limit answer options to two) and "Flip the question" (that is change the question). In each scenario the final decision again rests on the individual, that is, whether to accept the suggestions made by the audience, the friend or select from a reduced number of options. Similarly in *Indian Idol*, individuals compete through different music rounds. Three (on average, though there may be more members on the jury) judges evaluate the performances and offer their comments and preferences before candidates face public voting—to be eliminated from the show or be promoted to the next round of competition. The test of an individual's performance is however more than his singing talent. He must also appeal, to judges and viewers alike, in terms of "personality" (including manner of speech, dressing, body language etc.) and prove his potential to become a celebrity worthy of glossy magazines and lifestyle-product endorsement deals.

   Camera angles, lighting, sitting arrangements, musical accent and other creative aspects of the production also emphasize the individual—and moments of dramatic anxiety, euphoria or failure on the individual's face. In the intimacy of close up camera shots what matters is qualities like decisiveness, confidence and agency of individual players. The background is darkened as the individual performs under the spotlight in the studio, camera zooms in on close shots and our attention is fixed on an individual's tryst with destiny. The historical and social contexts of the individual's action fade away; instead the private space of the individual's talent and agency towards lifestyle aspirations, maximizing happiness and optimizing success is emphasized. In a narrative centered around personal responsibility, self discipline, free choice and self sufficiency, the contestants and their actions are measured against "the order of the self" (Murray and Ouellette, 2004).

Certain performance rounds in *Indian Idol* require singing in duets. But candidates are evaluated for individual contribution, whereby the drama often emerges from the individual's talent and ambition being frustrated by a team member who either lacks initiative, discipline, talent or requisite personality. There may be a noticeable kinship between participants on the show due to shared experiences but performing in any collective is understood to be inhibitive. Similarly on *KBC*, special episodes for festivals may feature teams of two (couples, or father and daughter, or young woman with her grandmother, or simply two friends) in celebration of family values and togetherness. But traditional norms of social relations confront the modern need to find an individual voice in order to win. When Manmohan, an engineer from New Delhi, sat on the "hot seat" as a participant along with his young daughter it was announced that if they win he would decide how to spend the money. The family hierarchy is thus undisturbed, and if anything it is reasserted in the context of negotiation. But Ruchika, the daughter, constantly "agrees" or "disagrees" with her teammate – her father – on the questions posed to them. She overrides her father's decisions on occasions, projects her educated and informed capabilities in doing so and suggests her sense of being comfortable with the times, while her father sits back and lets the new generation answer. By bringing to the fore the modern social realities, the show also gains favor of younger audiences—many of whom, like Ruchika, are from the young urban professional middle class and are learning to make decisions on their own with much on stake. Without alienating the existing norms of social relations a new order is introduced in which the human "will" to succeed is asserted as necessary and progressive in order to navigate the rules of changing times.

Central to neoclassical economics, which is the foundation of the theory of the social in neoliberal thought, is the idea of rational, self-interested individual as the basis of all economic activity. Only the individual is recognized as the legitimate actor, whether it is dealing with companies, trade unions or families. Bourdieu argues that this allows neoliberal discourse to "embark on a program of methodical destruction of *collectives*" (Bourdieu, 1998, pp. 95–6, original emphasis). In the 2001 budget, for instance, the then Finance Minister proposed de-protecting organized labor. Companies with less than 1000 workers (versus the existing cap of less than 100) could hire contractual employees without any obligation to provide permanent positions; could sack employees without government consent; and could be sold or liquidated with greater ease. The arguments supporting such positions claimed that dismantling the trade unions "clamoring for rights" will free private enterprise and create more growth opportunities (Barman, 2001). But as state services are privatized, public-sector units are disinvested, and companies cut jobs or offer contractual positions to stay competitive, the sense of unrest that emerges from being disconnected from the securities of life must be redefined in terms of a new system of thought. Reality game shows enable rearticulation and reimagination in terms of the opportunities (spectacular prize monies), values (focus on winning at all costs), actors (individual players) and strategies (competitive formats) of a market-driven society. A social milieu emerges in which the state's role in regulating socioeconomic activities is considered inhibitive of individual ambition; while market competition provides the logic for social relations.

Competition over participation

Reality shows feature competition as the means to a projected end. The dramatic tension arising from the individual's struggle to stay competitive and pursue success with a "do-or-die" spirit sustains a show's appeal. In *Indian Idol* season 3 for instance, the final contestants are often referred to as "*yuddhas*" (warriors) in a make or break "*mukabala*" (contest). News reports of the highly popular finale episode were also titled as the "biggest battle of this year" in media outlets (CNN-IBN special report, 2007). Both the finalists came from socioeconomically humble backgrounds from the northeastern states of India. The northeast shares a geographically, socially and politically distant, neglected—and often strained—relationship with mainland India. It was therefore remarkable that both participants in the finale came from the region for a show, which was out to find "*Bharat ki shaan*" (Pride of India). Both finalists also shared a special friendship, which was highlighted throughout the show as their spirit for healthy competition. But there was no ambiguity over what was at stake for them: winning the *Indian Idol* title and the Rupees 10 million music-recording contract with Sony was their one shot at redefining their lives. So compete they must.

Embedded in the framework of competition is the idea that resources (or prize monies) are limited and scarce; there can be only one winner (others must lose); it is necessary to fight for the top spot (struggle and sacrifice must be endured); and that the fittest will survive (while the weakest must accept their failing merit). In a country where bureaucratic control, corruption and social hierarchy have been systemized, the transparent and merit-based appeal of competition signifies opportunity and change. Merit or reward for one who earns and deserves it are associated with liberal notions of competition and individual ambition; while corrupt and inhibitive ways are associated with the state and notions of collective administration. The de-historicized, de-socialized and hence unshackled and liberated individual must be allowed to compete (and win or lose) based on his or her individual competencies and merit. Market-driven values of individual ambition, risk taking, losing or winning and playing with no guarantees are accommodated into everyday life on entertainment television.

It must be clarified though that viewers are often aware that the reality presented on "reality shows" is a result of manipulations at different levels (such as editorial decisions by producers, dictates of program sponsors, predetermined settings or targeted voting campaigns organized by "fan-following" or communities driven by parochial sentiments). Hence, it is implicitly understood and explicitly discussed on media reports that the most "deserving" contestant may not always win. But studies show that audiences are concerned less with "actuality" or "reality rendition" and more with how certain elements are depicted as real (Corner cited in Murray and Ouellette, 2004). Analytically, what matters is not what is real or not, but how certain elements are depicted as real and how such depictions interact with participant–viewer agency to render new social imaginaries meaningful.

In *Indian Idol* season 3, media reports revealed how regional ties were invoked to organize voting campaigns. The winner, Prashant Tamang's Nepali background prompted aggressive voting from Nepalese people both within and across India's border; in Nepal the timings of the domestic talent-hunt-reality show *Nepali Tara* (Nepal's Star) was changed to allow Nepalese people watch a fellow Nepali (though Indian citizen) compete in *Indian Idol* (Bamzai, 2007). In a society marked with socio-cultural differences (including class, language, region, religion, caste, ethnicity etcetera), reality-game shows in India have often provoked communities to mobilize support for "their" candidates. But the display of social ties does not challenge or negate the framework for action: that is, competition. On the contrary, community support for the success of a single individual reiterates the idea that individual ambition and rigors of competition must be celebrated as rewarding and forward looking. Those chasing individual dreams have a chance at fame and profit; those seeking collective rights—political, social or economic—are behind the times. The web site for the production company behind *Indian Idol* announces the show as "an incredible prospect for the youth of India to compete with each other" (Miditech press release, 2007). Competition is the new framework for participation.

Rewards and risks

Reality shows offer a reward structure that is laden with potential pitfalls of choice-and-risk taking. Strategic use of individual agency and competency can earn the ultimate prize but the path to the final reward must be navigated through a series of risky choices. In *Indian Idol* contestants must select the "right" song to find the popular pulse and motivate voting in their favor. If they are required to sing particular songs they must be lucky enough to get a song that "works" for their individual voice and personality.

In *KBC* the element of risk taking is more pronounced and deliberate: contestants begin a game of question–answer rounds with small amounts of money. The sum of money is approximately doubled at each subsequent question round till it reaches the final jackpot amount of Rupees 10 million. The prize money is however not cumulative which makes it necessary for the participant to decide whether she is going to gamble losing the sum she may have already earned by attempting the next question or not. Playing the game requires risk taking. But the opposite is also true: taking risks, itself, signals participation. Risking taking is necessary if one is to progress; simultaneously refusing to risk reflects lack of ambition to move forward.

In *KBC* II, Surinder Mittal, a software engineer from Mumbai participating on the show, was faced with the choice to either leave the game with the Rupees 50 thousand he had earned or continue playing. In the next round, if he answered correctly he could double his prize money, otherwise lose the entire amount. He decides to take a chance. His argument for doing so: "*aaj ke zamane mein risk lenna parta hai – nahi to aage kaise barenge?*," that is, "one has to take risks these days – otherwise one can not move ahead in life."

Outside the studio, Surinder Mittal's real-life decisions follow similar patterns. In an era of fluid capital and venture capitalists, concepts such as job-for-life and secured pension plans are being replaced by a worldview of "risk-taking." There are no guarantees anymore but there is the promise of possibility. Alongside, the rhetoric of deregulation, liberalization and privatization as a necessary risk, if India is to compete in the global economy, resonate with similar logic. On prime time entertainment television, however, the world of reality shows allows risks to emerge as a matter of choice and not compulsion. Risk taking can be viewed without addressing the imperatives of the political and economic order that shape it. A new cultural ethos of risk taking emerges as naturalized and common sense, while the liberal tendency—and political need—to de-historicize and de-socialize visions of the social world (Bourdieu, 1998) recedes into the background.

Common man and uncommon consumption

Reality shows invoke the idea of ordinary individuals surmounting extraordinary challenges. But the end goal is always determined in terms of the monetary and consumer rewards, whether in cash prizes, in luxury goods or professional–financial contracts. Irrespective of the hybrid genre (for example, game shows, quiz shows, dramatic narratives, and talent searches, etc.) what remains central to "reality shows" is the idea that real people can participate on the show to earn real money. Social distinction is defined in terms of private consumption, and vice versa. In *Indian Idol* for instance, the winners of season 1 and 2 are featured in season 3 to showcase the difference in their lifestyle. One of the winners from the previous season takes viewers for a tour of his newly acquired palatial house in Mumbai. He says to the camera, "*pahela mere pass kuch bhi nahi tha, ab eah sab hai*" ("earlier I did not have anything, now I have all this"). Success is directly evaluated in terms of the new material possessions: a new house in a city with one of the highest real estate prices in the world reflects the difference between being a "common man" and a respectable singer; while the finalists of the season 3 are showcased at shopping malls where media events are organized to reveal the preferred brands of the budding celebrities.

On special episodes of *KBC*, celebrities may play the game for "charitable causes" but the focus again is on how big an amount can they accumulate, and how much can they give. In season III, the film star Shah Rukh Khan who hosts the show expressed his empathy for a participant who wins many rounds of questions but loses at the final round by taking off an expensive luxury watch from his wrist and thrusting it into the hands of the contestant as a "consolation" prize. The following day media reports discuss the superstar's generosity along with details on the brand of the watch, its cost and style quotient. The premium world of private consumption is thus made accessible for the ordinary individual, not only by winning or participating on reality show but also by viewing and learning. New set of competencies are offered for the viewer that define identity formation in terms of consumption patterns. Simultaneously, PricewaterhouseCoopers 2006 report on Indian entertainment and media industry invites transnational corporations to invest by stating the market potential: "In India's urban areas, the consumer mindset is changing due to increased exposure to global influence via media and other interactions leading to higher aspirations which have provided a further fillip to leisure related spending" (PricewaterhouseCoopers report, 2006, p. 4).

Consumption and citizenship has been analytically linked so that consumption, as a selection of goods and appropriation of goods, is defined by what we consider valuable and how we want to integrate and distinguish ourselves in society (See Luke earlier in the volume for similar conceptualization). A new form of citizenship is created through the consumption patterns and answered in the private realm of commodity consumption and the mass media, more than in the abstract rules of democracy or collective participation in public spaces (Garcia-Canclini, 2001). Reality shows provide new aspirations centered on the market and consumption, both on screen and beyond. Media reports attribute reality shows for sparking a "luck-and-buck" "craze" behind the growing phenomenon of quizzes, scratch-card freebies, online punting and lottery schemes being offered by consumer markets with the purchase of products (Ray, 2000). The article goes on to cite a psychiatrist explaining the phenomenon as: "This is a change which Indians are experiencing over the last decade or so. Unlike the previous socialist-driven environment wherein giving up was considered a thing of style, the current system encourages acquisition as the call of the day. You need almost anything and everything to remain in control of your situation" (Ray, 2000, p. 40). A new socio-cultural framework emerges at the level of everyday practices that mediates the shift towards a liberal market economy.

Conclusion

Analysis of reality shows provide a point of entry into understanding India's social transformations towards a market-oriented society. Reality shows articulate certain discourses of reality, representation and change at

a moment of national transition. Analysis of the shows *KBC* and *h.*
and discussions on the public sphere (identified in terms of news re‌p
opinion pieces, talk shows), suggest correspondences between the discourses
of social change on the reality shows and political–economic policy shifts in
India. Cultural forms and practices, such as reality shows on India's thriving
private television networks, facilitate new frameworks to make sense of, and
accept the social changes.

The high 9 percent growth rate of the Indian economy (in the last few
years); the pool of skilled professionals and entrepreneurial energy that
promises continued growth for the Indian market has caught the attention
of the world. But India also labors under contradictions: 27 percent of the
population or 301 million people live below the poverty line at less than
one dollar a day, while the top 20 percent earns more than all others put
together (Aiyar, 2007). It remains to be seen whether the new cultural forms
can mediate the stark differences in material and socio-cultural power to
sustain social and national cohesion. But in the meantime analysis of reality shows suggest that new material and ideational frameworks appear on
prime time entertainment television to render changing realities as familiar
and meaningful.

16
"The Power to Narrate": Film Festivals, a Platform for Transnational Feminism?

Jasmine Champenois

> Black women have been silent for too long. Are they now beginning to find their voices? Are they claiming the right to speak for themselves? Is it not high time that they discovered their own voices ...?
>
> —*Awa Thiam (1986, p. 11)*

Scholars and activists of "third wave feminism"[1] have now accepted the idea of difference and multiple identities. This has fragmented their political discourse, as Lovenduski (1993) notes: "once the diversity of women is recognised and privileged over their commonality, no appeal to collective action can be addressed to common womanhood" (p. 91). Feminism's complex and diverse theoretical frame has thus come to mean little in terms of a unified political agenda. "A central problem within feminist discourse has been our inability to either arrive at a consensus of opinion about what feminism is or accept definition(s) that could serve as points of unification" (Hooks 1984).

Despite these observations, alternative strategic coalitions across class, ethnicity and national boundaries do exist, and it is my aim to identify and explore them as evidence of emerging transnational sites of feminist advocacy.

When Black Sisters speak out[2]

In the late 1970s, non-Western feminists began criticizing the women's movement and its scholarship for being racist and overly concerned with white middle-class women's issues. They argued that the form of theorizing found in second wave feminists' writings had reinforced the image of non-Western women in negative ways. Mohanty has summed it up powerfully:

> Third World women as a group or as a category are automatically and necessarily defined as: religious (read "not progressive"), family oriented (read

"traditional"), legal minors (read "still-not-conscious-of-their-rights"), illiterate (read "ignorant"), domestic (read "backward") and sometimes revolutionary (read "their country-is-in-a-state-of-war, they must fight!"). This is how the Third World difference is produced. (1988, p. 214)

Spivak (1988) has also elaborated on the "colonised woman" as a "subject of investigation" for biased Western feminists whom she sees as patronizing. "What can I do for her?" they ask, and not "what can we do together?"

Given this tension between self-representation and representation by others, critics like Carby, Spivak, and Mohanty encourage non-Western women to insert themselves into mainstream feminist discourse by speaking for themselves, particularly concerning traditions and customs such as early marriage, polygamy and Female genital mutilation (FGM). This, indeed, they have done, especially on the fraught issue of female genital assaults.

A divisive issue: FGM

Cutting of female genitalia has persisted for generations and, in some areas, is becoming more widespread and violent. According to the World Health Organisation (1996), about 130 million women are circumcized, and thousands die each year, as a result, in childbirth or from infections and hemorrhaging. The United Nations has recognized FGM and early marriage as violence to girls and women and has labeled them "harmful traditional practices." Several UN conventions see them a violation of human rights and injurious to the health, rights and well-being of women and girls (Heinonen 2001).[3]

In spite of this global concern, accounts of women who have undergone FGM show that the practice is deeply embedded, implying that change will be slow. Mackie explains this situation by the "process of reactance": "when a freedom to act is threatened or actually denied, reactance motivates attempts to protect or to regain the freedom of action" (1999, p. 3). Therefore, what may be perceived as Western-inspired exhortations has been known to elicit a defensive hostility that actually promotes the practice, rationalized as beneficial because it fulfils (misunderstood) religious obligations, ensures hygiene, guarantees proper sexual conduct and preserves family "honour." As Paula Heinonen notes, "Wherever it is practiced, FGM is not perceived as harmful to girls. It bestows social acceptance and high status not only [on] the girls but [on] the family as well" (2001, p. 10). Therefore although the Bamako Declaration, the Inter-African Committee and the Maputo Protocol all call the cutting "barbaric"—and these are African documents and institutions—care should be taken to avoid fuelling accusations of Western racist influence on attitudes towards abolition. For instance, some Egyptian religious leaders favorable to FGM accuse Western feminists fighting FGM of plotting the destruction of Muslim family structures and customs (Memri 2003).

Nonetheless struggles against FGM take place not only in international forums, but also among local populations, notably in Africa (MEMRI 2003; Heinonen 2001; Mackie 1999) where women's movements are active. As a matter of fact, "les mouvements féminins en Afrique militent ouvertement en faveur de l'abolition des mutilations sexuelles (...) la lutte se poursuit dans toute l'Afrique, que ce soit sur le plan politique, littéraire ou artistique." [Women's movements within Africa campaign actively against FGM. The fight goes on everywhere on the continent and includes politics, literature and artistic creation].[4]

Creative methods of fighting against harmful practices have gained a new momentum. For example, films, songs and plays are widely used in Sub-Saharan Africa to raise awareness among rural populations.[5] Documentaries including *La Duperie* (Burkina Faso) or *Ma fille ne sera pas excisée* (Bourema Niwema), produced by local activist groups are shown in villages. These educational programmes are subsidized by international organizations (WHO, UNICEF) but have not (yet) had the expected impact (Mackie 1999; Herzberger-Fofana, 2005).

Pioneering artistic work by Malian filmmaker Cheikh Omar Sissoko[6] has had more success in raising awareness of the harmful effect of FGM. Released internationally in 1989, his fictional film (*Finzan*) has encouraged other voices within Africa. Notably, in 1994, documentary films by Zara Mahamat Yacoub, *Dilemme au Féminin* (Chad) and Anne-Laure Folly's *Femmes aux yeux ouverts* (Togo) are now recognized as major contributions to African cinema[7] and the discourse on FGM. Both creative and political, these types of documentaries enable African women to speak for themselves to both African and international audiences.

Women's voices in international film festivals

> Power and status are signified through spatial and temporal dimensions of exhibition, a central process through which media help constitute and reflect social and religious difference[s] in [the] nation-state.
>
> Ginsburg, Abu-Lughod, and Larkin (2002, p. 7)

In 1992, Anne-Laure Folly, an international lawyer from Togo, decided to make films in order to "enlighten people about the African continent." She thought that African culture was too often unknown to or stereotyped by Westerners[8] and hoped to encourage more Africans to express themselves because "power comes from those who say things."[9] *Femmes aux Yeux Ouverts* (*Women with Open Eyes*) is her documentary portraying contemporary African women from Burkina Faso, Mali, Senegal and Benin. The complex and self-reflexive narration of their daily lives enables the protagonists to discuss issues such as marital rights, reproductive health and FGM, women's role in the economy and their political rights. These women organize themselves at the grassroots levels and thus challenge the stereotypical portrayal of African women as passive and victimized females.

Dilemme au féminin (Chad) by Zara Mahamat Yacoub raises the same issues and uses oral testimonies from women involved in the practice of FGM. Unlike speakers in *Women with Open Eyes*, Yacoub had to film her subjects veiled to protect their anonymity. In Yacoub, images are also deliberately violent, emphasizing the pain induced by such practices. Removal of a little girl child's clitoris is filmed. No discourse is necessary in light of such powerful visuals.

Where these films were shown interests us as much as their content. As Ginsburg states above, the dimensions of display frame both the discourse and its reception. The site of exhibition becomes not only a platform, a stage to raise voices, but also a site of resistance that gives power to narrate.

Interestingly both films won prestigious prizes in Western film festivals and have enabled the two African women directors to gain international recognition. The prestigious Pan African Film Festival, *Fespaco*, held in Ouagadougou in 1995, awarded Yacoub the "Club du Sahel" prize, an honor that brought the filmmaker to the attention of smaller film festivals like *Blackmovie* in Geneva which in turn organized discussions on the issue of FGM. Folly's and Yacoub's movies are also shown in American and European university classrooms and at the occasion of public conferences. In interviews, both women filmmakers expressed their commitment to use cinema as a medium to talk about the experience of girls and women from their countries.

Both documentaries have also been screened in West Africa at the Centres Culturel Français (French Cultural Institutes) and cinematic tours to villages have been sponsored by NGOs. After receiving international acclaim and prizes, Chad aired *Dilemme au féminin*. As the Fatwa enacted against Yacoub demonstrates, the screenings generated vigorous debate. Her life continues to be threatened many years after her documentary's release on national television. Nonetheless she stated later: "No matter what problems I encounter, what is essential is to convey a message. And the message is delivered. That is what was crucial for me. This is my role, it was my duty."[10]

When asked about the importance of film festivals in Europe and in the US, both Folly and Yacoub stress the benefits: "African films are viewed in large festivals, in large cinema houses with larger and larger audiences. Now, when one speaks of cinema, African cinema cannot be ignored, and that is a good thing."[11] An international film festival is usually an entertaining event featuring major productions but also independent films outside commercial distribution channels. It also draws in a significant number of journalists and marketing sites for films (posters, premiere, press conferences, etc.). Now, festivals vary according to their objectives and institutional category. Major events like Cannes and Venice are notably renowned for glamour and film competitions. African cinema is also represented in these international fairs under a "Southern films" or "world cinema" flag. At the 2004 Cannes festival, for instance, African director Ousmane Sembène won the selective prize "Un Certain Regard" for his fiction film entitled *Moolaadé* which condemns FGM. Community festivals are usually smaller and are targeted at a specific audience and, indeed, there are too many festivals devoted to African films in Europe and in the US to count. What is problematic, however, as the African film festival of New York illustrates, is the fact that these community events attract mainly a Western audience curious about otherness and authorship.

Although these events are not without faults, they have indubitably become a significant site of transnational cultural gatherings. Press coverage can be local, national and international and competition films may attract film critics and buyers from afar. It is not unusual, for instance, to find professionals such as filmmakers, producers, TV programmers and technical industry agents travelling all year long from festival to festival, meeting in February in Ouagadougou (Burkina Faso), May in Cannes (France) and November in Sundance (the US). For independent filmmakers, the festival circuit is the most effective alternative global distribution network.

Thus festivals also enable women filmmakers from Africa to gather, receive information and get publicity. Directors are invited by the festival organizers to promote their films. Film festivals like the Fespaco (Burkina Faso, 1995), Festival Francophone de Namur (Belgium, 2002), Festival International du Film d'Amiens (France, 2003) organized workshops aimed specifically at women filmmakers in order to train them and enable them to forge networks.[12] "We meet at festivals. Each woman knows where she wants to go and what she wants to say and do."[13]

Following the successful example of Burkina Faso's film festival (Fespaco), others are now being created in Sub-Saharan African countries like Benin, Senegal, Ivory Coast, Mali, South Africa, and Zanzibar.[14] These festivals are intended mostly to connect local African film directors with other African television producers and encourage movie productions not necessarily intended for Western audiences. It is too early to know what will be the place for women film directors within this new circle.

In any event, because African films remain poorly distributed, festivals are crucial to all filmmakers, male and female. The format of these events often allows a space for directors to talk with their audiences. Political agendas sometimes emerge: for instance, during *Les Journées du Cinéma Africain et Créole* of 1999 (Montreal), a group of women involved in the media (Yacoub among them) published a common statement, aimed at strengthening their involvement in promoting human rights and freedom of speech.[15]

Collective activism involving women from different countries is not rare. Cockburn describes cases of women's coalitions for peace in Bosnia-Herzegovina and of groups like Women in Black (Israel/Palestine).[16] For her, "transversal politics is a conceptual move to get around and above the immobilising contradiction ... between a dangerous belief in universal sisterhood and a relativist stress on difference that dooms us to division and fragmentation" (1998, p. 8). Co-operative actions are driven not by homogeneity but by recognition of participants' specific positioning. In the case of filmmakers, women directors are concerned not only with their own careers, but also with voices they release among marginalized people. Yet, as Spivak points out: what matters is not [only] who speaks but also who listens. Transversal dialogues can lack neutrality: women's discourse captured on camera may trigger further misunderstanding induced by the state of *being looked at*.

The gaze that matters: The power to look

> Now I am not only given ... permission to open up and talk, I am also encouraged to express my difference. My audience expects and demands it; otherwise people would feel they have been cheated: We did not come to hear a Third World member speak about the First (?) World [.] We came to listen to that voice of difference likely to bring us what we can't have and to divert us from the monotony of sameness.
>
> Trinh Minh-ha (1989, p. 88)

In Freudian thought, the gaze denotes voyeurism and exhibitionism.[17] Images of FGM may well appeal to voyeuristic tendencies, the necessarily violent footage offensive to some African women. Once again, the continent where genital torture takes place appears backward and barbarian; stereotypes are reinforced. Such images therefore risk achieving the opposite of their intent: allowing the West to bask in its own civility, modernity, and superiority. Edward Said has shown how the definition of a periphery enables the West to be defined as the centre. This also resonates in the ongoing discourse between white and black feminisms, West versus East or first versus third world, and helps us to understand the reaction of African residents of the US who criticized the activist Alice Walker. Her video against FGM was said to be "emblematic of the Western feminist tendency to see female genital mutilation as the gender oppression to end all oppressions ... a gauge by which to measure distance between the West and the rest of humanity."[18]

Thus the power to narrate seems to be in tension with the power "to look at." A new form of relationship emerges between the viewers and the viewed, and negative consequences may prove deleterious to feminist alliance across cultures. Nonetheless diversity of sex, class and racial backgrounds, once recognized, can still generate political involvement.

A need for "coalition politics"[19]: Transnational solidarity

> In Africa, there is a tendency to reject everything that comes from the outside that puts one's "culture" in question. This makes our role even

more important. But this does not mean that we Africans must exclude our European and America sisters from this struggle. Because of immigration, female genital mutilation is practiced just about everywhere in the world. Thus social awareness about it and the struggle against it must not be limited only to African countries.

> Zara Mahamat Yacoub, in Ellerson (2000, p. 345)

Although women increasingly express their differences, they are also inclined to articulate "connectedness"[20] in creative ways such as music, art and collective endeavor. Film festivals exemplify platforms open for debate and encounters with the "other." Folly and Yacoub have demonstrated that an issue like female genital mutilation can be discussed by communities from varied backgrounds. Both have found a way not only to express them internationally and locally, but also to give voice to marginalized women in Africa.[21]

Although Mohanty has criticized Western feminist thought for stereotyping "third world women," she also stresses the political necessity of strategic coalitions across class, ethnic and national boundaries. The union does not need spring from a common experience as women but from the need for political solidarity (1994, pp. 196–219). What is now called transnational feminism is therefore a collective strategy of resistance that acknowledges power asymmetries.

A coalition of this new type has arisen around the issue of FGM. After the United Nations Conferences in Cairo and Beijing, major international donors and UN agencies (such as WHO, UNICEF, UNAIDS and the World Bank) began to support non-governmental organizations in their campaigns against female genital mutilation. FGM is now at the core of international texts arguing for women's sexual and reproductive health and rights, for instance in the United Nations Declaration for the Elimination of Violence against Women (1993).

International advocacy groups have also flourished in major African capitals. The Inter-African Committee based in Addis-Ababa and the Foundation for Women's Health and Development (FORWARD) in London are raising awareness at national and international levels to prevent FGM, early marriages, and harmful practices. The use of short-film and documentaries has been one way to raise awareness not only locally on the African continent, but also in the main capitals of Europe. Levin (1999; 2000), by working with immigrant populations who import harmful practices from their home nations, has shown the importance of placing FGM on the human rights agenda of Western countries. The video catalogue distributed by FORWARD is the central pillar of this necessary dissemination of information in the main educational institutions of the UK.

In order to stimulate awareness internationally, most advocacy groups encourage the distribution of publications, videos, lectures and workshops on FGM.[22] In many African countries, for instance Ethiopia, female lawyers, doctors and activists have formed autonomous organizations, which prioritize women's and children's issues by means of education.

Needless to say, this "coalition politic" needs to hear and provide a platform to those who practice and follow custom, for their experience is undoubtedly key to solving the problem. And Pierrette Herzerber-Fofana was correct to add: "Les mouvements africains saluent tout acte de solidarité émanant des pays du Nord, mais sont unanimes pour se démarquer de toute ingérence à tendance raciste ou publicitaire qui donne la primauté aux images chocs et au ton agressif." [African movements welcome any act of solidarity from Northern Countries, but unanimously reject racist or publicity-seeking propaganda that uses shocking images and aggressive tones.] [23]

Filmmakers like Folly and Yacoub aim to stimulate debate at an international level. Anne-Laure Folly continues her struggle by producing documentaries against religious extremism (*Femmes du Niger*) and violence against women in time of war (*Les Oubliées*). Zara Mahamat Yacoub has been concerned with children in time of war (*Les Enfants de la guerre*) and street children (*Les Enfants de la rue*). These two directors illustrate the strength and abilities of women from "beyond the West" to express their views through courageous statements and portrayals of activism in so-called developing countries. Film festivals allow them a "room of their own" where messages are conveyed through artistic work. Both sides of the screen are offered a space for debate and disagreement. This expansion of the discourse on women's rights challenges the boundaries between public and private, national and international. More than mere crossings, these interactions may establish and promote international feminist synergies.

Acknowledgements

I especially want to thank Dr. Paula Heinonen and Dr. Tobe Levin for their constructive comments on the draft. I am grateful to Shirley Ardener and the International Gender Studies Center of the University of Oxford for providing me with guidance and support.

Notes

1. Formalized in 1992, with the creation of the movements Women's Action Coalition and Third Wave.
2. From the title of Awa Thiam's book against FGM (1986), *Black Sisters, Speak Out! Feminism and Oppression in Black Africa* (*La Parole aux Négresses*), London, Pluto Press.
3. For instance, The Convention on the Rights of the Child (1989) was ratified by 191 countries but not by the US and Somalia.
4. Pierrette Herzberger-Fofana, *Excision et mouvements féminins*, available at www.arts.uwa.edu.au/AFLIT/MGFG.html, last visited in January 2005. Personal translation.

5. One example from among many: Sini Sanuman/Healthy Tomorrow produces music CDs and music videos in Mali (www.StopExcision.net) (accessed January 25, 2005).

6. Former Minister of Culture in Mali and ardent defender of cinema from Africa.

7. The term African cinema deserves more attention as it is rejected by some film-makers as a categorization. We use it here to address the work of those who explicitly describe themselves as African filmmakers.

8. Interview with Africultures 1999, available at www.africultures.com (accessed January 25, 2005).

9. Interview with Ellerson (2000, p. 95).

10. Interview with Ellerson (2000, p. 345).

11. Ibid., p. 350.

12. See for instance Femmimages, available at www.fiff.namur.be (accessed January 25, 2005) or l'Union Nationale des Femmes de l'Image du Burkina Faso, unafib@yahoo.fr (accessed January 25, 2005).

13. Folly, Interview with Ellerson (2000, p. 100).

14. See www.africaonline.co (accessed January 25, 2005) for more details on these African festivals.

15. Réseau d'information sur le développement et la démocratie en Afrique, *Les femmes du cinéma et des médias dans la promotion des droits et libertés*, 1999.

16. Women from Israel and from Palestine stood together silently in protest of the war. This form of mobilization took place all over the world in favor of peace.

17. The gaze has been analyzed since then by feminists like Laura Mulvey *Visual Pleasure and Narrative Cinema* (1989) to explore the assumed gaze of male hero and male director who render females the objects of male desire.

18. Seble Dawit and Salem Merkuria in Levin (1999, p. 242).

19. Term used by Chilla Bulbeck (1998).

20. Concept used by Bulbeck (1998) to express the gathering of ideas among feminists.

21. It is relevant to note at this point that Folly and Yacoub do not seem to declare themselves feminist activists.

22. For details on the various advocacy groups and international activism, see *Guidelines on the Prevention of FGM* (1996), Ministry of Foreign Affairs, Denmark and Paula Heinonen (2001), *Report on Early, Forced Marriages, Abduction (efma) and Their Links to Custom/Tradition, FGM, Poverty and HIV/Aids*.

23. Personal translation.

17
Everyday Cultural Politics, Syncretism, and Cultural Policy

Dennis Galvan

Cultural *policy*, designed and engineered by elites and states, should be understood in relation to an underlying cultural *politics*, processes of ongoing contestation implicating many actors, at all levels, in transformations of meaning, symbols, habits, values, and identity. As noted elsewhere in this volume, the politics of culture (let alone something as formal as cultural policy) has long been shackled to an essentialist, static, primordialist notion of culture itself, as a hard-wired cognitive and semiotic script, which undergirds human action and taken-for-granted routine. This is true in "old school" anthropology (Geertz, 1973), more "cutting edge" thinking on action and reflexivity (Bourdieu, 1977), the classics of political culture (Almond and Verba, 1963), mainstream institutionalism (Powell and DiMaggio, 1991), and the latest reincarnations of modernization theory in studies of global convergence (Inglehart and Welzel, 2005).

In the arena of cultural policy, we understand as a kind of truism that culture is not static, primordial, quasi-genetic or so ingrained in early childhood socialization that it cannot change or become the object of political contestation. We nod appropriately in the direction of the basic insights into the social construction of reality (Berger and Luckman, 1966) and the discursive turn in the humanities and social sciences (Saussure, 1966; Foucault, 1977; Sewell 1992). Yet we sometimes have a particular way of rethinking culture that can shade towards the apolitical.

In particular, recent work on postcolonialism and globalization encourages us to think of culture as open to the emergence, especially under late capitalism, of hybrid practices, values and identities (Garcia Canclini, 1995; Kraidy, 2005; Appadurai, 1996; Bhabha, 1994; Mulcahy, Chapter 13 and Champenois, Chapter 16). Hybridity, I argue, should make us pause as political scientists, for it inadvertently replaces one structuralism with a new one, and can sell short the human agency at the heart of a politics of culture.

As a botanical metaphor, hybridity suggests the emergence of new, blended species, varieties, forms, or bodies from formerly distinct origin types. But notice that within the hybridity discourse, the origin types remain extant, unperturbed, pure. Mendel's nineteenth-century hybrid peas and mice in no way impact their pure (and in his view, superior) origin varieties. Urbanization and industrialization may result in a proliferation of mixed race families, but how are whiteness, blackness, or other origin categories affected by this process? Recent contributions in critical race theory recognize the reification of dominant and prior pools or categories implicit in the hybridization discourse (Bruyneel, 2007, Sexton, 2008).

Moreover, the politics of agency within hybridity are elitist. What does it mean to make hybrids? How exactly does an abstraction like "globalization" induce hybridization? Hybrids may emerge "in nature," but here we eschew a theory of agency completely. Hybrids may be made, but this is the work of someone with special position, the ability to single out origin forms, remove them from their natural context ("cut them out and turn them over," for de Certeau) and deliberately mix them in a controlled way. In science, this is elite and distinctive power, in the hands of the botanist or now the geneticist. In culture, race, and identity, who does this work? Who holds this privileged position? Is it only those with elite authorial and artistic position?

The goal of deconstruction is to show that authorship and artistry are not only elite domains, but are ubiquitous, widespread, everyday. The artistry of creativity and mixing is not limited to the literati or the aesthetically well trained, but is somehow part of life and is something we the *hoi polloi* do as well. But the discourse of hybridity, with its implicit reifications and unintended elitism, gets in the way. We need a framing that entails a more complete and small-d democratic theory of action.

The creativity of action, cultural change and syncretism

Here John Dewey (2002 [1922]) and Michel de Certeau (1984) can help, pointing us in the direction of syncretism as an alternative way of thinking about cultural change and cultural politics. Dewey's notion of deliberation anchors a small-d democratic theory of action in which life itself entails creativity. When we act, we don't necessarily know our ends and choose the appropriate means. We act in light of a repertoire of prior and partially salient habits. These are not routines or mindless repetitions for Dewey. Habits are prior solutions that we or others have used to deal with problems that have more or less the same shape as the one that we face in the moment.

When we think about acting, about walking across the street to pet a dog, or sawing a piece of wood, or cutting costs in lean times, or offering a kiss, action emerges in light of a wide range of possible habits, ways we know that this situation has been dealt with before. These are often partial models. We instinctively and very rapidly look these over, consider how they work as a course of action, and cobble together what to do in the moment by combining bits and pieces from this or that prior model or habit. In so doing we lay down a new solution, a new model, a new habit. This becomes part of a socially shared repertoire of relevant prior habits, salient in the next action, the next similarly shaped problem. This applies from the mundane (Do I jaywalk just here to get to the cute puppy in time? How do I coo or click to get its attention?) to the profound (Does the budget crisis require all of these layoffs? Is furlough or jobshare an option here? Can we forego new computers another year to save one job?). Dewey teaches us that action itself is inherently creative (see also Rosenstein essay in this volume on Dewey).

You might say that de Certeau shares this phenomenological account of the creativity of action but "updates" it to take into account the weight of twentieth-century structuralisms, exemplified by the extreme case Foucault. Back to Dewey for a moment. He knew that life was not, as it could be, an endless stream of everyday artistic creativity. He attributed this to the short-circuiting of the deliberative process (the "normal" functioning of habit described in the previous paragraphs) by forms of education centered on rote repetition and authoritarian politics that to reserve deliberation to elites and convince masses to live only by mindless routine (pp. 64–74). Foucault would look at this Deweyian notion and see it as quaintly dewy-eyed. For him, the disciplinary structure of modernity itself meticulously and necessarily reproduces rote repetition, mindless routine, and the impossibility of deliberation as the taken-for-granted normalities that organize our existence. Although extreme in its totalization, Foucauldian structuralism is analogous to most twentieth-century structuralist accounts, from culture as unchanging primordial motivator of action (old Geertz, 1973 as much as North, 1981 on ideology), to cognitive schema and scripts as parameters of social behavior (more determinative in Powell and DiMaggio, 1991, looser in March and Olsen, 1989), to normal-times lock-in of path-dependent historical institutionalism (Pierson, 2004; Collier and Collier, 1991).

De Certeau says, yes, fine, much of social life is determined by those who occupy a distinct spatial position of power, from which they establish a "proper" ideal of the nature and order of action, which they then seek to extend over a domain of human activity. These "strategies" use the power to spatially order the sequence of action to gain control over time and by extension, action. Knowing where to place ourselves and what actions to take in particular spaces and times ensures that we understand and perform our predetermined roles in an order of military action, production, commuting, recreating, passive consumption, or political docility.

To this essentially Foucauldian (or if you will, institutionalist, or culturalist) account of the order or action, de Certeau adds the idea of tactics as a normal feature of everyday existence. We improvise. When we act, we have memories, lots of them. We may not have a spatial position of power or an ideal of the "proper" that we can expand – indeed, that's the normal reality of modernity. But we can piece together from a surplus of memory, of temporal resources, a clever remark, an improvisation, an alternative, a blow that is just right in the moment, even if it by itself may not change the order of things. We cook in light of structured predetermined recipes, but we improvise in the moments, throwing cumin in the oatmeal cookies because on that afternoon the cumin jar happens to be in front of the lazy Susan. We manage an organization in light of rules, roles and expectations, but effective managers improvise and experiment on the fly long before they codify and routinize (Weick, 2000). When we read, we read predetermined, authorially "strategic" texts. But we poach them into memory, reading out of order, or making associations with utterly irrelevant (from the author's point of view) ideas or experiences or feelings as we lay down a memory trace of the text in our minds. Reading is really a creative act of *experiencing* a text, not just following the strictures of the order of paragraphs, sentences, letters, ideas established by the necessarily strategic vision of the author. For de Certeau, that which started out as a strategic grid, a clear order, becomes, in light of ongoing tactical action, in light of lived experience, a torn and ruptured fabric, a sieve order.

Even if we cannot change the world, even if the power to make hybrids is kept from us, by being alive we engage in tactical action all the time. By being alive, we can and do deliberate and thus perturb, even just a little bit, the prior habits, institutions, norms, values, cultures in which we find ourselves. Thus, if cultural *policy* is for de Certeau strategic, life itself is an ongoing cultural *politics*. Cultural change is thus ubiquitous, but not as a function of the high artistry of the designer or the engineer, but as a function of the widely available, small-d democratic artistry embedded in the creative nature of action.

For these reasons, I find the imagery, discourse and connotations of syncretism, borrowed from religious anthropology,[1] useful in thinking about agency and the politics of culture. To act syncretically is to decompose extant forms and recombine them to make something novel. The origin forms are transgressed, violated, poached, taken apart, turned into raw material for the making of the syncretic alternative, whether it is Santeria or jazz. Syncretic agency is Deweyian and de Certeauian in precisely this sense of decomposition, recombination, transgression and play as central attributes of the process of change. Like Dewey's notion of habit or De Certeau's sieve order, the syncretic idea is cumulative: yesterday's syncretism shapes today's supposed orthodoxy (repertoire of habits; particular structure of the sieve order), and thus becomes the backdrop and raw material for tomorrow's next syncretic act.[2]

Syncretism thus accomplished three tasks, illustrated by empirical examples presented below from my ongoing fieldwork in Senegal, West Africa, and Central Java, Indonesia. First, it reconciles the structural/semiotic and agency/practice aspects of both culture and institutions by highlighting everyday creativity as actors take apart and pragmatically recombine systems of meaning, narrative structures, rules and organizations in an ongoing process of crafting new cultural and institutional forms. Second, syncretism undermines "one-size-fits-all" models of change, suggesting instead that cultural policies that promote "human rights," "electoral democracy," "free markets" and other vectors of "modernity" will, if they are to take root at all, be locally transformed in a syncretic process of sense-making that grounds these and other institutions in local notions of culture and historical memory. Finally, syncretism calls our attention as political scientists to a politics of contestation over meaning, struggles to define "authentic" culture, local "tradition" and legitimate "historical memory" as efforts to control the symbolic resources that actors use as they build syncretic forms of culture and institutions.

Syncretism in practice in Senegal and Indonesia

Four brief illustrations of syncretic institutional and cultural change, three derived from my two decades of research in Senegal, one from more recent work in Central Java, Indonesia, offer some empirical illustration of the kind of cultural politics described above.

First, in the early twentieth century, the French colonial regime in Senegal saw individuation of property relations and a free market in alienable land as essential to making Africans efficient producers of cash crops (peanuts, in this case). But farmers in a particular part of rural Senegal resisted privatization and alienability of land, largely, they say, because it would undermine soil fertility, ensure the end of rainfall, destroy farming, and thus, wipe out civilization as they knew it. Why this reactive traditionalism in the face of the modernization of land tenure?

In this part of rural Senegal, land had historically been neither individually owned nor communally held, but "managed" by a customary political leader/resource manager/shaman/adjudicatory authority known as a "master of fire." The original master of fire was a migrant who first settled the area, lighting a brush-clearing fire to open space for building houses and farming. He did this, local cosmology insists, with the help of key ancestral and allied spirit-beings with whom he and his descendants were expected to maintain good relations. In return, these spirit beings ensured the fertility of the soil, regularity of rains, and viability of agriculture. By the early twentieth century, masters of fire still managed access to land, determined how much space would be planted in various crops, controlled field rotation, and set aside fallow areas. During the growing season, they coordinated the pasturing of livestock on fallow fields both to keep cows and goats from trampling crops, and to make sure that livestock manure helped refertilize the soil. Thus, Serer farmers say they resisted private property because if the land were broken up into parcels, the link between the masters of fire and the ancestral spirits would be broken, with the calamitous results mentioned above.

Rather than accept what outsiders considered land tenure "modernization," or reactively defend local "tradition," Serer farmers in the early twentieth century concocted land pawning, a new, syncretic institution of exchange.

Someone who controlled a field (master of fire or his designate) would grant *revocable use rights* of a piece of land to an individual who needed the space in exchange for a one-time lump sum cash payment. When the original field proprietor (or his heir) wanted to reclaim the field, the field taker would accept back the cash payment, without interest, and return the field. The return of a field was not merely a mechanical market exchange among parties to a contract. It entailed particular, ritualized acts, everyday performances of symbolic importance. The party returning the field must accept the cash without condition, uttering the semi-ritualized "*jange o qol of*," or "take back your field," as a means to replay the new version of master of fire custodianship of land embedded in pawning as improvised, syncretic practice.

Pawning blended the free market's flexibility and on-demand reallocation of the crucial element of agricultural capital (land) with a Serer ontology of "traditional" property relations. Pawning worked, permitting the Serer to intensify their agricultural system when they needed to grow peanuts for cash. In spite of commodification and pressures for individuation, pawning also ensured (and depended on) the economic, political, and social centrality of the institution of the master of fire.

The second example builds on the first, and is situated in the same locale in rural Senegal, but in more recent years. Since 1972, the Senegalese government has put in place democratically elected Rural Councils to implement a land reform and manage local development. Thirty years of analysis of these Rural Councils makes possible a quasi-experiment within a geographically bounded case setting: when democratically elected local councils were syncretically adapted to function as "neo-masters of fire," they proved more politically legitimate, and more effective with regard to their primary goal (authoritative land and natural resource management). When efforts at syncretic adaptation of these local councils were cut short, actors found them less legitimate, and became more likely to resist, ignore or sabotage the efforts of these councils to manage land and other resources. Interview respondents are clear that they expect "the state (the Rural Councils) to be the new masters of fire," in remaining proximate to the economic needs of families and willing, on a year-by-year basis to make adjustments in land allocation that reflect a holistic approach to governance.

This syncretic adaptation has not resulted in a singular reinterpretation of democratic local councils in light of a unitary historical memory or notion of tradition. Rather, syncretism has opened the door to creative, messy and diverse forms of agency, resulting in the fractal multiplication of various, divergent riffs on the Rural Councils, and riffs on the riffs. For many, making the Rural Councils the new masters of fire means a kind of kin representation, in which one gains access to land or to justice *because* a Rural Councilor is a kinsman. This leads to fairly open debate about the nature of kinship, and claims that those of low caste (praise singers, blacksmiths, ex-slaves), who had historically been economically dependent, are in fact ill-defined extended kin of those in power. Subordinates are tactically (in the de Certeau sense) redeploying what we often take to be a hard and fast structural given of culture – kinship – in a way that creatively repositions them and seeks to refashion the institutions of governance. The multiplicity of such institutional possibilities should lead us to consider how this diversity of new syncretic institutional forms may eventually yield more widespread and sometimes dominant new institutional results via identifiable, politically contested processes of selection and promulgation.[3]

The third example grows from the observation that Senegal stands out as an unusual case in Africa for its remarkably low level of ethnic conflict (outside the southern, geographically isolated Casamance enclave). I have argued elsewhere (Galvan, 2006) that pan-ethnic, syncretic, informal institutions of cooperation represent an important ingredient in accounting for the low level of identity-based tension in much of Senegal, and the relatively consolidated nature of national political identity. In particular, a practice known locally as "joking kinship" plays an important role in this regard.

Joking kinship as practiced in Senegal (and many other parts of Africa) generally consists of widely held notions of perceived relatedness that may link large extended families (patrilineal and sometimes matrilineal clans), or ethnic groups. As observed in the founding colonial anthropological works on the subject,[4] and in more recent scholarship,[5] joking kinship typically centers on regularized patterns of mutual ribbing, insulting and teasing, with primary themes of historic subordination/slavery and food insecurity.

For example, upon meeting a person of the Serer ethnic group, a person from the Tukolor ethnic group might include among the usual greetings a jab like "Oh, you're a Serer? Then you're my slave." To which it would be appropriate for the Serer person to retort, "No, no, all Tukolors are the slaves of the Serer." Or Serer neighbors with last name Faye and Diouf, also understood to have a joking kinship, might follow this exchange: "Diouf? Diouf, you all eat too much." "Oh, you Fayes, you can't invite a Faye over to your house, because you will never have enough food to feed him." Both parties might continue this type of mutually insulting banter for a short time, and greetings aside, move on to everyday conversation or the particular subject that brings them together.

Beyond these regularized insults, the rhetoric of joking kinship also prohibits open conflict between these metaphorical cousins. Joking kin are usually expected, in spite of the teasing, to show special willingness to support or provide material resources when their "cousins" are in need. Moreover, it is widely expected that joking kin are especially suited to intervene in the internal conflicts of the group with whom they are paired as cousins.

Joking kinship has changed over the course of its documented history. It is not a script or a structuralist feature of "primordial" African culture. It is improvisational and syncretic. Origin stories root it in founding alliances between progenitors of ethnic groups. But as these groups have fragmented, migrated, and shifted, joking kinships have been transformed too, with new alliances popping as groups find themselves in new circumstances. Rafäel Ndiaye (1992) argues that joking kinships linking major families in the old empire of Mali can be matched to the migration patterns and adoption of new names as these powerful families left Mali and moved westward to present-day Senegal and southward to what is now Côte d'Ivoire. Thus, Traorés, once allied in joking kinship in Mali with Coulibalys, became Diops when they made it to Senegal, and took up joking kinship with Falls, themselves linked to the Coulibalys of Mali. The presence of the joking kinship practice at many social levels fraught with potential tension (inter-ethnic, inter-clan, between spouses and their in-laws, between grandchildren and grandparents) also suggests mutability and transformation. Moreover, as Serer people have become more urbanized, they have taken advantage of the fact that many Wolofs (Senegal's dominant ethnic group) have Serer surnames. This has enabled them to build surname-based joking kin with Wolof people they meet in the cities, even though historically there never was joking kinship between Wolof and Serer ethnic groups. Likewise, in recent years, political elites and cultural entrepreneurs, especially in Senegal, Mali and Burkina Faso, have publicly promoted joking kinship as an explanation for why these countries have not suffered the fate of Rwanda, and as a means to promote nation building and consolidation of a "genuinely African" basis for political community.

Finally, in Central Java, Indonesia, the Sultan of the city-state of Yogyakarta was once the emblem of Javanese history and pre-colonial pride, but was transformed during the 1940s independence struggle into a symbol of national unity. This itself reflected creative syncretism, but of an elite kind. As Dutch forces hunted down Sukarno and the leaders of the independence struggle, they took refuge in Yogyakarta, a city considered so central to Javanese cultural pride that it was unlikely the Dutch would destroy it. The Sultan went one step further and declared his palace grounds, the Kraton, a university, in which the first enrolled students were the leaders of the independence struggle (Kahin and George, 1952).

While this was clearly a strategic (in the de Certeau sense), elite act of cultural policy, it had ramifications in the realm of cultural politics through the ensuing decades. The Sultan emerged in popular imagination as a symbol not just of Javanese pride, but also of Indonesian national unity and national identity. Indeed, this was why this Sultan was the only monarch allowed to retain office after the establishment of independent Indonesia in 1949. Yogyakarta was consequently given special status as a city-scale province in the new Indonesia, whose elected governor has always been the ruling Sultan.

Minority groups, especially the economically powerful but much reviled Chinese community, did not fail to take notice of the Sultan as a new symbol of Indonesian, not Javanese pride and unity. Along with minority Christians, the Chinese community became chief promoters of the rhetoric and image of this Sultan as a living symbol of "ancient" Javanese virtues of tolerance, circumspection, deference, and inclusivity. These virtues, however, ancient, are said to define contemporary Indonesianness and set the terms for tolerance and inclusion of all Indonesian citizens, regardless of ethnic or religious origin. The Sultan remains the living embodiment of these ideals and practices, according to the novel reinterpretation of culture much promoted by Chinese and Christians. Thus, to this day, the minorities syncretically poach and redeploy the "traditional" values and most important political symbol of the majority Javanese Muslims in the name of recognition and inclusion. The majority acquiesces to this redeployment.

The Sultan emerges as the embodiment of practices and values that in turn smooth market relations, disputes over school curriculum, turmoil between neighbors, and children's squabbles. Indeed, more than ten years after the social unrest that brought down Suharto and led to anti-Chinese violence across much of Indonesia, this story of the Sultan's role in protecting peace is still much recounted. Rioters were looting Chinese shops and attacking Chinese people in the neighboring city of Surakarta. Rioters were gathering at the edge of Yogyakarta, with similar goals in mind. The Sultan drove out of his palace to meet them on the street, got out of limousine, stood on it, and gave a speech in which he implored the crowd to refrain from violence. He invited them to an interfaith prayer service at his palace, which included Muslims, Christians, Buddhists and others. The riots never came to Yogyakarta, and the Chinese minority was not attacked there.

The Sultan himself added a new chapter to the syncretic redefinition of his office and his cultural significance. He made himself the center of the "City of Tolerance" image, which was widely discussed and promoted with regard to Yogyakarta. It has also become a major theme in the Sultan's current campaign for the Indonesian presidency. A large majority of people in Yogyakarta recognize this formula as the basis for not just low levels of conflict, but the emergence of a new form of identity that at once transcends ethno-religious difference and at the same time is built on a link to a perceived-traditional past. This heritage, once Javanese, has been reworked to become the "neo-heritage" of multicultural Yogyakarta as "City of Tolerance."

Shifting methods and policy: The politics of contestation over meaning

The Sultan of Yogyakarta or Senegalese joking kinship as bases for national political community are constructs, particular syncretic forms of particular use to certain actors at particular times. The same can be said of land pawning in early twentieth-century rural Senegal, and various versions of the Rural Councils promoted in the same region.

Syncretism, fundamentally about grassroots creativity in the ongoing reinterpretation and transformation of culture and institutions, opens the door to variation and contestation. Syncretism undermines universalistic and teleological notions of "cultural change," and demands three fundamental changes in how we design and make sense of cultural policy. First, syncretism demands an adjustment of scale. Following the logic of Scott (1998), one-size-fits-all solutions in reworking culture to support goals like nation building or inclusive citizenship are destined to fail because they do not harness the "ramshackle" processes of grassroots creative adaptation. Policy makers and analysts must thus develop design, implementation, and tracking tools to see and understand the diversity of new cultural forms that proliferate at the most local of levels.

Second, syncretism demands a rehabilitation of methods once associated with ethnomethodology (Garfinkel, 1967), updated to take into account the dynamics of social constructivism. Operating at very local, micro-scales, syncretism requires those who design and assess policy to understand myriad local histories, cultures and memories of institutions. This will entail a massive new undertaking of political ethnographic analysis (which can and should employ large numbers of already trained but underemployed social scientists from the locales under study). But this new political ethnography can not be rooted in old fantasies about "tribe," "tradition," or primordialist notions of "culture or overly reified and elitist concepts like hybridity." It must recognize that what we call tradition, indigeneity, cultural memory, or the customs of a people is subject to grassroots reinvention, and reformulation as a feature of everyday life and therefore as a site for political contestation over the content of memory and its relevance in the present day.

Thus, the political ethnography of syncretism requires a dynamic analysis of competing versions of historical memory of culture and tradition, mobilized by actors with identifiable interests and social-structural position, to advance particular claims or goals. This opens the door to a new, micro-level political science of the small-scale forms of contestation over culture, symbol and myth, the deployments of these structures of neo-tradition in political struggle, and the ways in which these sometimes-coherent systems of meaning enmesh actors and in turn help shape, constrain and structure actors' own identities and interests.

Finally, syncretism demands deep and meaningful decentralization. The kinds of reforms associated with the Rural Councils in Senegal beginning in 1972, or with various versions of federalism and power sharing in Nigeria, India, former Yugoslavia, or contemporary Iraq are not enough. Delivering on the real promise of decentralization means giving local-level bodies the power to interpret national legal and policy principles in ways that make cultural sense in local contexts. Only by granting this power to adapt and syncretically transform the institutions of development, governance, and representation will it become possible to bridge the longstanding legitimacy gap that divides the state from society. It is the power to syncretically transform culture that has the potential to rebuild a link between postcolonial society and state, and thus tap the much-discussed but ever-elusive mobilizational potential of "traditional" social relations.

Notes

1. For a thorough review of the etymology and origins of the term, see Stewart and Shaw (1994) and Stewart (1999).
2. For my own more complete exploration of the nature of institutional and cultural syncretism and how people in rural Senegal have used it to respond to a century of land tenure and local governance changes, see Galvan (2004). For theoretical overviews to the concept, see Berk and Galvan, (2009), and Galvan and Sil, (2007). For similar deployments of the concept to make sense of the incorporation of new organizational structures in Japanese firms in the postwar period, see Sil (2002), and to present trade associations as alternatives to perfect market competition and regulated monopoly in early twentieth-century US industrialization, see Berk (1994). For parallel conceptualizations which share the basic logic of institutional syncretism (decomposability of structure, creativity and reflexivity of agency) but do not use that phrase, see Stark, D. and Bruszt, L. (1998) on "recombinant property" in Eastern Europe after the Cold War, Sabel and Zeitlin (1997) on "institutional intercurrence," Herrigel and Zeitlin (1999) on the mutability of institutional forms in Germany and Japan under US occupation (1999), and Anderson (1974) on the "concatenation of modes of production." For earlier, but conceptually rather different, efforts to deploy to "syncretism" in political contexts, see Haas (1997) and Di Palma (1978).
3. For a complete account of the syncretic adapation of these locally elected bodies, see Galvan (2007).
4. The anthropological classics on joking kinship from the era of colonial codification of culture include A. R. Radcliffe-Brown, "On Joking Relationships," *Africa*, 13:3, July 1940, pp. 195–210; Marcel Griaule, "L'Alliance Cathartique," *Africa*, 18:4, October 1948; pp. 242–58; A. I. Richards, "Reciprocal Clan Relationships among the Bemba of NE Rhodesia," *Man*, 37:222, December 1937; Denise Paulme, "Parenté à plaisanterie et alliance par le sang en Afrique Occidentale," *Africa*, 12:4, 1939, 433–44; M. H. Labouret, "La parenté à plaisanterie en Afrique Occidentale," *Africa*, 2, 244–53; Marcel Maus, "Parentés à plaisanteries," Ecole pratique des hautes etudes, section des sciences religieuses, annuaire, 1927–8.
5. See for example, Sten Hagberg, "The Politics of Joking Relationships in Burkina Faso," Papers presented at the workshop on *Friendship, Descent and Alliance*, December 16–18, 2002, Max Planck Institute for Social Anthropology, Allemagne.

Bibliography

Acheson, K. and Maule, C. (February 1998). "International Agreements and the Cultural Industries," *North American Outlook*, vol. 6, no. 4.

ACSA (2008). "The Mécénat Report 2008." Tokyo: Association for Corporate Support of the Art, Japan.

Adam, S. and Kriesi, H. (2007). "The Network Approach." In P. A. Sebatier (ed.), *Theories of the Policy Process*, 2nd edn, pp. 129–54. Boulder, CO: Westview Press.

Adesara, H. (2004, August 14). "Sony's 'Indian Idol' Dream Run Starts 17 August." [Online]. Retrieved April 17, 2008 from http://www.indiantelevision.com/mam/headlines.

Agger, B. (1990). *The Decline of Discourse: Reading, Writing and Resistance in Postmodern Capitalism.* New York: Falmer Press.

Africultures (1997) "Interview with Anne-Laure Folly." Retrieved January 8, 2004 from www.africultures.org.

Aiyar, S. (2007). "Inclusive Inequality," *India Today*, September 24, 42–5.

Aiyar, V. S. and Chopra, A. (2000). "The Great Gamble," *India Today*, July 17, 48–54.

Alderson, E., Blaser, R. and Coward, H. (eds.) (1993). *Reflections on Cultural Policy Past, Present and Future.* Atlantic Highlands, NJ: Humanities Press International.

Alexander, N. (1995). "Core Culture and Core Curriculum in South Africa." In Jackson and Solis, (eds.), *Beyond Comfort Zones in Multiculturalism.* Westport, CT: Bergin and Garney.

Almond, G. A. and Verba, S. (1963). *The Civic Culture.* Princeton: Princeton University Press.

Amariglio, J. (1988). "The body, economic discourse, and power: An economists' introduction to Foucault," *History of Political Economy*, 20(4), 583–613.

Anderson, B. (1983). *Imagined Communities: Reflections on the Origin and Spread of Nationalism.* London: Verso.

Anderson, P. (1974). *Lineages of the Absolutist State.* London: N. L. B.

Anglim, J. M. (2004). "Crossroads in the Great Race: Moving beyond the International Race to Judgment in Disputes over Artwork and Other Chattels," *Harvard International Law Journal*, 45(1), 239–301.

Anheier, H. and Isar, Y. R. (eds.) (2008). *The Cultural Economy. The Cultures and Globalization Series 2.* Los Angeles: Sage.

Appadurai, A. (2004). "The Capacity to Aspire: Culture and the Terms of Recognition." In V. Rao and M. Walton (eds.), *Culture and Public Action.* Palo Alto: Stanford University Press.

Appadurai, A. (ed.) (2000). *Public Culture: Globalization.* Durham: Duke University Press.

Appadurai, A. (1996). *Modernity at Large: The Cultural dimensions of Globalization.* Minneapolis, MN: University of Minnesota.

APSARA (2004). "Résultats du questionnaire sur les itinéraires des visiteurs dans le parc d'Angkor." Siam Reap, Cambodia.

APSARA (2003). "Seconde conférence intergouvernementale pour la sauvegarde et le développement d'Angkor." France, Paris.

Arango, T. (December 1, 2008). "World Falls for American Media, Even as It Sours on America." *New York Times.* Available at http://www.nytimes.com/2008/12/01/business/media/01soft.html?_r=1and ref=usand pagewant.

Armstrong, K. (2002). *Islam: A Short History.* New York: Modern Library Paperback.

Ashcroft, B. (2001). *On Post-Colonial Futures: Transformations of Colonial Culture.* New York: Continuum.

Balassa, C. (2008). *America's Image Abroad: The UNESCO Cultural Diversity Convention and U.S. Motion Picture Exports.* Vanderbilt University (CE2213).

Balassa, C. (February 4, 1998). "International Cooperation to Improve Trade Rules,"*North America Outlook*, vol. 6, no. 4.

Balassa, C. (1981). "Trade Issues in the Motion Picture Industry." Office of the United States Trade Representative.

Balfe, J. (ed.) (1993). *Paying the Piper: Causes and Consequences of Arts Patronage.* Minnesota: University of Minnesota Press.

Bamzai, K. (2007). "Real Politics," *India Today*, October 8, 62–4.

Barakat, H. (1993). *The Arab World: Society, Culture and State.* Berkeley: University of California Press.

Barghoorn, F. C. (1960). *The Soviet Cultural Offensive: The Role of Cultural Diplomacy in Soviet Foreign Policy.* Princeton, NJ: Princeton University Press.

Barman, A. and S. Guha R. (June 4). "Unshackling the Locked Gates," Outlook India, June 4. http://www.outlookindia.com/article.aspx?211871.

Barnett, C. (2001). "Culture, Policy, and Subsidiarity in the European Union: From Symbolic Identity to the Governmentalization of Culture," *Political Geography*, 20(4), 405–26.

Barnett, M. and Raymond D. (eds.) (2005). *Power in Global Governance.* Cambridge, UK: Cambridge University Press.

Barney, D. (2000). *Prometheus Wired: The Hope for Democracy in the Age of Network Technology.* Sydney, AU: University of New South Wales Press.

Bartelsen, J. (1993). *A Genealogy of Sovereignty.* Stockholm: University of Stockholm. Diss.

Barthes, R. (1972). *Mythologies.* New York: Hill and Wang.

Basu, A. (1995). "Introduction." In A. Basu (ed.), *The Challenge of Local Feminisms: Women's Movements in Global Perspective.* Oxford: Westview Press.

Baudrillard, J. (1996). *The System of Objects.* London: Verso.

Beaudreau, B. C. (2006). "Identity, Entropy and Culture," *Journal of Economic Psychology*, 27(2), 205–23.

Beck, U. (1994). "The Reinvention of Politics: Towards a Theory of Reflexive Modernization." In U. Beck, A. Giddens, and S. Lash (eds.), *Reflexive Modernization: Politics, Tradition and Aesthetics in the Modern Social Order*, pp. 1–55. Oxford: Polity Press.

Beckmann, C. and Gedak, A. (2006). "Kultur und die Fonds für Strukturentwicklung der Europaischen Union." Bonn, Germany: Institut für Kulturpolitik der Kulturpolitischen Gesellschaft e. V.

Beer, S. H. (1973). "Modern Political Development." In S. H. Beer, A. B. Ulam, S. Berger, Goldman (eds.), *Patterns of Government: The Major Political Systems of Europe*, 3rd edn., pp. 1–68. New York: Random House.

Belfiore, E. and Bennett, O. (2008). *The Social Impact of the Arts: An Intellectual History.* Basingstoke: Palgrave Macmillan.

Bennett, T. (2003). "Culture and Governmentality." In J. Z. Bratich, J. Packer and C. McCarthy (eds.), *Foucault, Cultural Studies, and Governmentality*, pp. 47–63. Albany: State University of New York Press.

Bennett, T. (2001). "Differing Diversities: Transversal Study on the Theme of Cultural Policy and Cultural Diversity." In T. Bennett (ed.), *Differing Diversities: Transversal Study on the Theme of Cultural Policy and Cultural Diversity, Followed by Seven Research*

Position Papers, pp. 7–70. Strasbourg: Cultural Policy and Action Department, Council of Europe Publishing.

Bennett, T. (1998). *Culture: A Reformer's Science*. London: Sage.

Berger, P. and Luckmann, T. (1966). *The Social Construction of Reality: A Treatise in the Sociology of Knowledge*. New York: Anchor Books.

Berk, G. (1994). *Alternative Tracks: The Constitution of American Industrial Order, 1865–1917*. Baltimore: Johns Hopkins University Press.

Bernier, I. (2005). "Trade and Culture." In P. F. J. Macrory, A. W. E. Appleton and M. G. Plumeder (eds.), *The World Trade Organization: Legal, Economic and Political Analysis*. New York: Springer.

Bhabha, H. K. (1994). *The Location of Culture*. New York: Routledge.

Bianchini, F. (1993). "Remaking European cities: the role of cultural policies," Franco Bianchini and Michael Parkinson (eds.). *Cultural policy and urban regeneration: The West European Experience*, pp. 1–20. Manchester: Manchester University Press.

Bianchini, F. and Parkinson, M. (eds.). *Cultural Policy and Urban Regeneration: The West European Experience*, pp. 199–213. Manchester: Manchester University Press.

Bizet, B. (2000). "Eléments de politique culturelle et touristique pour le Cambodge." Banque Mondiale.

Bogason, P. (1996). "Changes in Local Government and Governance." In P. Bogason (ed.), *New Modes of Local Organizing: Local Government Fragmentation in Scandinavia*, pp. 1–13. Commack, NY: Nova Sciences Publishers, Inc.

Bogost, I. (2006). "Playing Politics: Videogames for Politics, Activism, and Advocacy," *First Monday*, 11(9). Available at www.firstmonday.org/issues/special11_9/bogost/index.html.

Bourdieu, P. (1999). *Pascalian Meditations*. Cambridge: Polity.

Bourdieu, P. (1998). "Neo-Liberalism, the Utopia (becoming a reality) of Unlimited Exploitation." In P. Bourdieu and R. Nice (eds.), *Acts of Resistance: Against the Tyranny of the Market*, pp. 94–105. New York: The New Press.

Bourdieu, P. (1993). *The Field of Cultural Production*, ed. R. Johnson. New York: Columbia.

Bourdieu, P. (1988). *Homo Academicus*. Cambridge: Polity Press.

Bourdieu, P. (1984). "A Social Critique of the Judgment of Taste," Richard Nice (trans.). *Distinction: A Social Critique of the Judgment of Taste*, pp. 9–96. Cambridge, MA: Harvard University Press.

Bourdieu, P. (1984). *Distinction: A Social Critique of the Judgment of Taste*. Cambridge: Harvard University Press.

Bourdieu, P. (1977 [1972]). *Outline of a Theory of Practice*. Cambridge: Cambridge University Press.

Braman, S. (2009). "Globalizing Media Law and Policy." In D. Thussu (ed.), *Internationalizing Media Studies*. London: Routledge.

Braman, S. (2008). "Theorizing the Impact of IT on Library-State Relations." In G. Leckie and J. Buschman (eds.), *Information Technology in Librarianship: Critical Approaches*, pp. 105–26. Westport, CT: Libraries Unlimited.

Braman, S. (2008). "International Treaties and Art," *International Journal of Cultural Policy*, 14(3), 315–33.

Braman, S. (2007). *Change of State: Information, Policy, and Power*. Cambridge, MA: MIT Press.

Braman, S. (2002). "Informational Meta-Technologies, International relations, and Genetic Power: The Case of Biotechnologies." In J. N. Rosenau and J. P. Singh (eds.), *Information Technologies and Global Politics*: *The Changing Scope of Power and Governance*. Albany, NY: State University of New York Press.

Braman, S. (2000). "The Constitutional Context: Universities, New Information Technologies, and the US Supreme Court," *Information, Communication and Society*, 3(4), 526–45.

Braman, S. (1998). "The Right to Create: Cultural Policy in the Fourth Stage of the Information Society," *Gazette: The International Journal of Communication Studies*, 60(1), 77–91.

Braman, S. (1996). "From Virtue to Vertu to the Virtual: Art, Self-Organizing Systems, and the Network Economy," *Readerly/Writerly Texts: Essays on Literature, Literary/ Textual Criticism, and Pedagogy*, 3(2), 149–66.

Braman, S. (1996). "Art in the Information Economy," *Canadian Journal of Communications*, 21, 179–96.

Braman, S. (1994). "Art Policy for the Net," *Undercurrent*, 1(1), Spring. Available at http://darkwing.uoregon.edu/~heroux/home.html.

Braman, S. (1991). "Contradictions in Brilliant Eyes," *Gazette: The International Journal of Communication Studies* 47(3), 177–94.

Braman, S. (1990). "Trade and Information Policy," *Media, Culture and Society*, 12, 361–85.

Brancusi v. United States, 54 Treas. Dec. 428 (Cust. Ct. 1928).

Brightman, R. (1995). "Forget Culture: Replacement, Transcendence, Relexification," *Current Anthropology*, 10(4), November, 509–46.

Brooks, David (November 10, 2005). "Gangsta, in French," *New York Times*. <http://select.nytimes.com/2005/11/10/opinion/10brooks.html>

Brown, R. H. (1998). *Toward a Democratic Science: Scientific Narration and Civic Communication*. New Haven: Yale University Press.

Bruyneel, K. (2007). *The Third Space of Sovereignty: The Postcolonial Politics of Indigenous Relations*. Minneapolis: University of Minnesota Press.

Bryson, B. (1996). "Anything but Heavy Metal: Symbolic Exclusion and Musical Dislikes," *American Sociological Review*, 61, 884–99.

Bulbeck, C. (1998). *Re-Orienting Western Feminisms, Women's Diversity in a Post-Colonial World*. Cambridge, UK: Cambridge University Press.

Burton, L. and Ruppert, D. (1999). "Bear's Lodge or Devils Tower: Inter-Cultural Relations, Legal Pluralism, and the Management of Scared Sites on Public Lands," *Cornell Journal of Law and Public Policy*, 8, 201–47.

Cameron, J. B. and Becker, W. B. (eds.) (1993). *Photography's Beginnings*. Albuquerque, NM: University of New Mexico Press.

Carby, H. V. (1997). "White Woman Listen! Black Feminism and the Boundaries of Sisterhood." In R. Hennessy and C. Ingraham (eds.), *Materialist Feminism*, pp. 110–28. London and New York: Routledge.

Cassierer, E. (2000). *The Logic of the Cultural Sciences*. New Haven: Yale University Press.

Cassierer, E. (1955–57). *The Philosophy of Symbolic Forms*. New Haven: Yale University Press.

Castells, M. (2004). "Informationalism, Networks, and the Network Society: A Theoretical Blueprint." In M. Castells (ed.), *The Network Society: A Cross-Cultural Perspective*, pp. 3–51. Cheltenham and Northampton: Edward Elgar Publishing Limited.

Catlin, S. (1980). "Political Iconography in the Diego Rivera Frescoes at Cuernavaca, Mexico." In Millon and Nochlin (eds.), *Art and Architecture in the Service of Politics*. Cambridge, MA: MIT Press, 1980.

Cawelti, J. G. (1978). "The Concept of Artistic Matrices," *Communication Research*, 5(3), 283–304.

Center for Strategic and International Studies (1975). "International Information Education and Cultural Relations: Recommendations for the Future." Washington, DC.

Chakrabarti, P. (2007). "Dream Merchants," *The Indian Express*, New Delhi, March 19, 2007, 6.

Chechi, A. (2004). "Cultural Matters in the Case Law of the European Court of Justice," *Art Antiquity and Law*, 9(3), 281–98.

Cherbo, J. M., Vogel, H. L. and Wyszomirski, M. J. (2008). "Toward and Arts and Creative Sector." In J. M. Cherbo, R. A. Stewart and M. J. Wyszomirski (eds.), *Understanding the Arts and Cultural Sector in the United States*. New Brunswick, NJ: Rutgers University Press.

Clifford, J. (1988). *The Predicament of Culture: Twentieth-Century Ethnography, Literature, and Art*. Cambridge, MA: Harvard University Press.

CNN-IBN Special Report (2007, September 21). "Biggest Battle This Year: Report on Indian Idol finale." Broadcast on CNN-IBN September 21, 2007.

Cockburn, C. (1998). *The Space between Us: Negotiating Gender and National Identities in Conflict*. London and New York: Zed Books.

Cody, E. and Shin, A. (2009). "WTO Ruling Could Further Open China to U.S. Entertainment Industry," *Washington Post*, August 13, 2009. Available at http://www.washingtonpost.com/wp-dyn/content/article/2009/08/12/AR2009081202971.html (accessed September 2, 2009).

Collier, R. B. and David C. (1991). *Shaping the Political Arena: Critical Junctures, the Labor Movement, and Regime Dynamics in Latin America*. Princeton, NJ: Princeton University Press.

Commission of the European Union (2006). *The Economy of Culture in Europe*. Brussels: Directorate-General for Education and Culture.

Comor, E. (2008). *Consumption and the Globalization Project: International Hegemony and the Annihilation of Time*. Basingstoke: Palgrave Macmillan.

Comor, E. (2002). "New Technologies and Consumption: Contradictions in the Emerging World Order." In J. N. Rosenau and J. P. Singh (eds.), *Information Technologies and Global Politics: The Changing Scope of Power and Governance*. Albany, NY: State University of New York Press.

Convents, G. (2003). "L'Afrique? Quel Cinéma!" Anvers: EPO.

Cook, J. (1993, February). "Division of cultural property as Slovakia splits," *The Art Newspaper*, vol. 15, Record number 6176.

Council of Europe (1997). *In from the Margins: A Contribution to the Debate on Culture and Development in Europe*. Strasbourg: Council of European Publishing, European Task Force on Culture and Development.

Cowen, T. (2006). *Good and Plenty*. Princeton, NJ: Princeton University Press.

Cowen, T. (2002). *Creative Destruction: How Globalization is Changing the World's Cultures*. Princeton: Princeton University Press.

Cowen, T. (1998). *In Praise of Commercial Culture*. Cambridge, MA: Harvard University Press.

Crean, S. (2000). "Looking Back to the Future: Creators and Cultural Policy in the Era of Free Trade," *Journal of Canadian Studies*, 35(3), 199–211.

Critical Art Ensemble. (CAE) (2001). *Digital Resistance: Explorations in Tactical Media*. Brooklyn, NY: Autonomedia.

Cummings, M. C., Jr. (2003). *Cultural Diplomacy and the United States Government: A Survey*. Washington, DC: Center for Arts and Culture. Available at www.culturalpolicy.org.

Cummings, M. C. and Katz, R. S. (eds.) (1987). *The Patron State: Government and the Arts in Europe, North America and Japan*. New York: Oxford University Press.

Cunningham, C. B. (2001). "In Defense of Member State Culture: The Unrealized Potential of Article 151(4) of the EC Treaty and the Consequences for EC Cultural Policy," *Cornell International Law Journal*, 34(1), 119–63.

D'Angelo, M. and Vespérini, P. (1998). *Cultural Policies in Europe: A Comparative Approach*. Strasbourg: Council of Europe Publishing.

D'Angelo, M. and Vespérini, P. (1999). *Cultural Policies in Europe: Method and Practice of Evaluation*. Strasbourg: Council of Europe Publishing.

Dallmayr, F. (1984). *Language and Politics*. Notre Dame: University of Notre Dame Press.

Dalton, K. (2001). Personal communication, July 17.

Dannatt, A. (2000). "Global Missile Systems as Artistic Muse," *The Art Newspaper*, 107, *Record Number 4611*.

Danner, M. (2008). "Obama and Sweet Potato Pie," *New York Review of Book*, 55(18), 12–20.

Davila, A. (1997). *Sponsored Identities: Cultural Politics in Puerto Rico*. Philadelphia: Temple University Press.

De Certeau, M. (1984). *The Practice of Everyday Life*. Berkeley: University of California Press.

De Schoutheete, P. (2006). "The European Council." In J. Peterson and M. Shackleton (eds.), *The Institutions of the European Union*, 2nd edn., 37–59.

Deibert, R. J. (2002). "Circuits of Power: Security in Internet Environment." In J. N. Rosenau and J. P. Singh (eds.), *Information Technologies and Global Politics: The Changing Scope of Power and Governance*. Albany, NY: State University of New York Press.

Deibert, R. J. (1997). *Parchment, Printing, and Hypermedia: Communication and World Order Transformation*. New York: Columbia University Press.

Derne, S. (2005). "The (Limited) Effect of Cultural Globalization in India: Implications for Culture Theory," *Poetics*, 33, 33–47.

Deutsch, R. (1996). *Evictions: Art and Spatial Politics*. Cambridge, MA: MIT Press.

Dewdney, C. (1998). *Last Flesh: Life in the Transhuman Era*. New York: Harpercollins Canada.

Dewey, P. (2008). "Transnational Cultural Policymaking in the European Union," *Journal of Arts Management, Law and Society*, 38 (2), 99–118.

Dewey, P. (2007). "Introduction," *Journal of Arts Management, Law, and Society*, 37(1), 3–9.

Dewey, J. (2002 [1922]). *Human Nature and Conduct*. Amherst, NY: Prometheus Books.

Dewey, J. (1959 [1934]). *Art as Experience*. New York: Perigee Books.

Di Palma, G. (1978). *Political Syncretism in Italy: Historical Coalition Strategies and the Present Crisis*. Berkeley: Institute of International Studies, University of California.

DiMaggio, P. (1991). "Social Structure, Institutions, and Cultural Goods: The Case of the U.S." In P. Bourdieu and J. S. Coleman (eds.), *Social Theory for a Changing Society*, pp. 133–55. Boulder, CO: Westview Press.

Dosse, F. (1999). *Empire of Meaning: The Humanization of the Social Sciences*. Minneapolis: University of Minnesota Press.

Du Gay, P., Hall, S., Janes, L., Mackay, H. and Negus, K. (1997). *Doing Cultural Studies: The Story of the Sony Walkman*. Thousand Oaks, CA: Sage.

Duelund, P. (2003). *The Nordic Cultural Model*. Copenhagen: Nordic Cultural Institute.

Duelund, P. (2003). "The Nordic Cultural Model: Summary." In P. Duelund (ed.) *The Nordic Cultural Model: Nordic Cultural Policy in Transition*, pp. 479–529. Copenhagen: Nordic Cultural Institute.

Duncan, C. (1995). *Civilizing Rituals: Inside Public Art Museums*. London: Routledge.

Dungarembga, T. (1988). *Nervous Conditions*. Seattle, WA: Seal Press.

Dzuverovic-Russell, L. (2003). "The Artist and the Internet: A Breeding Ground for Deception," *Digital Creativity*, 14(3), 152–8.

Edelson, S. D. (1984). "Concerted International Effort in the Trade of Cultural Property," *Law and Policy in International Business*, 16(4), 1249–73.

Ekeh, P. (1975). "Colonialism and the Two Publics in Africa: A Theoretical Statement," *Comparative Studies in Society and History*, 17(1), 91–112.

Ellerson, B. (2000). *Sisters of the Screen: Women of Africa on Film, Video, and Television*. Trenton, NJ: Africa World Press. Documentary presented at Fespaco, 2003.

Epstein, S. B. and Mages, L. (2005). *Public Diplomacy: A Review of Past Recommendations*. Washington, DC: CRS Report for Congress.

Escobar, A. (1995). *Encountering Development: The Making and Unmaking of the Third World*. Princeton: Princeton University Press.

Esposito, J. and Mogahed, D. (2008). *Who Speaks for Islam: What a Billion Muslims Really Think*, New York, NY: Gallup Press.

Europa (2007). "Communication from the Commission on a European Agenda for Culture in a Globalizing World." Available at http://www.ec.europa.eu/culture/eac/communication/pdf_word/COM 2007242_en.pdf (accessed December 1, 2007).

Europa (2006). "The Economy of Culture in Europe." Available at http://www.ec.europa.eu/culture/eac/sources_info/studies/economy_en.html (accessed December 1, 2007).

European Commission (2002). *A Community of Cultures: The European Union and the Arts*. Brussels: Directorate-General for Press and Communication Publications.

European Union (2007). "Directive 2007/65/EC of the European Parliament and of the Council of 11 December 2007." Retrieved November 22, 2008 from http://eur-lex.europa.eu/LexUriServ/LexUriServ.do?uri=CELEX:32007L0065:en:NOT

Fanon, F. (1968) *The Wretched of the Earth*. New York: Grove.

Farhi, P. (October 26, 1998). "Pepco's Starpower Venture to Sign Cable TV Pact with D. C." *Washington Post*, F25.

Farhi, P. and Rosenfeld, M. (October 25, 1998). "American Pop Penetrates Worldwide; Nations With New Wealth, Freedom Welcome Bart Simpson, Barbie and Rap," *Washington Post*, A01.

Farr, J. (2004). "Social Capital: A Conceptual History," *Political Theory*, 32(1), 6–33.

Faulkner, S. (2003). "Asylum Seekers: Imagined Geography and Visual Culture," *Visual Culture in Britain*, 4(1), 93–114.

Fawcett, L. (2005). "Regionalism from an Historical Perspective." In M. Farrell, B. Hettne and L. Van Langenhove (eds.), *Global Politics of Regionalism: Theory and Practice*, pp. 21–37. London and Ann Arbor, MI: Pluto Press.

Federation of Indian Chambers of Commerce and Industry–Pricewaterhouse Coopers Report (2007). "The Indian Entertainment and Media Industry: A Growth Story Unfolds." Available at www.pwc.com/india.

Federation of Indian Chambers of Commerce and Industry–Pricewaterhouse Coopers Report (2006). "India, the Fastest Growing Free Market Democracy: Entertainment and Media Industry Report." (In collaboration with India Brand Equity Foundation). Available at www.pwc.com/india.

Feigenbaum, H. (June 2005). "Hollywood: From Flexible Specialization to Globalized Production," *Economia della Cultural*, 2, 221–228. http://translate.google.com/translate?hl=en&sl=it&u=http://www.mulino.it/edizioni/riviste/scheda_fascicolo.php%3Fisbn%3D10374&ei=GGX4SpzgHcmTlAeU0cXxCg&sa=X&oi=translate&ct=result&resnum=4&ved=0CBIQ7gEwAw&prev=/search%3Fq%3Dfeigenbaum%2Beconomia%2Bdella%2Bcultura%2B2005,%2Bno.%2B2%26hl%3Den%26client%3Dfirefox-a%26rls%3Dorg.mozilla:en-US:official%26sa%3DG

Feigenbaum, H. (2004). "Is Technology the Enemy of Culture?" *International Journal of Cultural Policy*, 10(3), 251–63.

Feigenbaum, H. (March 2003). "Digital Entertainment Jumps the Border," *Scientific American*, 288 (3), 78–83.

Ferguson, J. (1990). *The Anti-Politics Machine: Development, Depoliticization, and Bureaucratic Power in Lesotho*. Cambridge: Cambridge University Press.

Finnemore, M. (1996). *National Interests in International Society*. Ithaca, NY: Cornell University Press.

Fischer, F. (2003). *Reframing Public Policy: Discursive Politics and Deliberative Practices*. Oxford: Oxford University Press.

Fishman, J. J. (1977). "The Emergence of Art Law," *Cleveland State Law Review*, 26, 481–97.

Fiumiara, G. C. (1995). *The Metaphoric Process: Connections between Language and Life*. London: Routledge.

Fletcher-Tomenius, P. and Forrest, C. (2000). "Historic Wreck in International Waters: Conflict or Consensus?," *Marine Policy*, 24(1), 1–10.

Florida, R. (2004). *The Rise of the Creative Class: And How It's Transforming Work, Leisure, Community and Everyday Life*. New York: Basic Books.

Florida, R. (2002). *The Rise of the Creative Class*. New York: Basic Books.

Folgarait, L. (1998). *Mural Painting and Social Revolution in Mexico, 1920–1940*. Cambridge: Cambridge University Press.

Folly, A. (dir.) (1994). *Femmes Aux Yeux Ouverts*. BetaCam, 52 mn. Togo.

Forrest, A. (1994). "A New Start for Cultural Action in the European Community: Genesis and Implications of Article 128 of the Treaty on European Union," *Cultural Policy*, 1(1), 11–20.

Folly, A. (2000). Interview. In B. Ellerson (ed.) *Sisters of the Screen: Women of Africa on Film, Video, and Television*, pp. 94–108. Trenton, NJ: Africa World Press.

Foucault, M. (2002a). *The Archaeology of Knowledge*. London and New York: Routledge.

Foucault, M. (2002b). "The Subject and Power." In J. D. Faubion (ed.), *Power: Essential Works of Foucault 1954–1984*, Volume 3, pp. 326–48. London: Penguin Books.

Foucault, M. (1994). *The Order of Things: An Archaeology of the Human Sciences*. New York: Vintage Books.

Foucault, M. (1991). "Governmentality." In G. Burchell, C. Gordon, and P. Miller (eds.), *The Foucault Effect: Studies in Governmentality*, pp. 87–104. Chicago: The University of Chicago Press.

Foucault, M. (1980). "Two Lectures." In C. Gordon (ed.), *Power/Knowlegde: Selected Interviews and Other Writings 1972–1977*, pp. 78–108. New York: Pantheon Books.

Foucault, M. (1980). *Power/Knowledge: Selected Interviews and Other Writings*. New York: Pantheon.

Foucault, M. (1979). "Omnes et Singulatim: Towards a Criticism of 'Political Reason'". Stanford University, October 10/16, 1979. In S. McMurrin (ed.), *Tanner Lectures on Human Values*. Salt Lake City: University of Utah Press.

Foucault, M. (1977 [1975]). *Discipline and Punish: The Birth of the Prison*. New York: Vintage.

Foucault, M. (1970). *The Order of Things*. New York: Vintage.

Freire, P. 1970/2000. *Pedagogy of the Oppressed*. New York: Continuum.

Frey, B. S. (2000). *Arts and Economics: Analysis and Cultural Policy*. Berlin: Springer.

Fulbright, J. W. (August 5, 1951). "Open Doors, Not Iron Curtain," *The New York Times Magazine*, pp. 26. http://74.125.113.132/search?q=cache:J8cIQJHOM5IJ: www.culturalpolicy.org/pdf/Schneider.pdf+%27open+doors,+not+iron+curtain%27 +fulbright&cd=1&hl=en&ct=clnk&gl=us&client=safari

Fyall, A. and Leask, A. (2006). *Managing World Heritage Site*. UK: Elsevier

Gaimster, D. (2004). "Measures against the Illicit Trade in Cultural Objects: The Emerging Strategy in Britain," *Antiquity*, 78(301), 699–707.

Galperin, H. (2004). *New Television, Old Politics: The Transition to Digital TV in the United States and Britain*. New York: Cambridge University Press.

Galperin, H. (1999). "Cultural Industries Policy in Regional Trade Agreements: The Cases of NAFTA, the European Union and MERCOSUR," *Media, Culture and Society*, 21(5), 627–48.

Galvan, B. D. G. (December 2, 2009). "How and When People Remake Institutions: A Field Guide to Creative Syncretism," *Theory and Society*.

Galvan, D. and Sil, R. (2007). "The Dilemma of Institutional Adaptation and the Role of Syncretism." In Galvan and Sil (eds.), *Reconfiguring Institutions across Time and Space: Syncretic Responses to Challenges of Political and Economic Transformation*. New York: Palgrave Macmillan.

Galvan, D. (2007). "Syncretism and Local-Level Democracy in Rural Senegal." In Galvan and Sil (eds.), *Reconfiguring Institutions across Time and Space: Syncretic Responses to Challenges of Political and Economic Transformation*. New York: Palgrave Macmillan.

Galvan, D. (2006). "Joking Kinship, Nation-Building and Constructivism in Senegal," *Cahiers d'Etudes Africaines*, XLVI (3–4), No. 183–4.

Galvan, D. (2004). *The State must be Our Master of Fire. How Peasants Craft Culturally Sustainable Development in Senegal*. Berkeley, University of California Press.

Galvan, D. (1997). "Institutional Syncretism and the Articulation of Modes of Production in Rural Senegalese Land Tenure Relations," *African Rural and Urban Studies*, 4(2–3), 59–98.

Gamble, S. (ed.) (2000). *The Routledge Companion to Feminism and Postfeminism*, pp. 1–52. London and New York: Routledge.

Gandy, O. (1993). *The Panoptic Sort: A Political Economy of Personal Information*. Boulder, CO: Westview.

Garcia Canclini, N. (1995/2005). *Hybrid Cultures: Strategies for Entering and Leaving Modernity*. Minneapolis, MN: University of Minnesota Press.

Garcia Canclini, N. (2001). *Consumers and Citizens: Globalization and Multicultural Conflicts*. Minneapolis and London: University of Minnesota Press.

Garfinkel, H. (1967). *Studies in Ethnomethodology*. Cambridge, UK: Polity Press.

Geertz, C. (1976). "Art as a Cultural System," *Modern Language Notes*, 91(6), 1473–99.

Geertz, C. (1973). *The Interpretation of Cultures*. New York: Basic Books.

Giddens, A. (1984). *The Constitution of Society: Outline of the Theory of Structuration*. Berkeley, CA: University of California Press.

Giedion, S. (1948). *Mechanization Takes Command: A Contribution to Anonymous History*. Oxford: Oxford University Press.

Gilley, B. (2001). "Lowered Sites," *Far Eastern Economic Review*, 164(1), 60–2.

Ginsburg, F. D., Abu-Lughod, L. and Larkin, B. (2002) (eds.). *Media Worlds*. Berkeley: University of California Press.

Global Hunger Index (2006). "A Basis for Cross Country Comparison," Report Published by International Food Policy Research Institute and German Agro Action.

Goff, P. M. (2007). *Limits to Liberalization: Local Culture in Global Marketplace*. Ithaca, NY: Cornell University Press.

Goff, P. M. (2000). "Invisible Borders: Economic Liberalization and National Identity," *International Studies Quarterly*, 44, 533–62.

Goodwin, C. (2006). "Art and Culture in the History of Economic Thought." In V. A. Ginsburgh and D. Throsby (eds.), *Handbook of the Economics of Art and Culture*. (Handbooks in Economics 25). Amsterdam: North-Holland.

Gordon, C. (2007). "Culture and the European Union in a Global Context," *Journal of Arts Management, Law and Society*, 37(1), 11–30.

Gottlieb, Y. (2005). "Criminalizing Destruction of Cultural Property: A Proposal for Defining New Crimes under the Rome Statute of the ICC," *Penn State International Law Review*, 23, 857–96.

Gowing, L. (ed.) (1995). *A History of Art*. New York: Barnes and Noble Books.

Goyder, J. (1997, January). "Nothing to do with art?," *The Art Newspaper*, vol. 66, Record number 1011.

Grabher, G. & Stark, David (eds.) (1997). *Restructuring networks in post-socialism: legacies, linkages, and localities*. New York, NY: Oxford University Press

Gramsci, A. (2008). *Selections from the Prison Notebooks*. New York: International Publishers.

Grasstek, V. (2005). "Treatment of cultural goods and services in international trade agreements." Presented to the UNESCO Expert Meeting for Policy Leaders and Decision Makers in the Broadcasting and Audio-visual Industry in Asia, Singapore, February, 2006.

Greaves, T. (ed.) (1994). *Intellectual Property Rights for Indigenous Peoples: A Sourcebook*. Oklahoma City, OK: Society for Applied Anthropology.

Greenfeld, L. (2001). *Spirit of Capitalism: Nationalism and Economic Growth*. Cambridge, MA: Harvard University Press.

Greenfeld, L. (1992). *Nationalism: Five Roads to Modernity*. Cambridge, MA: Harvard University Press.

Greffe, X. (2003). "La valorization économomique du patrimoine," *La Documentation Française*, France.

Greffe, X. (2004). "La valorisation économique du patrimoine." [The Economic Value of Heritage], *BBF*, 2, 141–2. [Online]. Available at http://bbf.enssib.fr/ (accessed November, 2009).

Griaule, M. (1948). "L'Alliance cathartique," *Africa*, 18(4), October, 242–58.

Grover, S. F. (1992). "The Need for Civil-Law Nations to Adopt Discovery Rules in Art Replevin Actions: A Comparative Study," *Texas Law Review*, 70, 1431–67.

Guéguen, D. (2006). *The New Practical Guide to the EU Labyrinth*, 9th edn. Brussels: Europe Information Service Publishing.

Haas, E. (1997). *Nationalism, Liberalism and Progress: The Rise and Decline of Nationalism*, Volume I. Ithaca: Cornell University Press.

Habermas, J. (1989). *The Structural Transformation of the Public Sphere: An Inquiry into a Category of Bourgeois Society*. Cambridge, MA: MIT Press.

Habermas, J. (1987). *The Philosophical Discourse of Modernity*. Cambridge, MA: MIT Press.

Hacking, I. (1999). *The Social Construction of What?* Cambridge, MA: Harvard University Press.

Hagberg, S. (2002). "The Politics of Joking Relationships in Burkina Faso," Papers presented at the workshop on Friendship, Descent and Alliance, December 16–18, 2002, Max Planck Institute for Social Anthropology, Allemagne.

Hall, S. (1997). "The Work of Representation." In S. Hall (ed.), *Representation: Cultural Representations and Signifying Practices*, pp. 13–74. London: Sage Publications.

Halonen (2005). "'Fishing for a Good Program': Public Sector Cultural Producers in Search of Justification." Nordisk Kulturpolitisk Tidskrift, *Nordic Journal of Cultural Policy*, vol. 8, no. 2, 50–79.

Hannerz, U. (1992). *Cultural Complexity: Studies in the Social Organization of Meaning.* New York: Columbia University Press.

Hannerz, U. (1996). *Transnational Connections.* London: Routledge.

Hanson, G. H. and Xiang, C. (May 2007). "International Trade in Motion Picture Services." Available at http://irpshome.ucsd.edu/faculty/gohanson/TradeinServicesNBER2008.PDF

Hardt, M. and Negri, T. (2000). *Empire.* Cambridge, MA: Harvard University Press.

Hart, J. A. (2009). "Video on the Internet: The Content Question." In D. Gerbarg (ed.), *Television Goes Digital.* New York: Springer.

Hart, J. A. (2004). *Technology, Television, and Competition.* New York: Cambridge University Press.

Harvey, D. (2006). *Spaces of Global Capitalism.* London: Verso.

Harvey, D. (1989). *The Condition of Postmodernity.* Oxford: Blackwell.

Haywood, D. (1995, December). "Who needs UNESCO?," *The Art Newspaper*, vol. 54, Record number 8259.

Heard-Lauréote, K. (2005). "Transnational Networks: Informal Governance in the European Political Space." In W. Kaiser and P. Starie (eds.), *Transnational European Union: Toward a Common Political Space*, pp. 36–60. New York: Routledge.

Heinonen, P. (2001). "Report on Early, Forced Marriages, Abduction (efma) and Their Links to Custom/Tradition, FGM, Poverty and HIV/Aids, A Womankind Worldwide Background Document." Retrieved January 8, 2004 from www.fourliteracy.com.

Hennessy, A. (1971). "Artists, Intellectuals and Revolution," *Journal of Latin American Studies*, 3, May 1971, 71–88.

Herrigel, G. and Zeitlin, F. J. (2004). *Americanization and Its Limits: Reworking US Technology and Management in Post-war Europe and Japan.* Oxford: Oxford University Press.

Herzberger-Fofana, P. (2005). "Excision et mouvements féminins." Accessed January 25, 2005 from www.arts.uwa.edu.au/AFLIT/MGFG.html.

Herzfeld, M. (2001). *Anthropology: Theoretical Practice in Culture and Society.* London: Blackwell.

Hesmondhalgh, D. (2007). *Cultural Industries*, 2nd edn. London: Sage Publications.

Hillman Chartrand, H. and McCaughey, C. (1989). "The Arm's Length Principle and the Arts: An International Perspective—Past, Present and Future." In M. C. Cummings and J. M. Schuster (eds.), *Who's to Pay for the Arts? The International Search for Models of Arts Support*, pp. 43–80. New York: ACA Books.

Hindu Business Line (August 13, 2005). "KBC 2 Boosts Star Ratings." [Online]. Retrieved November 30, 2006 from http://www.blonnet.com/2005/08/13/stories/2005081302530800.htm.

Hindustan Times (December 20, 2007). "Future's Digital." *Hindustan Times*, 1. New Delhi.

Hobsbawm, E. and Ranger, T. (eds.) (1983). *The Invention of Tradition.* Cambridge, Cambridge University Press.

Hogan, P. (2000) *Colonialism and Cultural Identity: Crises of Tradition in the Anglophone Literatures of India, Africa, and the Caribbean.* Albany: State University of New York Press.

Hogwood, B. W. and Gunn, L. A. (1984). *Policy Analysis for the Real World.* Oxford, UK: Oxford University Press.

Holden, P. (2006). "Rajaratnam's Tiger: Race, Gender and the Beginnings of Singapore Nationalism," *Journal of Commonwealth Literature*, 41(1), 127–40.

Hooks, B. (1984). *Feminist Theory from Margin to Centre.* Boston: South End Press.

Horkheimer, M. and Adorno, T. W. (1976). *Dialectic of Enlightenment.* New York: Continuum.

Huntington, S. P. (1998) *The Clash of Civilizations.* New York: Simon and Schuster.

Huntington, S. (1996). *The Clash of Civilizations and the Remaking of World Order.* New York: Simon and Schuster.

Huntington, S. (2004). *Who Are We? The Challenges to America's National Identity.* New York: Simon and Schuster.

Hutchinson, J. (1987). *The Dynamics of Cultural Nationalism: The Gaelic Revival and the Creation of the Irish Nation State.* London: Allen and Unwin.

Indiantelevision.com (July 28, 2004). "Sony Unveils 'Indian Idol' Plans; Winner to be Crowned in February." [Online]. Retrieved April 17, 2008 from http://www.indiantelevision.com/headlines/y2k4/jul/july190htm.

Inglehart, R. and Welzel, C. (2005). *Modernization, Cultural Change and Democracy.* Cambridge: Cambridge University Press.

Innis, H. (1950). *Empire and Communications.* Oxford: Clarendon Press.

Ivey, W. (2008). *Arts, Inc.: How Greed and Neglect Have Destroyed Our Cultural Rights.* Berkeley: University of California Press.

Jackson, M. R. (2008). "Art and Culture Participation at the Heart of Community Life." In J. A. Cherbo, R. A. Stewart and M. J. Wyczomirski (eds.), *Understanding the Arts and Creative Sector in the United States.* New Brunswick, NJ: Rutgers University Press.

Jackson, S. and Solis, J. (eds.) (1995). *Beyond Comfort Zones in Multiculturalism.* Westport, CT: Bergin and Garney.

Jacobs, J. (2004). *Dark Age Ahead.* New York: Random House.

Jameson, F. (1992). *Postmodernism, or the Cultural Logic of Late Capitalism.* Durham: Duke University Press.

Jayme, E. (2005). "Globalization in Art Law: Clash of Interests and International Tendencies," *Vanderbilt Journal of Transnational Law*, 38(4), 927–45.

Johannisson, J. and Trépagny, V. (2006). "Förändringar i kulturpolitikens geografi: Ett forskningsprojekt om relationen mellan olika politiska nivåer" [Changes in the Geography of Cultural Policy: A Research Project on the Relations between Different Levels of Government]. Application submitted to the Swedish Arts Council 2006-10-20.

Johannisson, J. (2008). "The Geography of Cultural Policy: Regional Cultural Policy in Sweden." Paper presented at The Fifth International Conference on Cultural Policy Research (ICCPR 2008), August 20–24, 2008, Yeditepe University, Istanbul.

Johannisson, J. (2006). "Det lokala möter världen: Kulturpolitiskt förändringsarbete i 1990-talets Göteborg" [The Local Meets the World: Cultural Policy (Re)construction in the City of Göteborg during the 1990s]. Borås: Valfrid. Diss.

Johansson, J. (2004). "Regionförsök och demokrati: Demokratisk legitimitet och regionalt utvecklingsarbete i Skåne och Västra Götaland" [Regional Experiments and Democracy: Democratic Legitimacy and Regional Development in Skåne and Västra Götaland]. Halmstad: Högskolan i Halmstad.

Johansson, J. (2000). "Regionalisation in Sweden." In Gidlund, Janerik and M. Jerneck (eds.), *Local and Regional Governance in Europe: Evidence from Nordic Regions*, pp. 125–59. Cheltenham: Edward Elgar.

Kahin, G. (1952). "Nationalism and Revolution in Indonesia." Ithaca: Cornell University Press.

Kangas, A. (2003). "Cultural policy in Finland." In P. Duelund (ed.), *The Nordic Cultural Model: Nordic Cultural Policy in Transition*, pp. 79–112. Copenhagen: Nordic Cultural Institute.

Kangas, Mangset. P., Dorte, A. and Vestheim, G. (2008). "Introduction: Nordic Cultural Policy," *International Journal of Cultural Policy*, 14(1), 1–5.

Katzenstein, P. J. (ed.) (1996). *The Culture of National Security: Norms and Identity in World Politics*. New York: Columbia University Press.

Kawashima, N. (2006a). "Audience Development and Social Inclusion in Britain," *International Journal of Cultural Policy*, 12(1), 55–72.

Kawashima, N. (2006b). "Governance of Nonprofit Organizations: Missing Chain of Accountability in Nonprofit Corporation Law in Japan and Arguments for Reform in the US," *UCLA Pacific Basin Law Journal*, 24(1), 81–124.

Kawashima, N. (2003). "Businesses and the NPO Sector in Japan: Development and Prospects." In S. Osborne (ed.), *The Voluntary and Non-Profit Sector in Japan: The Challenge of Change*, pp. 102–17. London and New York: Routledge.

Kawashima, N. (2001). "The Emerging Nonprofit Sector in Japan: Recent Changes and Prospects," *The Nonprofit Review*, 1(1), 5–14.

Kawashima, N. (1997). "Theorising Decentralisation in Cultural Policy: Concepts, Values and Strategies," *The International Journal of Cultural Policy*, vol. 3, no. 2, 341–59.

Keck, M. E and Sikkink, K. (1998), *Activists Beyond Borders: Advocacy Networks in International Politics*. Ithaca, NY: Cornell University Press.

Keohane, R. O. (1989). "International Institutions: Two Approaches." In R. O. Keohane (ed.), *International Institutions and State Power: Essays in International Relations Theory*, pp. 158–79. Boulder, CO: Westview Press.

King, J. (1972). *Science and Rationalism in the Government of Louis XIV, 1661–1683*. New York: Octagon Books.

Kittler, F. (1999). *Gramophone, Film, Typewriter*. Stanford: Stanford University Press.

Kraidy, M. (2005). *Hybridity, or the Cultural Logic of Globalization*. Philadelphia: Temple University Press.

Kratochwil, F. V. (1991). *Rules, Norms, and Decisions: On the Conditions of Practical and Legal Reasoning in International Relations and Domestic Affairs*. Cambridge, UK: Cambridge University Press.

Kohut, A. and Stokes, B. (2006). *America against the World*. New York: Times Books.

Kommittédirektiv 1992:86. *En regionberedning*. Stockholm: Civil departementet.

Krishna, S. (2007, January 24). "Star Power: King Khan gives KBC III a Fair Start," *Economic Times*, p. 4.

Labadi, S. (2005). "A Review of Global Strategy for a Balanced, Representative and Credible World Heritage List 1994–2004," *Conservation and Management of Archaeological Sites*, 7(2), 89–102.

Labouret, M. H. (1929). "La parenté à plaisanterie en Afrique Occidentale," *Africa*, 244–53.

Lakoff, G. and Johnson, M. (2003). *Metaphors We Live By*. Chicago: University of Chicago Press.

Laqueur, W. (1994). "Save Public Diplomacy," *Foreign Affairs*, 73(5).

Lash, S. (1993). "Pierre Bourdieu: Cultural Economy and Social Change." In C. Calhoun, E. LiPuma and M. Postone (eds.), *Bourdieu: Critical perspectives*, pp. 193–211. Chicago, IL: University of Chicago Press.

Latour, B. (2004). *The Politics of Nature: How to Bring the Sciences into Democracy*. Cambridge, MA: Harvard University Press.

Latour, B. (1987). *Science in Action*. Cambridge, MA: Harvard University Press.

Lee, J. T. T. (2004). "Treaties, Time Limits and Treasure Trove: The Legal Protection of Cultural Objects in Singapore," *Art, Antiquity and Law*, 9(3), 237–80.

Lefebvre, H. (1984). *Everyday Life in the Modern World*. New Brunswick, NJ: Transaction.

Lenschow, A. (2006). "Europeanisation of Public Policy." In J. Richardson (ed.), *European Union Power and Policymaking*, pp. 55–71. New York: Routledge.

Lessig, L. (2005). *Free Culture: The Nature and Future of Creativity*. New York: Penguin.

Levin, T. (2000). "Ill at Ease with Mariam, Gloria Naylor's Infibulated Jew." In Dorethea Fisher-Hornung and Heike Raphael-Hernandez (eds.), *Holding Their Own: Perspectives on the Multi-Ethnic Literatures of the United States*, pp. 51–66. Tübingen: Stauffenberg.

Levin, T. (1999). "Alice Walker, Activist. Matron of FORWARD." In M. Diedrich, H. Louis Gates Jr. and C. Perdersen (eds.), *Black Imagination and the Middle Passage*, pp. 240–54. Oxford, UK: Oxford University Press.

Lewis, J. and Miller, T. (2002). *Critical Cultural Policy Studies: A Reader*. London: Blackwell.

Littoz-Monnet, A. (2007). *The European Union and Culture: Between Economic Regulation and European Cultural Policy*. Manchester and New York: Manchester University Press.

Littoz-Monnet, A. (2005). "The European Politics of Book Pricing," *West European Politics*, 159–81.

Lord, K. M. (2008). *Voices of America: U.S. Public Diplomacy for the 21st Century*. Washington, DC: Brookings Institution.

Lovenduski, J. and Randall, V. (1993). "Difference, Identity and Equality." In *Contemporary Feminist Politics, Women and Power in Britain*, pp. 57–92. Oxford, New York: Oxford University Press.

Lowenthal, L. (1961). *Literature, Popular Culture and Society*. New York: Prentice-Hall.

Lufkin, M. (2006b, March). "The view from Eastern Europe," *The Art Newspaper*, vol. 167, Record number 21153.

Luke, T. W. (2002). *Museum Politics: Power Plays at the Exhibition*. Minneapolis: University of Minnesota Press.

Luke, T. W. (1992). *Shows of Force: Power, Politics, and Ideology in Art Exhibitions*. Durham, NC: Duke University Press.

Luke, T. W. (1989). *Screens of Power: Ideology, Domination, and Resistance in Informational Society*. Urbana: University of Illinois Press.

Luke, T. W. (1985). *Ideology and Soviet Industrialization*. Westport, CT: Greenwood Press.

Luke, T. W. (1983). "Informationalism and Ecology," *Telos*, 59–73.

Lyon, D. (2001). *Surveillance Society: Monitoring Everyday Life*. Buckingham: Open University Press.

Lyotard, J. F. (1984). *The Postmodern Condition: A Report on Knowledge*. Minneapolis: University of Minnesota Press.

Mackie, G. (1999). "Female Genital Cutting: The Beginning of the End." In B. ShellDuncan and Y. Hernlund (eds.), *Female "Circumcision": Multidisciplinary Perspectives*. Boulder: Lynne Riener.

Macmillan, M. (2003). *Paris 1919: Six Months that Changed the World.* New York: Random House Paperbacks.

Magder, T. (September 2004). "Transnational Media, International Trade and the Idea of Cultural Diversity," *Continuum: Journal of Media and Cultural Studies*, 18(3).

Mahalingham, T. V.(2006). "Hot Seat Just Got Hotter: Can KBC III Rake In The Ratings Like Before?," *Business Today*, December 31, 74. http://archives.digitaltoday.in/businesstoday/20061231/current5.html

Mahamat, Y. Z. (2000). Interview. In B. Ellerson (ed.) *Sisters of the Screen, Women of Africa on Film, Video, and Television*, pp. 343–50. Trenton, NJ: Africa World Press.

Mahamat, Y. Z. (1994). *Dilemme au féminin.* BetaCam, 25mn, Tchad.

Malmström, C. (1998). *Regions, Power and Glory: Regional Parties in West Europe.* Stockholm: SNS. Diss.

Mankekar, P. (1993). "National Texts and Gendered Lives: An Ethnography of Television Viewers in a North Indian City," *American Ethnologist*, 20(3), 543–63.

March, J. G. and Olsen, J. P. (1989). *Rediscovering Institutions: The Organizational Basis of Politics.* New York: The Free Press.

Marcuse, H. (1964). *One-Dimensional Man: Studies in the Ideology of Advanced Industrial Society.* Boston: Beacon Press.

Mariño, M. (2006). *Borderlands. Presented to the Conference Constant Capture.* Milwaukee, WI: University of Wisconsin-Milwaukee.

Martorella, R. (1996). "Japanese Corporate Collectors: A Social and Industrial Elite." In R. Martorella (ed.), *Art and Business: An International Perspective on Sponsorship*, pp. 203–9. Westport, CT and London: Praeger.

Marx, G. T. (forthcoming). *Windows into the Soul: Surveillance and Society in an Age of High Technology.* Chicago: University of Chicago Press.

Massey, D. (1999). *Power-Geometries and the Politics of Space-Time.* Heidelberg: Department of Geography, University of Heidelberg.

Massey, D. (1994). *Space, Place and Gender.* Cambridge: Cambridge Polity Press.

Mattelart, A. (2005). "Cultural Diversity Belongs to Us All." *Le Monde Diplomatique.* Retrieved from http://mondediplo.com/2005/11/15/15unesco.

Mattelart, A. (2003). *The Information Society.* London: Sage.

Mattern, M. (1999). "John Dewey, Art and Public Life," *The Journal of Politics*, 61(1), 54–75.

Maus, M. (1927). "Parentés à plaisanteries." *Ecole pratique des hautes etudes.* Section des sciences religieuses. Annuaire.

Mbembe, A. (2001). *On the Post Colony.* Berkeley: University of California Press.

McChesney, R. (2002). "The Global Restructuring of Media Ownership." In M. Raboy (ed.), *Global Media Policy in the New Millennium.* Luton, UK: University of Luton Press.

McCormick, J. (2008). *The European Union: Politics and Policies.* Boulder, CO: Westview Press.

McDowell, S. D. (1997). "Globalization and Policy Change: Television and Audio-Visual Service Policies in India," *Media, Culture and Society*, 19(2), 151–72.

McGuigan, J. (2004). *Rethinking Cultural Policy.* London: Open University Press.

McGuigan, J. (1996). *Culture and the Public Sphere.* London: Routledge.

McLuhan, M. (1964/1994). *Understanding Media: The Extensions of Man.* Cambridge, MA: The MIT Press.

McLuhan, M. (1962). *In The Gutenberg Galaxy: The Making of Typographic Man.* Toronto: University of Toronto Press.

McPherson, C. (2000). "EU Policy Inconsistency, Market Concentrations and Satellite Television: A Specific Case with Pan-business Implications," *European Business Review*, 12(2), 100–9.

Melkote, S. R., Sanjay, B. P. and Ahmed, S. A. (1998). "Use of Star TV and Doordarshan in India: An Audience Centered Case Study of Chennai City." In S. R. Melkote, P. Shields and B. C. Agrawal (eds.), *International Satellite Broadcasting in Asia*, pp. 157–77. Lanham, MD: University Press of America.

MEMRI, The Middle East Media Research Institute (2003). "La controverse sur l'excision en Egypte." *Enquête et Analyse, 52*. Retrieved January 16, 2004, from http://memri.org.

Merryman, J. H. (1986). "Two Ways of Thinking About Cultural Property," *American Journal of International Law*, 80, 831-52.

Metcalf, C. (2004). *Changing Ways in Uganda*. Retrieved from www.oneworld.org/patp/vol6_1/p19.hml.

Miditech (2007). "About Indian Idol 3." Press release Retrieved from http://www.miditech.tv/content.aspx?page=about_indian_idol_3.

Miller, T. and Yúdice, G. (2002). *Cultural Policy*. London, Thousand Oaks and New Delhi: Sage.

Millon, H. A. and Nochlin, L. (1980). *Art and Architecture in the Service of Politics*. Cambridge, MA: The MIT Press.

Mills, S. (1997). *Discourse*. London: Routledge.

Minh-ha, T. T. (1989). *Woman, Native, Other*. Bloomington and Indianapolis: Indiana UP.

Ministry of Foreign Affairs, Danida (1996). *Guidelines on the Prevention of FGM*. Ministry of Foreign Affairs: Denmark.

Mitchell, R. (2003). "Nordic and European Cultural Policies." In P. Duelund (ed.), *The Nordic Cultural Model*, pp. 437–78. Copenhagen: Nordic Cultural Institute.

Mitchell, T. (1988). *Colonising Egypt*. Cambridge: Cambridge University Press.

Mohanty, C. T. (1988). "Under Western Eyes: Feminist Scholarship and Colonial Discourse." In P. Williams, and L. Chrisman (ed.), *Colonial Discourse and Post-Colonial Theory, A Reader*, pp. 196–219. London: Pearson Education.

Monten, L. M. (2004). "Soviet World War II Trophy Art in Present Day Russia: The Events, the Law, and the Current Controversies," *DePaul University Journal of Art and Entertainment Law*, 15, 37–98.

Moussis, N. (2005). *Guide to European Policies*. Rixensart, Belgium: European Study Service.

Mulcahy, K. V. and Wyszomirski, M. J. (1995). *America's Commitment to Culture: Government and the Arts*. Boulder, CO: Westview Press.

Mumford, L. (1971). *Myth of the Machine: Technics and Human Development*. New York: Harcourt Brace Jovanovich.

Murray, S. and Ouellette, L. (2004). *Reality TV: Remaking Television Culture*. New York and London: New York University Press.

Myers, F. (2004). "Ontologies of the Image and Economies of Exchange," *American Ethnologist*, 31(1), 5–20.

Ndiaye, R. (1992). "Correspondances Ethno-Environnement Africain III Patronymiques et Parenté Plaisantante," *Une Problématique D'intégration à Large Echelle*, 97–128.

Nhan, L. (2008). *Sustainable Tourism in Cultural Heritage Sites and Developing Countries-an Angkor/Siem Reap Case Study*. Paris: ESCP-EAP.

Ninkovich, C. F. (1965). *The Neglected Aspect of Foreign Affairs*. Washington DC: Brookings Institution.

Noland, M. and Pack, H. (2003). *Industrial Policy in an Era of Globalization: Lessons from Asia*. Washington, DC: Peterson Institute.

North, D. C. (1990). *Institutions, Institutional Change and Economic Performance*. New York: Cambridge University Press.

North, D. C. (1981). *Structure and Change in Economic History*. New York: Norton Norwegian Institute for Cultural Heritage Research.

Nugent, N. (2006). *The Government and Politics of the European Union*. Durham, NC: Duke University Press.

Nye, J. S., Jr. (2004). *Soft Power: The Means to Succeed in World Politics*. New York: Public Affairs.

Nye, J. S., Jr. (2002). *The Paradox of American Power*. Oxford: Oxford University Press.

Obuljen, N. (2004). *Why We Need European Cultural Policies: The Impact of EU Enlargement on Cultural Policies in Transition Countries*. Amsterdam: European Cultural Foundation.

Ocampo, M. (2006). *Methodology for the Development of a Sustainable Community-Based Ecotourism Operation: Action Research-Development of the "Enchanted Forest."* Kompong Phluk village-Angkor Parc. Master's Thesis: Staffordshire University.

OECD (2009). *The Impact of Culture on Tourism*. Paris: Organization of Economic Cooperation and Development.

Office of the United States Trade Representative (USTR) (1998). "Foreign Trade Barriers Report: Europe," p. 18. Available at http://www.ustr.gov/assets/Document_Library/ Reports_Publications/1998/1998_National_Trade_Estimate/asset_upload_file841_ 2758.pdf (accessed December 4, 2008).

Ong, A. (1999). *Flexible Citizenship: The Cultural Logics of Transnationality*. Durham: Duke University Press.

Øresund Region (2008). Retrieved from http://www.oresundsregionen.org.

Palumbo, A. C. (1995). "'Averting "Present Commotions': History as Politics in Penn's Treaty," *American Art*, 9(3), 28–55.

Pathania, G. (1998). "Responses to Transnational Television in a STAR-Struck Land: Doordarshan and Star TV in India." In S. R. Melkote, P. Shields and B. C. Agrawal (eds.), *International Satellite Broadcasting in Asia*, pp. 157–77. Lanham, MD: University Press of America.

Patin, V. (2005). *Tourisme et Patrimoine* France: La Documentation Française.

Patterson, T. E. (2007). *Creative Destruction: An Exploratory Look at News on the Internet*. Boston: Harvard University Press.

Paulme, D. (1939). "Parenté à plaisanterie et Alliance Par le Sang en Afrique Occidentale," *Africa*, 12(4), 433–44.

Pavlic, B. and Hamelink, C. J. (1985). *The New International Economic Order: Links Between Economics and Communications*. UNESCO.

Peters, B. G. (2005). *Institutional Theory in Political Science: The "New Institutionalism."* New York: Continuum.

Peterson, J. and Shackleton, M. (2006). *The Institutions of the European Union*. New York: Oxford University Press.

Peterson, R. and Kern, R. (1996). "Changing Highbrow Taste: From Snob to Omnivore," *American Sociological Review*, 61, 900–7.

Peterson, R. A. and Simkus, A. (1992). "How Musical Tastes Mark Occupational Status Groups." In M. Lamont and M. Fournier (eds.), *Cultivating Difference: Symbolic Boundaries and the Making of Inequality*, pp. 152–86. Chicago: University of Chicago Press.

Pierson, P. (2004). *Politics in Time: History, Institutions, and Social Analysis*. Princeton, NJ: Princeton University Press.

Petit, M. (2005). "UNESCO Approves the Convention on Cultural Diversity." In *Broadcasting Regulation and Cultural Diversity*. Retrieved from http://www.brcd.net/ cac_brcd/AppPHP/modules.php/name+blogand sec=8andd_op=showcom.

Pine, J. P. and Gilmore, J. H. (1999). *The Experience Economy: Work is Theatre and Every Business a Stage*. Boston: Harvard Business School Press.

Pollock, M. A. (2005). "Theorizing EU Policy-Making." In H. Wallace, W. Wallace, and M. Pollack (eds.), *Policy-Making in the European Union*, pp. 13–48. New York: Oxford University Press.

Porter, M. (1990). *The Competitive Advantage of Nations*. New York: Basic Books.

Portes, A. (1998). "Social Capital: Its Origins and Applications in Modern Sociology," *Annual Review of Sociology*, 24, 1–24.

Postman, N. (1985). *Amusing Ourselves to Death: Public Discourse in the Age of Show Business*. New York: Penguin Books.

Powell, W. W. and DiMaggio, P. J. (1991). *The New Institutionalism in Organizational Analysis*. Chicago: University of Chicago Press.

Pressouyre, L. (1996). *The World Heritage Convention, Twenty Years Later*. Paris: UNESCO.

Pricewaterhouse Coopers. (2006). "FICCI–PricewaterhouseCoopers forecast Indian Entertainment and Media Industry to Grow 19% CAGR through 2010." Retrieved from http://www.pwc.com/extweb/ncpressrelease.nsf.

Prott, L. V. (1997, January). "For and against Unidroit," *The Art Newspaper*, vol. 66, Record number 3008.

Putnam, R., and Feldstein, L. (2003). *Better Together: Restoring the American Community*. New York: Simon and Shuster.

Putnam, R. (2000). *Bowling Alone: The Collapse and Revival of American Community*. New York: Simon and Shuster.

Pye, L. and Verba, S. (1965). *Political Culture and Political Development*. Princeton: Princeton University Press.

Rabinow, P. (1996). *Essays on the Anthropology of Reason*. Princeton: Princeton University Press.

Radcliffe-Brown, A. R. (1940). "On Joking Relationships," *Africa*, 13(3), 195–210.

Rajagopal, A. (2001). *Politics After Television: Religious Nationalism and the Reshaping of the Indian Public*. Cambridge: Cambridge University Press.

Rauch, J. E. and Trindade, V. (2005). *Neckties in the Tropics: A Model of International Trade and Cultural Diversity*. Cambridge: National Bureau of Economic Research Working Paper No. W11890.

Ray, S. G. (2000). "The Bettor Nationality: Quizzes, Scratch-Card Freebies and Online Punting Whet India's Hunger for More," *Outlook India*, 38–40.

Rectanus, M. W. (2002). *Culture Incorporated: Museums, Artists, and Corporate Sponsorships*. Minneapolis and London: University of Minnesota Press.

Region Skåne (2004). "A Dynamic Skåne: A Vision for Development," Regional Development Program for Skåne. Allkopiering / AM-tryck & reklam, Hässleholm, 9. Available at http://www.skane.se/upload/Webbplatser/RU/Dokument/RUP_Kortversion_ENG.pdf (accessed November 15, 2008).

Region Skåne (2003). "Växa med kultur: Region Skånes kulturpolitiska program" [Growing with Culture: Cultural Policy Program for Region Skåne]. Available at http://iccpr2008.yeditepe.edu.tr/papers/Johannisson_Jenny.doc.

Region Västra Götaland (2005). "Kulturpolitik för Västra Götaland" [A Cultural Policy for Västra Götaland]. Available at http://iccpr2008.yeditepe.edu.tr/papers/Johannisson_Jenny.doc.

Region Västra Götaland (2005). "Vision Västra Götaland: A Good Life." Available at http://iccpr2008.yeditepe.edu.tr/papers/Johannisson_Jenny.doc.

Remer, G. (1999). "Political Oratory and Conversation: Cicero versus Deliberative Democracy," *Political Theory*, 27(1), 39–64.

Réseau d'information sur le Développement et la Démocratie en Afrique (1999). "Les Femmes Du Cinéma et des Médias Dans la Promotion des Droits et Libertés," *Journées du Cinéma Africain et Créole*. Montréal.

Richards, A. I. (December, 1937). "Reciprocal Clan Relationships among the Bemba of NE Rhodesia," *Man* 37, 188–93.

Richardson, J. (2006). "Policymaking in the EU: Interests, Ideas and Garbage Cans of Primeval Soup." In J. Richardson (ed.), *European Union Power and Policymaking*, pp. 3–30. New York: Routledge.

Richmond, Y. (2003). *Cultural Exchange and the Cold War*. University Park, PA: Pennsylvania State University Press.

Rifkin, J. (2004). *The European Dream: How Europe's Vision of the Future is Quietly Eclipsing the American Dream*. New York: Penguin.

Rigal, L. (2000). Framing the Fabric: A Luddite Reading of Penn's Treaty with the Indians, *American Literary History*, 12(3), 557–84.

Robertson, R. (1992). *Globalization: Social Theory and Global Culture*. Newbury Park, CA: Sage.

Robinson, J. and Filicko, T. (2000). "American Public Opinion about the Arts and Culture: The Unceasing War with Philistia." In J. Cherbo and M. Wyszomirski (eds.), *The Public Life of the Arts in America*, pp.151–74. Newark: Rutgers University Press.

Rochfort, D. (1998). *Mexican Muralists: Orozco, Rivera, Siqueiros*. New York: Chronicle Books.

Rorty, R. (2000). "Universality and Truth." In R. B Brandom (ed.), *Rorty and His Critics*, pp. 1–30. Malden, MA: Blackwell.

Rorty, R. (1979). *Philosophy and the Mirror of Nature*. Princeton, NJ: Princeton University Press.

Rosenau, J. N. (2003). *Distant Proximities: Dynamics beyond Globalization*. Princeton, NJ: Princeton University Press.

Rosenstein, C. (2004). "Conceiving Artistic Work in the Formation of Artist Policy: Thinking Beyond Disinterest and Autonomy," *Journal of Arts Management, Law and Society*, 34(1), 59–77.

Ross, M. H. (1997). "Culture and Identity in Comparative Political Analysis." In M. I. Lichbach and A. S. Zukerman (eds.), *Comparative Politics: Rationality, Culture, and Structure*. New York: Cambridge University Press.

Rothstein, B. (2001). "Välfärdsstat, förvaltning och legitimite" [The Welfare State, Administration and Legitimacy]. In B. Rothstein (ed.), *Politik som organisation: Förvaltningspolitikens grundproblem*, pp. 49–8). Stockholm: SNS Förlag.

Ruffolo, G. and Parliamentary Group of the PSE, European Parliament (2001). "The Unity of Diversities: Cultural Co-Operation in the European Union." Firenze, Italy: Angelo Pontecorboli Editore.

Ruggie, J. G. (1993). "Territoriality and Beyond: Problematizing Modernity in International Relations," *International Organization*, vol. 17, pp. 139–74.

Sabel, C. F. and Zeitlin, J. (1997). *World of Possibilities: Flexibility and Mass Production in Western Industrialization*. Cambridge: Cambridge University Press.

Said, E.(1994). *Culture and Imperialism*. New York: Vintage, 1994.

Said, E. (1993). *Culture and Imperialism*. New York: Knopf.

Said, E. (1979). *Orientalism*. New York: Pantheon.

Sandholtz, W. (2005). "The Iraqi National Museum and International Law: A Duty to Protect," *Columbia Journal of Transnational Law*, 44(1), 185–240.

Sarikakis, K. (2007). "Introduction: The Place of Media and Cultural Policy in the EU." In K. Sarikakis (ed.), *Media and Cultural Policy in the European Union: European Studies*, pp. 13–21. Amsterdam: Rodopi.

Saussure, F. (1966). *Course in General Linguistics*. New York, NY: McGraw-Hill.

Sauvé, P. and Steinfatt, K. (2001). "Towards Multilateral Rules on Trade and Commerce: Protective Regulation or Efficient Protection," in Productivity Commission (ed.),

Achieving Better Regulation of Services 323, at 327 (2001). Available at http://www. cid. harvard.edu/cidtrade/Papers/Sauve/sauveculture.pdf (accessed December 4, 2008).

Schiller, D. (2000). *Digital Capitalism: Networking the Global Market System*. Cambridge, MA: MIT Press.

Schneider, C. P. and Nelson, K. (2008). *Mightier than the Sword: Arts and Culture in the U.S.-Muslim World Relationship*. Washington, DC: Brookings Institution.

Schneider, C. P. (2007). "Culture Communicates: U.S. Diplomacy that Works." In *The New Public Diplomacy: Soft Power in International Relations*. Basingstoke, UK: Palgrave Macmillan.

Schuster, J. M. (2002). *Informing Cultural Policy: The Research and Information Infrastructure*. New Brunswick, NJ: Center for urban Policy Research.

Schuster, J. M. (1997). "Book Review of Martorella *Art and Business*," *Journal of Cultural Economics*, 21, 153–6.

Scott, J. (2002). "World Heritage as a Model for Citizenship: The Case of Cyprus." *International Journal of Heritage Studies*, (8)2, 99–115.

Scott, J. (1998). *Seeing Like the State: How Certain Schemes to Improve the Human Condition Have Failed*. New Haven: Yale University Press.

Seikaly, Z. A. (July–August, 1989). "It's Possible: A Joint Exhibition of Palestinian and Israeli Art." *Middle East Report*, 159, July–August, 45. Available at http://74.125.47.132/ search?q=cache:0Iviw4TcLTcJ:www1.georgetown.edu/grad/cct/artandpower.pdf+ middle+east+report+159+(45)+%27it%27s+possible:+a+joint+exhibition+of+palesti nian+and+israeli+art%27&cd=1&hl=en&ct=clnk&gl=us&client=safari.

Sen, A. (2006). *Identity and Violence: The Illusion of Destiny*. New York: W. W. Norton.

Sewell, W. H. (1999). "The Concept of Culture." In V. Bonnell and L. Hunt (eds.), *Beyond the Cultural Turn: New Directions in the Study of Society and Culture*. Berkeley: University of California Press.

Sewell, W. H. (July, 1992). "A Theory of Structure: Duality, Agency and Transformation." *American Journal of Sociology*, 98(1), 1–29.

Sexton, J. (2008). *Amalgamation Schemes: Antiblackness and the Critique of Multiracialism*. Minneapolis: University of Minnesota Press.

SFS (1996). *Lag om försöksverksamhet med ändrad regional ansvarsfördelning*. Stockholm: Fritze.

Shore, C. (2000). *Building Europe: The Cultural Politics of European Integration*. New York: Routledge.

Sil, R. (2002). *Managing "Modernity": Work, Community, and Authority in Late-Industrializing Japan and Russia*. Ann Arbor: University of Michigan Press.

Singh, J. P. (2010). *The Arts of Globalization*. New York, NY: Columbia University Press.

Singh, J. P. (2008a). *Negotiation and the Global Information Economy*. Cambridge, UK: Cambridge University Press.

Singh, J. P. (2008b). "Paulo Freire: Possibilities for Dialogic Communication in the Information Age, Key Thinkers in the Information Age," *Information, Communication, Society*, 11(5), August, 699–726.

Singh, J. P. (2008c). "Between Cooperation and Conflict: International Trade in Cultural Goods and Services." In J. M. Cherbo, R. A. Stewart and M.J. Wyszomirski (eds.), *Understanding the Arts and Cultural Sector in the United States*. New Brunswick, NJ: Rutgers University Press.

Singh, J. P. (2007). "Culture or Commerce? A Comparative Assessment of International Interactions and Developing Countries at UNESCO, WTO, and Beyond," *International Studies Perspectives* 8: 36–53.

Singh, J. P. (2002). "Introduction: Information Technologies and the Changing Scope of Power and Governance." In James N. Rosenau and J. P. Singh (eds.), *Information Technologies and Global Politics: The Changing Scope of Power and Governance.* Albany, NY: State University of New York Press.

Singhal, A. and Rogers, E. M. (2001). *India's Communication Revolution: From Bullockcarts to Cybermarts.* New Delhi and Newbury Park, CA: Sage.

Sinha, N. (2007). *India Profile.* Retrieved from http://www.museum.tv/archives/etv/I/htmll/india/india.htm.

Skot-Hansen, D. (1999). "Culture of the Times: Strategies in Local Cultural Policy," *Nordic Journal of Cultural Policy,* 2(1), 7–27.

Smelser, N. (1976). *Comparative Methods in the Social Sciences.* Englewood Cliffs, NJ: Prentice-Hall.

Smith, M. P. (2001). *Transnational Urbanism: Locating Globalization.* Oxford: Blackwell.

Smith, S. (2004). "Singing Our World into Existence: International Relations Theory and September 11," *International Studies Quarterly,* 48(3), 499–515.

Soja, E. (1980). "The Socio-Spatial Dialectic," *Annals of the Association of American Geographers,* 70(2), 207–25.

Somers, M. (1995). "The Narrative Constitution of Identity: A Relational and Network Approach," *Theory and Society,* 23, 605–49.

SOU (1995). *Regional Framtid.* Stockholm: Fritze.

Soyinka, W. (November 28, 2000). Comments Made at the White House Conference on Cultural Diplomacy. Washington, DC: Executive Office of the President.

Spivak, G. C. (1997). "French Feminism in an International Frame." In S. Kemp and J. Squires (eds.), *Feminisms, Oxford Readers,* pp. 51–5. Oxford and New York, Oxford University Press.

Spivak, G. C. (1988). "Can the Subaltern Speak?" In W. Patrick and C. Laura (eds.), *Colonial Discourse and Post-Colonial Theory, A Reader,* pp. 66–111. London: Pearson Education.

Spruyt, H. (1996). *The Sovereign State and its Competitors.* Princeton, NJ: Princeton University Press.

Stalder, F. (2005). *Open Cultures and the Nature of Networks.* Novi Sad: Futura publikacije.

Stalder, F. (2001). "The End of an Era: The Internet Hits Ground." Retrieved from http://felix.openflows.org/html/endofera.html.

Stark, D. and Bruszt, L. (1998). *Postsocialist Pathways: Transforming Politics and Property in East Central Europe.* New York: Cambridge University Press.

Stark, D. (1996). "Recombinant Property in East European Capitalism," *American Journal of Sociology,* 101, 993–1027.

Starks, M. (2007). *Switching to Digital Television: UK Public Policy and the Market.* London: Intellect Books.

Stevenson, D. (2004). "Civic Gold Rush: Cultural Planning and the Politics of the Third Way," *International Journal of Cultural Policy,* 10(1), 119–31.

Stewart, C and Shaw, R. (1994). *Syncretism/Anti-Syncretism: The Politics of Religious Synthesis.* London: Routledge.

Stewart, C. (1999). "Syncretism and Its Synonyms," *Reflections on Cultural Admixture. Diacritics,* 29(3), 40–62.

Stienstra, D. (2000). "Cutting to Gender: Teaching Gender in International Relations," *International Studies Perspectives,* 1(3), 233–44.

Stokes, B. (1991). Tinseltown Trade War, *National Journal,* February 23, 434, at 438.

Swedish Arts Council (2008). "Swedish Arts Council – Kulturradet." Retrieved from http://www. Kulturradet.se (accessed November 15, 2008).

Swedish Arts Council (2006). *Culture in Figures 2006:3: Public Expenditures 2005 in a Regional Perspective.* Stockholm: Statens kulturråd.

Swedish National Council for Cultural Affairs (1997). *Cultural Policy in Practice.* Stockholm: Statens kulturråd.

Swidler, A. (1986). "Culture in Action: Symbols and Strategies," *American Sociological Review*, 51(2), 273–86.

Swidler, Anne. (1995). Cultural Power and Social Movements. In H. Johnston and B. Klandermans (eds.), Social Movements and Culture, (pp. 25–40). Minneapolis: University of Minnesota Press.

Szalai, G. and Frater, P. (2009). "U.S. prevails in WTO case against China," *Hollywood Reporter*, August 12.

Tepper, S. (2005, 23 May). "Television Most-Watched Programs," *International Herald Tribune*, p.10.

Tepper, S. (2002). "Creative Assets and the Changing Economy," *Journal of Arts Management, Law and Society*, 32(2), 159–68.

Thiam, A. (1986). *Black Sisters, Speak Out: Feminism and Oppression in Black Africa.* London: Pluto Press.

Thorsell, J. (2003). "World Heritage Convention: Effectiveness 1992–2002 and Lessons for Governance." Gland, Suisse/Gatineau, Québec: UICN/Parks Canada.

Throsby, D. (2001). *Culture and Economics.* Cambridge: Cambridge University Press.

Throsby, D. (1999). "Cultural Capital," *Journal of Cultural Economics*, 23, 3–12.

Tobin, B. F. (2007). "Native Land and Foreign Desire: William Penn's Treaty with the Indians," *American Indian Culture and Research Journal*, 19(3), 87–119.

Toman, J. (1996). *The Protection of Cultural Property in the Event of Armed Conflict.* Surrey, UK: Ashgate Publishing Co.

Törnqvist (1998). *The Renaissance of Regions: On Technology and the Conditions of Social Communication.* Stockholm: SNS.

Trépagny (2003). "The Design of Regions: Identity Production in Cultural Policy Information." In H. Egeland and J. Johannisson (eds.), *Kultur, plats, identitet: Det lokalas betydelse i en globaliserad värld*, pp. 65–89. Nora: Nya Doxa. SISTER Skrifter från 9.

Tuch, H. (ed.) (1994). *Communicating with the World in the 1990's: A Commemorative Symposium.* Washington DC: US Information Agency Alumni Association: Public Diplomacy Foundation.

UNESCO (2007). *Patrimoigne mondial-défit pour le millénaire.* Paris, France: UNESCO.

UNESCO (2005). *Convention on the Protection and Promotion of the Diversity of Cultural Expressions.* Retrieved http://portal.unesco.org/culture/en/ev.php-URL_ID=33232&URL_DO=DO_TOPIC&URL_SECTION=201.html#III (accessed October 1, 2009).

UNESCO, (2005). *Masterpieces of the Oral and Intangible Heritage of Humanity-Proclamations 2001, 2003 and 2005.* CLT/CH/ITH/PROC/BR3. Available at http://unesdoc.unesco.org/images/0014/001473/147344e.pdf (accessed Nov. 27, 2009).

UNESCO (2005). *Orientation devant guider la mise en œuvre de la Convention du patrimoine mondial.* Paris, France: UNESCO.

UNESCO (2002). *La Convention du patrimoine mondial Vingt ans après.* Paris, France: UNESCO.

UNESCO (2002). *Patrimoine mondial 2002-Héritage partagé, responsabilité commune.* Paris, France: UNESCO.

UNESCO (1998). *Action Plan on Cultural Politics for Development.* Stockholm: UNESCO.

UNESCO (1995). *Our Creative Diversity: Report of the World Commission on Culture and Development.* Paris: UNESCO.

UNESCO (1972). *Convention concernant la protection du patrimoine mondial, culturel et naturel adopté par la Conférence général de l'UNESCO à sa dix-septième session.* Retrieved from http://portal.unesco.org/fr/ev.php-URL_ID=13055&URL_DO=DO_TOPIC&URL_SECTION=201.html (accessed on August 1, 2008).

UNESCO Institute for Statistics (2005). *International Flows of Selected Cultural Goods and Services, 1994–2003.* Montreal, Quebec: UNESCO Institute for Statistics. Retrieved from www.uis.unesco.org/ev_en.php?ID=6372_201&ID2=DO_TOPIC (accessed October 1, 2009).

UN World Tourism Organization (2008). *Tourism Highlights 2008 Edition.* Madrid: WTO. Retrieved from www.world-tourism.org (accessed January 10, 2009).

US Government Printing Office (1984). *U.S. National Study on Trade in Services: A Submission by the United States Government to the General Agreement on Tariffs and Trade.* Washington DC.

US Mission to UNESCO (2005). *UNESCO Convention Could Limit Freedom of Cultural Expressions and Trade.* Paris, France.

US Department of State (2005). *U.S. Opposed "Deeply Flawed" U.N. Cultural Diversity Convention.* Bureau of International Information Programs (IIP). Retrieved from http://usinfo.state.gov/is/Archive/2005/Oct/21-870552.html (accessed January 10, 2009).

US Department of State (2005). *The Convention on the Protection and Promotion of the Diversity of Cultural Expressions.* Retrieved from http://www.state.gov/r/pa/prs/ps/2005/54690.htm (accessed January 10, 2009).

US Department of State (June, 2005). *Draft Convention on Cultural Diversity "Deeply Flawed," U.S. Says.* Bureau of International Information Programs. Retrieved from http://www.america.gov/st/washfile-english/2005/October/20051020170821GLnesnoM3.670901e-02.html (accessed January 10, 2009).

Veblen, T. (1998). *The Theory of the Leisure Class: An Economic Study of Institutions.* Amherst, NY: Prometheus Books.

Veron, L. (March 1999). "Hollywood and Europe: A Case of Trade in Cultural Industries, the 1993 GATT Dispute." CIAO Working Papers. Retrieved from http://www.ciaonet.org/wps/ve102.

Vestheim, G. (2008). "All Kulturpolitikk Er Instrumentell." In Beckman, Svante and S. Månsson (eds.), *KulturSverige 2009: Problemanalys och statistik.* Linköping: SweCult/Linköpings universitet.

Vestheim, G. (2001). "Democracy, Cultural Policy and Culture Institutions." Culture, Society and Market: The Swedish Research Seminar Held at Sigtuna, January 24–5, 2000, pp. 59–76. Stockholm: The Swedish National Council for Cultural Affairs and The Bank of Sweden Tercentenary Foundation.

Vestheim, G. (1995). "Models of Cultural Policy: The Scandinavian Experience," *Kulturpolitisk Tidskrift*, 2(4), 6–26.

Villanueva, R. H. (1995). "Free Trade and the Protection of Cultural Property: The Need for an Economic Incentive to Report Newly Discovered Antiquities," *George Washington Journal of International Law and Economics*, 29(2), 547–80.

Virilio, P. (1995). *The Art of the Motor.* Minneapolis: University of Minnesota Press.

Vogel, H. L. (2007). *Entertainment Industry Economics: A Guide for Financial Analysis.* Cambridge, UK: Cambridge University Press.

Volkerling, M. (1996). "Deconstructing the Difference-Engine: A Theory of Cultural Policy," *The European Journal of Cultural Policy*, 2(2), 189–212.

Von Eschen, P. M. (2000). "Satchmo Blows Up the World: Jazz, Race, and Empire in the Cold War." In R. Wagneileitener and E. T. Mary (eds.), *Here, There, and Everywhere: The Foreign Politics of American Popular Culture.* University Press of New England.

Voon, T. (2007). *Cultural Products and the World Trade Organization.* Cambridge, UK: Cambridge University Press.

Voon, T. (2006). "UNESCO and the WTO: A Clash of Cultures," *International and Comparative Law Quarterly*, Vol. 55, No. 3.

Wallace, H., Wallace, W. and Pollack, M. A. (2005). *Policy-Making in the European Union.* New York: Oxford University Press.

Wallerstein, I. (1990). "Culture as the Ideological Battleground of the Modern World-System." In M. Featherstone (ed.), *Global Culture: Nationalism, Globalization, and Modernity*, pp. 31–55. London: Sage Publications.

Walt, V. (1998, June 23). "Female Circumcision: A Village Issue," *International Herald Tribune*, p. 12.

Wang, D. (2003). "The Discourse of Unequal Treaties in Modern China," *Pacific Affairs*, 76(3), 399–425.

Weaver, R. K. and Rockman, B. A. (1993). *Do Institutions Matter? Government Capabilities in the United States and Abroad.* Washington, DC: The Brookings Institution.

Weick, K. (2000). *Making Sense of Organizations.* Malden, MA: Blackwell.

Williams, R. (1976). *Keywords: A Vocabulary of Culture and Society.* London: Fontana/Croom Helm.

Wilson, J. S. (1959, September 13). "Who is Connover? Only *We* Ask," *New York Times Magazine.*

Winter, T. (2007). *Post-Conflict Heritage, Postcolonial Tourism: In Culture, Politics and Development at Angkor.* Routledge, UK.

World Health Organization (1996). *Female Genital Mutilation: Information Pack.* Retrieved from www.who.int/frh-whd/FGM/infopack/English/fgm_infopack.htm (accessed November 15, 2008).

World Trade Organization (2005). Audiovisual Services: Information Note by the Secretariat. WTO.

World Trade Organization. (2000). Communication from the United States: Audiovisual and Related Services. WTO.

World Trade Organization (1998). Audiovisual Services: Background Note by the Secretariat. WTO.

World Trade Organization (1990). Matters Relating to Trade in Audiovisual Services: Note by the Secretariat. Working Group on Audiovisual Services. WTO, MTN.GNS/AUD/W/14.

Yoshimoto, M. (2008). "Bunka seisaku saiko (Rethinking cultural policy)," *Nissei Kisoken Shohou (Research reports of the Nissei Life-Insurance Research Institute)*, 51, 37–116.

Zakaria, F. (October 14, 2002). "Our Way", *The New Yorker.* Available at http://www.fareedzakaria.com/articles/nyer/101402.html (accessed December 15, 2008).

Zechenter, E. M. (1997). "In the Name of Culture: Cultural Relativism and the Abuse of the Individual," *Journal of Anthropological Research*, 53(3), 319–47.

Zolberg, V. (1993). "Remaking Nations: Public Culture and Post-Colonial Discourse. In Balfe," *Paying the Piper: Causes and Consequences of Arts Patronage.* Minnesota: University of Minnesota Press.

Index

abstract expressionism   104
Adorno, Theodor   5, 29
aesthetics   2, 64, 157
Africa   4, 7, 175, 196, 201, 207
African cinema   196–199
Albright, Madeleine   104
Algeria   160
Ali Shaheed Muhammad   107, 207
    (*see also* hip-hop)
American Sociological Association   3
Americanization   79, 109, 162
Anderson, Benedict   8, 46
Angkor temples   171 (*see also*
    Cambodia)
Appadurai, Arjun   8, 13, 30, 61
Arab and Islamic states   13, 105, 160
Arabic publishing   4
Armenia   43
art and treaties   29–36
artists   40, 48, 105, 129, 160
    cultural dialogue and   109
    revolutionary art   159–160
    state identity and   36, 50
arts
    corporate support for   140–151
    role of   105–109
    institutions   39
    lobbies   82
    marketing   148
    spending   82
Asia   80, 107, 175
Association of Cultural Economics
    International   3
audiovisual dispute   9, 84–94 (*see also*
    GATT, WTO)
Australia   51, 81, 96
Austria   41
authorship   64, 70, 73, 204

Barthes, Roland   29
Benin   198
Berlin   63
Beuys, Joseph   48 (*see also* artists)
Bhabha, Homi K.   32

Bollywood   9, 12
Bonaparte, Napoleon   42
Bourdieu, Pierre   29, 45, 188, 203
    (*see also* cultural capital)
Brookings Institution   109
Burkina Faso   210
Bush, George W.   106

cable and satellite networks   183–184
Cairo   107
Cambodia   14, 47, 168, 171, 175
Canada   10, 47–48, 77–78, 93
Canclini, Garcia   8
Castells, Manuel   71
Castro, Fidel   39
censorship   95 (*see also* human rights)
Chad   196
Chile   43
China   4, 31, 43, 47, 98, 184, 210–211
Chinese-American community   107
Chinese Taipei   92
clash of civilizations   162 (*see also*
    Huntington, Samuel)
Cold War   103–108
colonialism   7, 13, 79–91, 155, 161, 165
Committee on Culture and Education
    (CULT)   122
communication technology   56, 57, 14,
    80, 56, 33, 80, 81, 91, 102
communication theory   8
Communism   102
constructionism   64, 115 (*see also*
    cultural policy)
Copenhagen   63
copyright   2, 11, 64, 70, 73, 98
COREPER   122
corporate cultural politics   67 (*see also*
    Japan)
corporate social responsibility
    programs   146–147
Cote d'Ivoire   210
Council of Europe   12, 63, 116–120
Cousins, Norman   105
Cowen, Tyler   10, 78, 82

Creative Commons license   61, 73
  (*see also* copyright)
cross-cultural dialogue   106, 109
Cuban Missile Crisis   39
cultural capital   45 (*see also* Pierre
  Bourdieu)
cultural diplomacy   12, 101–110
  Report of the Advisory Committee on
    Cultural Diplomacy   103
cultural diversity   78, 81–83 (*see also*
  Cohen, Tyler)
cultural economics   5
cultural exception   88 (*see also* GATS)
cultural governance   64
cultural heritage   12, 12–13, 50–51,
    129, 158, 170, 174–176
  architectural   169
  national   41–43
  and tourism   169, 174 (*see also*
    tourism industry)
cultural identity   13, 87, 155, 157, 163
cultural industry   2–4, 9, 14, 30, 56–59, 80
  audiovisual   9, 79, 91
  creative   82
  film industry   4, 77–82
  media   102, 59, 57, 60, 58
  motion picture   80–97
  television   79
  tourism industry   4, 174 (*see also*
    cultural heritage)
cultural policy   63–72, 83, 115,
    120–127, 132–134, 203 (*see also*
    cultural heritage, cultural diplomcy,
    cultural voice, digital policy)
  conservation   12
  definition of   9, 65
  national   116
  quotas   81–89
  regional and local   127–138
  subsidies   2, 83
  tariffs   2, 44–45
  taste   66
  trade versus culture   84–99
cultural production   8, 13, 70, 103
cultural programs   107, 122
cultural property   41–47
cultural renaissance   13, 157–160
  (*see also* Mexico)
cultural revivalism   160–163 (*see also*
  Arab and Islamic states)

cultural sphere   117
cultural technologies   6, 14
cultural voice   9, 11–14
culture
  as cultural policy   73
  as high art   67
  as hybrid   73, 82 (*see* hybridization)
  as national heritage   158, 175
  as power   35, 79, 114 (*see also* power)
  as sustainable development   135
  digital culture   56–61
  governmentalization of   48 (*see also*
    Foucault, Michel)
Culture Action Europe   121
Czech Republic   42

Dangarembga, Tsitsi   1, 7
Denmak   51, 60, 131, 165
Dewey, John   5, 50, 113, 140, 204–212
digital policy   56–61
  digital culture   60, 69, 72, 81, 102
  Digital Millenium Copyright Act
    (DMCA)   61
  digital platforms   63–71
  digital rights management (DRM)   61
  digitized networking   68
Directorate General for Education and
    Culture (DGEAC)   121–122 (*see also*
    European Union)
discursive analysis   182
Doha Development Round   85, 90–95
  (*see also* WTO)

East Asia   61
East, the   101
Eastern Europe   104
economic liberalization   183 (*see also*
  India)
education   102
Education, Audiovisual, and Culture
    Executive Agency (EACEA)   120–122
Egypt   4, 43, 104, 108–109, 160, 196
Eisenhower, Dwight   104
Ethiopia   41
Europe   80, 93, 97, 166, 171, 175, 186
European Commission   80, 121 (*see also*
  European Union)
European Community   38, 45, 48
  (*see also* Euopean Union)
European conquests   160

European identity   10, 156
European Union   2, 10, 11–12, 48, 51,
    63, 81, 88–89, 93–94, 119, 129
  arts policy   38, 114–115, 123
  Audiovisual Media Services
    Directive   80
  Commission of the European
    Union   114
  Council of Ministers   119–122
  cultural identity   13
  cultural policy   11, 113–125
  Directorate General for Education and
    Culture   121–122
  European Commission   80, 121
  European Community   38, 45, 48
  European Court of Justice   38, 45, 81
  European Cultural Capitals
    program   117
  European Parliament   119–123
  European Youth Orchestra   117
  Lisbon Agenda   114, 121
Europeanization   115, 123–125, 157
    (*see also* cultural policy and cultural
    identity)

Fanon, Frantz   155
Female Genital Mutilation (FGM)
    195–198
feminism   109, 194–198
film festivals   9, 194–197, 201
  Middle East International Film Festival
    (MEIFF)   109
film industry   4, 77–82 (*see also* cultural
    industries)
Fisher, Frank   130
Florida, Richard   4, 30
Folly, Anne-Laure   196, 201
Foreign Affairs Reform and
    Restructuration Act of 1998   104
Foreign Trade Barriers Report 1998   90
Foucault, Michel
  discursive formations   65–71, 130,
    203–205
  governmentality   6, 34, 66
  power   30–31, 65, 69, 71 (*see also*
    power)
France   10, 13–14, 42, 46, 50, 77–78, 88,
    93, 107, 160, 166, 168, 170, 173, 198
freedom of expression   95, 129, 133
    (*see also* human rights)

Freire, Paulo   13, 113
Frey, Bruno   5
Fulbright, William   102
Fundamentalism   163

gaze   199
General Agreement on Tariffs and Trade
    (GATT)   9–10, 38–40, 85–92
General Agreement on Trade in Services
    (GATS)   88–90, 98
Georgetown University   107
Germany   31, 48, 50, 63
Gillespie, Dizzy   12, 105
globalization   9, 11, 14, 34, 36, 48,
    77–78, 102, 106, 127, 130, 162, 165,
    171, 203–204
Gramsci, Antonio   29, 161
Greenland   165

Habermas, Jurgen   79
Hall, Stuart   63, 66
hegemony   161 (*see also* Gramsci,
    Antonio)
Hesmondhalgh, David
  decentralized platforms   69
  Web 2.0 as disturbance   74
hip-hop   107–108
Hobbes, Thomas   80
Hollywood   4, 77, 81–82
Honduras   96
Hong Kong   92
Horkheimer, Max   5, 29
human rights   41, 43, 95, 109, 194–201
    (*see also* censorship, freedom of
    expression, women's rights)
Huntington, Samuel   31–33, 162
hybridity   7, 14, 82, 203–204 (*see also*
    Tyler, Cowen)

identity   107, 162, 113
  European   10, 156
  multiple identities   14, 194
  national identity   87, 91, 115,
    156–159
  regional identity construction   134
India   2, 12, 158, 181–193
Indonesia   207
information society   36, 68
informationalism   68
information technolgy   4, 91

International Conference on Cultural Policy Research (ICCPR) 127–128
International Council of Museums (ICOM) 50
International Criminal Tribunal 43
International Journal of Cultural Policy Research 128
international negotiations 7, 37–40, 84–99
Internet 57, 60, 69–73, 81
Iran 104, 161
Iraq 43, 104, 160
Iron Curtain 105–106
Islam 106, 157 (*see also* Muslim world)
Israel 40, 96
Italy 41–42, 82, 160
Ivory Coast 198

Jameson, Fredric 30
Japan 12, 47, 67, 77, 92, 141–151, 168
jazz 104–108 (*see also* cultural diplomacy)
Jean-Francois Lyotard 30
Jefferson, Thomas 109
Jordan 160

Kennedy, John F. 104
Klimt, Gustav 41
Korea 60
Kurds 161
Kyrgyzstan 107

Laqueur, Walter 104
Latin America 4–5, 157
Latin fusion 107 (*see also* hip hip-hop)
Latour, Bruno 30
Lebanon 160
Lessig, Lawrence 61
Liberia 96
Libya 160
Lowenthal, Leo 29
Lysistrata 13

Malaysia 108
Mali 4, 12, 196–198, 210
marine policy 38
Marx, Karl 5
McLuhan, Marshall 29
mesena 12, 141–151 (*see also* Japan)

Mexico 2, 13, 34, 92, 157–159 (*see also* cultural renaissance)
Middle East 101
Minh-ha, Trin 199
Mitterand, Francois 90
modernity 107
Morocco 14, 108, 160, 173–174
most favored nation (MFN) 10, 90, 98
Motion Picture Association of America (MPAA) 88
Motion Picture Report 85–87
Murdoch, Rupert 78
music 4, 12, 104–108
musicians 104–105
Muslim world, the 101, 106, 108
Muslims on Screen and Television (MOST): A Cross Cultural Resource Center 109
Mussolini, Benito 41

Nas 108 (*see also* hip-hop)
national conscience 105
National Endowment for the Arts (NEA) 11, 40
national identity 87, 91, 115, 156–159 (*see also* identity)
NATO 30–40 (*see also* NATOarts)
Netherlands, the 107
network society 68
New World Information and Communication Order (NWICO) 14
New York 63
New York Philharmonic 101
New Zealand 39
Nicaragua 96
Nigeria 212, 101, 104
non-government actors & organizations (NGOs) 106–108, 150, 197
Nordic countries 67–72, 129, 132
North America 166
North, Douglas 115
Nubia 170
Nuremberg Trials 42–43
Nye, Joseph 29, 143 (*see also* soft power)

Obama, Barack 19–20, 101
Obregon, Alvaro 159
online communities 103
Organization of African Unity (OAU) 38

Organization of European Cooperation
  and Development (OECD) 87
Orientalism 14, 161
Ottoman Empire 160–161
Ousmane, Sembene 7
Ozomatli 107–108

Pacific 175
Palestine 40, 107–108, 160
Paris 47, 107, 109
Paris Conference of 1815 42
Parsons, Talcott 79
Perry, William 101
piracy 61 (*see also* digital culture)
Plato 1
postcolonialism 11, 13, 103, 156–157
  (*see also* cononiality, cultural
  policies)
power 29, 65
  hegemonic 156
  in cultural policy 14, 64, 119
  individualizing 30–35 (*see also*
    Foucault)
  institutional 120
  instrumental 7, 40
  macro 74
  meta-power 4, 6–8
  micro 68, 72
  real 108
  soft power 8, 119, 102, 115, 143
  structural 45
propaganda 102
prosumption 70–72 (*see also* digital
  culture)
protectionism 83, 90
Protocol on Strategic Environmental
  Assessment 38
Protocol on Water and Health 38
public diplomacy 101–106
Puerto Rico 164
Pyongyang 101

Qatar 107
quotas 81–89 (*see also* cultrual policy)

Recording Industry Association of
  America (RIAA) 58
Rivera, Diego 160 (*see also* artists)
rock n' roll 107
Rorty, Richard 130

Rosenau, Jim 14
Russia 48, 102, 105, 164
Rwanda 210

Saban Center for Middle East
  Policy 109
Said, Edward 14, 156, 161, 166, 194
  (*see also* Orientalism)
satellite broadcasting services 8, 89
Sen, Amartya 14 (*see also* multiple
  identities)
Senegal 8, 14, 198, 207–121
Singapore 51, 92
Slovak republic 42
soap operas 109
social networking 108
soft law 115 (*see also*
  cultural policy)
soft power 8, 119, 102, 115, 143
  (*see also* power, Joseph Nye)
South Africa 198
South Korea 61
Southeast Asia 103
Soviet Union 31, 102–105
Soyinka, Wole 101
Spain 157
Sub-Saharan Africa 196
subsidies 2, 83 (*see also* cultrual
  policy)
Sudan 160
supra-national 11
Sweden 11–12, 127–138
Switzerland 47–48
syncretism 204–121 (*see also*
  Dewey, John)
Syria 43, 160–161

Taiwan 61
Talib Kweli 108 (*see also* hip-hop)
Tan, Amy 107
tariff, *see also* cultrual
  policy 2, 44–45
taste hierarchies 66 (*see also* Bourdieu,
  Pierre and cultural policy)
television shows 4, 109, 181–193
  (*see also* India)
Television Without Frontier Directive
  (TWF Directive) 88–90
  (*see also* EU)
Thiam, Awa 194

Throsby, David   5
Tibet   43
trade and culture   9, 37, 44, 77, 84–99
   (*see also* cultrual policy)
Transjordan   160
transnational governance   220–224
treaties   2 (*see also* EU)
   Treaty of Maastricht, the   37, 48,
      113–122
   Treaty of Rapallo   48
   Treaty of Rome, the   37, 39, 47
   Treaty of Waitangi   39
   World Heritage Treaty   43
Tribe Called Quest   107
Tunisia   160
Turkey   161
TV reality shows   190–193

Ukraine   164
Ulises Bella   107 (*see also* hip-hop)
UNESCO   9–14, 43, 48, 84, 85, 91, 95,
   116–117, 120
   Culture Sector   167
   Declaration on the Protection of
      Cultural Heritage   166
   World Heritage Center   167
   World Heritage List   167, 171
   World Heritage List of Humanity   173
UNESCO conventions
   Convention on the Means of
      Prohibiting and Preventing the
      Illicit Import Export and Transfer of
      Ownership of Cultural Property   50
   Convention on the Protection and
      Promotion of the Diversity of
      Cultural Expressions   10, 73, 78,
      83–85, 93–95, 116–117
   Convention on the Protection
      of the Underwater Cultural
      Heritage   38
   Convention on the Protection and
      Use of Transboundary Watercourses
      and International Lakes   38
   World Heritage Convention
      of 1972   37, 166, 169–170
UNICEF   196
Unidroit Convention on Stolen
   and Illegally Exported Cultural
   Objects   47, 50

United Kingdom   38, 42–43, 48, 51,
   107, 144, 150, 160
United Nations   14, 167, 195
United States   2–3, 11, 14, 34, 38, 40,
   43, 47, 60–63, 77–79, 82–98,
   106, 102, 108–109, 144,
   168, 186, 198
   U.S. Presidents   101, 104, 106, 109
   United States Department of
      State   91–96, 103, 107
   United States Information Agency
      (USIA)   103–104
   United States Objectives Paper   90–92,
      96–97
Uruguay Round   9, 84, 85,
   87–90, 92–93, 98 (*see also* GATT)
US-Islamic World Forum   109
US-Muslim world
   relationship   101

Valenti, Jack   88–90
Veblen, Thorsten   29
Vietnam   168, 170

Wallerstein, Immanuel   36
war of ideas   102, 106
Web 2.0   64, 72, 103
Williams, Raymond   63
women's rights   109, 194–201
World Health Organization
   (WTO)   195
World Heritage List   161, 171–173
World Tourism Organization   4
World Trade Center attacks   103
World Trade Organization (WTO)   4,
   9–10, 84, 89, 91, 85, 44
   audiovisual sector   91–98
   Doha Round negotiations   85,
      90–95
   WTO Group on Negotiating Services
      (GNS)   90
World War II   41, 67, 85, 96, 142
Wu, Tim   61

Yugoslavia   41, 43, 212

Zakharia, Fareed   102
Zanzibar   198
Zimbabwe   2, 4, 119

.